God, Country, and The Supreme Court

James K. Fitzpatrick

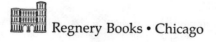 Regnery Books • Chicago

Manufactured in the United States of America.

Regnery Books is an imprint of Regnery Gateway, Inc. All inquiries
concerning this book should be directed to Regnery Gateway, Inc., 940 North
Shore Drive, Lake Bluff, IL 60044.

Library of Congress Cataloging in Publication Data.

Fitzpatrick, James K.
   God, country, and the Supreme Court.
   Bibliography: p.
   Includes index.
   1. Religious liberty—United States—History.
2. United States. Supreme Court—History.
3. Religion and state—United States—History.
I. Title.
KF4783.F58   1984   342.73'0852   84-18334
ISBN 0-89526-610-5   347.302852

To Evelyn Mangan Fitzpatrick

CONTENTS

Introduction

Society cannot exist unless a controlling power upon will and appetite be placed somewhere, and the less of it there is within, the more there must be without. It is ordained in the eternal constitution of things that men of intemperate minds cannot be free. Their passions forge their fetters.

—*Edmund Burke*

During our Bicentennial celebrations a few years back, Americans displayed a—to some—surprisingly vigorous patriotic fervor. And I am not at all inclined to tone it down. Nevertheless, it must be noted that, as history measures times, two hundred years is not that long a span. The American political system and our constitutional order—which will not have its Bicentennial until 1988—still must be considered what someone has called the "Great Experiment."

Our Founding Fathers, it must be remembered, were attempting to demonstrate to the Old World that something *new* in history was possible; that a successful social and political order could be built and sustained without a king or established church acting as guarantor of public virtue; that self-rule, a republican system of government, had become possible; that the pessimism of the defenders of European Old Regime authoritarianism was unwarranted. It was no longer necessary—and the people of the United States were to prove it unnecessary—for a society to pronounce beforehand in the highest law of the land *what kind* of people they intended to be, as was the fashion with the old European Christian monarchies.

We would not need, our Founding Fathers were convinced, the external legal superstructure of the medieval *res publica Christiana* to remain a just and virtuous society. We already were, as Willmoore Kendall phrased it, a "virtuous people." Perhaps our European forebears needed authoritarian regimes, but Americans did not. We were fit for self-rule, government by discussion. We had internalized those checks upon will and appetite that Burke spoke of.

But did the "Great Experiment" mean—as so many modern spokesmen for a secular understanding of life tell us—that the influence of the Christian religious convictions of the American people were to be denied a role in the formation of law and social policy? Quite the contrary, I insist. The record is clear. There were, it is true, certain influential Americans of a Jacobin stripe at the time of the Constitutional Convention interested in a new "religion of humanity." But they were a decided minority. Well over 90 percent of eighteenth-century Americans were members of church congregations which by today's standards would be considered fundamentalist and orthodox. They never would have consented to a constitution meant to make their society less conducive to a Christian way of life. In fact, it would not be an overstatement to say that the Constitution was designed to grant the early American Christian sects *increased* freedom to proceed unmolested with the task of forming the moral consensus—those inner moral checks without which a free society cannot remain a good society. We would be a virtuous society—and a Christian society since eighteenth-century American notions of virtue were Christian in origin—without "saying it" in our Constitution.

Rather than *telling* our people, as did Old Regime autocrats, in the highest law of the land *what* their historical identity ought to be, we would trust them with the task of forming "a more perfect union." Since they were a "virtuous people" what could go wrong? A republican system of government would not threaten Christian values. It would preserve them at least as well as any European king and his lords and cardinals. Righteous folk needed no ruling class of moral guardians.

Yet almost immediately a problem developed. The agreement not to publicly define ourselves as a Christian people, or to speak in law at all of a conceded national moral character, led American intellectuals and policymakers to argue as if the key political questions centered on the *methods* of government rather than on the ends. The great national debates proceeded as if the techniques of government—the process, the *how*—were the central questions for men of intelligence and good will. Questions of states' rights, federalism, strict or loose constructionism, etc., became the burning issues. Politicians, academicians, and journalists argued for the system which would be most likely to give directive power to people with views similar to their own or views that they considered the most high-minded.

But the point is that the arguments were developed as if the *system* were the primary concern. Indeed, listening to the debates one can quite easily get the impression that the participants were genuinely surprised at the *coincidence* that the approach to good government that they favored would result in their views gaining ascendancy. Hamilton wants an increase in the power of the federal government; Jefferson wants states' rights. In 1810, in the face of the embargo, New England shipping states argued the justice of states' rights and secession; the South disagrees. Thoreau talks of the legitimacy of civil disobedience in protest against slavery; J.C. Calhoun calls for "concurrent majorities" in the face of a developing national antislavery sentiment.

Yet think of what happens when the "outs" become the "ins." It is as if a collective amnesia settles over the land. That, or a stunning degree of disingenuousness. The states' righters become the centralizers; the loose constructionists warn that "power corrupts." Jefferson boldly assumes new federal powers to complete the Louisiana Purchase. The New England shipping states and the southern slaveholding states reverse their positions in the years before the Civil War. Arthur Schlesinger, the favorite mandarin of the Kennedy Camelot, begins writing of the dangers of the "Imperial Presidency" during the Nixon years. And it must be stressed, the new positions are defended with the same stance as the old. It is not that central power becomes trustworthy when the right people with the right views hold it, or is to be feared when there are scoundrels in office. No, the debate still centers on the mechanics of government. It is not *what* decisions our society makes, but *how* it makes them—that is the primary concern. We go on, as T.S. Eliot phrased it, trying "to escape the darkness without and within" by "dreaming of systems so perfect that no one will need to be good."

And what is so bad about that? Perhaps nothing in and of itself. But the fact is that Americans have allowed themselves to be taken from the original point—where the agreement was not to officially define our society *in law* as a Christian, or even a God-centered, society—to the situation of today: where Supreme Court decisions and ACLU court actions invalidate societal practices that give "aid and comfort" to a Christian lifestyle. Where the original constitutional "deal" called upon America's Christians to use their moral judgments when making law and social policy—as long as they did so in a republican manner and not through ecclesiastical mandate—Americans today are taught to view their moral convictions as unacceptable determinants of the way they vote; that is, if those convictions were shaped in a church congregation, and if those convictions do not happen to coincide with reigning secular liberal notions of social justice. I am sure you have noticed: A religious zeal for Cesar Chavez's union or against the war in Vietnam is one thing; the same for school prayer or against abortion is quite another.

American society, in other words, has found itself becoming increasingly "de-Christianized." The lack of Christian resistance to this turn of events forces one to reconsider the wisdom of the God-centered political order of Europe's Old Regime. Like it or not, the thought arises: Perhaps the scars of Original Sin are too deep for a society to remain virtuous and Christian without its members being constantly reminded of that responsibility in precise language in the law of the land. We must insert Burke's reminders at the heart of American political debate in the coming years. He was self-evidently correct. Societies cannot survive without checks upon will and appetite. Christianity was meant in the original scheme of things to provide the *inner* checks that would allow our republican system of government to function—a government with a minimum of checks from *without*. If the modern secular liberal understanding of the role of religious convictions in our society supplants the older understanding, we will have none of those inner disciplines. Checks from without will become necessary to give a sense of mission and purpose to our society. Who will provide those disciplines? Marxists are singing a siren's song. (The Cubans know why *they* went to Africa.) Other varieties of totalitarianism have made an appearance in this century in Europe. One would think the attractive alternative for Americans would be a revivification of the Christian consensus our Founding Fathers depended upon when they argued against the systems of the Old World autocrats; a freeing up of American Christians from the ACLU understanding of the separation of church and state.

There have been many moments in our country's history when this stress on the *how* of political life can be seen taking precedence over the *what*. Nine of the most noteworthy and instructive follow. Let us examine them once again, this time for the purpose of confronting the curious denaturing of society that results.

I

The First Amendment—Then and Now

If it is true that the Founding Fathers expected the American people to enact public policy reflective of their religious convictions—as long as there was no state-church as such—why has it become so questionable, so "undemocratic," a practice in our time? Why were not Americans before the last half century aware of that "wall of separation" between church and state that must be kept "high and impenetrable," in the Supreme Court's words? Why were not laws prohibiting abortions, pornography, and gay rights *always* understood to be an illegitimate imposition of religious belief, in clear violation of the First Amendment guarantees of religious liberty?

To be blunt, is the ACLU mentality in any way faithful to the spirit of the First Amendment? Or is its modern prevalence the result of a remarkably successful con job, a con job which has resulted in what, quite frankly, could be called a "secularist coup," a cunning de-Christianizing of America? Were the American intellectuals who issued the Humanist Manifesto in 1933—John Dewey was one—and the Humanist Manifest II in 1973 calling for an understanding of our social order in line with the intentions of the Founding Fathers when they openly proclaimed their determination to "free" men's minds from the influence of revealed religions which hold to a belief in a personal

God and a divinely-ordained code of conduct binding on human choice and behavior?

It is a crucial question. If the religious beliefs of the American people are to be permitted no meaningful role in the formation of law and public policy, the authors of the two *Humanist Manifestoes* find the way cleared for their efforts to weaken the Christian inner disciplines which allow the American constitutional order to go on without the need for Burke's "checks upon will and appetite . . . from without." This in a time when Marxist disciplines from without are singing that siren's song. (Are the secularizers in America aware of the possible nexus? Certainly one must imagine the Marxists to be. Probably many liberals are not.) Orthodox Christians and Jews are disarmed, left convinced that "good Americans" do not "impose" religious convictions on their fellow citizens; convinced the only serious political questions that good Americans can ask center on the machinery of politics (the *how*), while the enemies of traditional religion are left free to push ahead in pursuit of a political enactment of their ideological convictions. The realization of their social aims (the *what*), since they are "secular," is a laudable political objective. Thus we find it permissible for Christians, as Christians, with the active leadership of their priests and ministers, to mobilize against the war in Vietnam, to save the whales or the redwoods, to ban nuclear weapons, in support of a Cesar Chavez lettuce boycott (since the secular liberals seek these goals too); but, we are told, they are in violation of the First Amendment when they organize to stop abortion, close down a massage parlor on the same street with the local grade school, seek to deny tenure to a self-professed Marxist professor at the state college, or seek tax relief for church-related schools.

Is such a secularization of American life what the First Amendment was designed to accomplish? The record is clear. Nothing of the sort was intended.* In fact, as we shall see, the First Amendment was designed to promote not so much a freedom *of* religion as a freedom *for* religion. Indeed, it was meant to "free up" the Protestant denominations of the original thirteen states, to allow them to work unmolested and energetically at

---

* It is possible, it is true, to find indications in the writings of certain prominent early Americans—Thomas Paine and Benjamin Franklin, for example—of a Jacobin mentality, of a preference for a new "religion of humanity" to replace the ancient faith. But it would be wrong to picture such views as in any way representative of an early American consensus either in society at large or at the Constitutional Convention.

the task of Christianizing American life—at providing the inner disciplines which would allow the constitutional order to function. The Founding Fathers understood the Christian religion—at the very least the natural virtues and inner restraints it encouraged—to be necessary for the well-being of any government by discussion in North America.

Perhaps we should be a bit more stingy with our superlatives. They, at any rate, were less in error than the modern secularizers on this point. Perhaps as a result of man's fallen nature (the scars of Original Sin, as they used to say in less enlightened days), societies require more than a Constitution that *allows* religious authority to operate freely. Perhaps a reminder of man's contingent nature is needed in the highest law of the land to keep a people God-centered and good; perhaps there is a good deal more to the medieval synthesis than Americans would like to admit. Perhaps the ease with which the modern secularizers have twisted the meaning of the First Amendment into an anti-Christian mandate should lead Americans to a more critical view of the wording of the First Amendment and the philosophical outlook it represents. Perhaps the framers should have foreseen how that wording, lacking as it does a mention of God, could be manipulated. And perhaps, then, we can charge that they should have developed a Constitution more clearly God-centered if they were genuinely concerned with securing America's Christian roots. Perhaps they were too intellectually indebted to the Enlightenment. Perhaps Americans should become willing to think that thought in our time.

On the other hand, it could be that we should blame ourselves more. One cannot help but wonder if a Constitution written by the leaders of the Spanish Inquisition could have stopped the growth of the secularist counterculture permissiveness in America in the late 1960s and 1970s. Blaming our current plight on the absence of certain words in our Constitution would appear to be just what Eliot meant by "dreaming of systems so perfect that no one will need to be good."

The City on a Hill

The historical record is clear (so clear that one wonders how liberalizing scholars can pretend otherwise): American society in the late 1700s would have no part of legislation effected to de-Christianize society. That is not why they revolted from England. On one level the point can be made with remarkable ease; i.e., why did not the framers, at the behest of the urgent masses, lash out at the laws against public lewdness, fornication, blasphemy, etc., so common in the original thirteen states—laws clearly based on the religious teachings of the early American Christian churches?

Of course, such an approach is unsatisfactory—ineffective anyway—in the final analysis, since the secularizers argue that they are seeking to apply the wisdom of the Founding Fathers to situations that had not arisen during their lifetimes; that those who ratified the Constitution would agree, if they could be brought back to life, that their political theory is best expressed in our time by people who view American life with an ACLU mentality.

To counter such a charge, the first thing that must be understood is that Americans in the century before the ratification of the Constitution did not draw up their colonial charters and constitutions or write and speak in such a way as to imply that they wanted societies thoroughly Christian. No sir, they "implied" no such thing. They said it, pronounced it, wrote it down on paper in black and white; explicitly, incontrovertibly, period, plain, flat-out. If one wishes to impute a secularizing intention to the Constitutional Fathers in 1787–1788, one is obliged not only to show where they displayed such intent, but also why they desired such a radical departure from the societal traditions of their people up until that time.

To make the point let us begin at the beginning: the original Jamestown and Plymouth settlements. In both cases the colonists made explicit that they saw themselves as engaged in a specifically Christian task: the establishment of a community of believers where, above all else, the social order was to be constructed to improve upon the European record of helping men do God's work on earth, and to save their souls.

In the case of the Pilgrims at Plymouth, their departure from England was occasioned directly by their dissatisfaction with the religious and moral atmosphere which prevailed in England as a result of the Church of England's influence as the established church. Our schoolbooks and Thanksgiving mythology may lead us to believe that the Pilgrims left in protest over the lack of "freedom of worship" and "freedom of conscience," and that they sailed to America to establish a society where such religious orthodoxy would have no place; but nothing is further from the truth. They did not resent the "legislation of morality"; they resented the legislation of morality by a church they felt corrupt and insufficiently reformed. If their understanding of the Christian dispensation had been guiding the Stuart kings rather than an excessively "popish" one, they would have had no problem at all with the union of church and state. They underscored that point in the Mayflower Compact itself, a political covenant formed, they tell us, "in the presence of God" in order to launch a colony "in the name of God," a colony that would exalt "the Glory of God" and work for the "advancement of the Christian Faith." In fact, they continued to identify themselves as a community of subjects of a king who was "Defender of the Faith."[1]

How then have the secularizers been able to make the Pilgrims part of their tradition? Usually, by ignoring what the Mayflower Compact actually says. When they are confronted with the text, some interesting verbal gymnastics become the order of the day. Note the twists employed in *The Mayflower Compact: The First Democratic Document in America* by John E. Walsh. Now, admittedly, the author of this little book had no intention of writing a scholarly treatise. His goal was to write a short and easily read book, suitable even for high school students. But the basic language he employs only makes his dilemma more obvious. You can sense the rising discomfort as he attempts to squeeze the Pilgrim's frame of mind into the framework of accepted secular liberal thinking, lest young folks lose their respect for the Thanksgiving tradition. No doubt he believes himself to be engaged in a patriotic act. But he does admit to the problem.

> It is true that the exercise of these restrictions [legislated morality and an established church] was not prohibited by the document and, in framing of later laws, the restrictions did make an appearance under various guises. But such restrictions, now of course recognized as undemocratic, were part of the common belief of those times, and their employment at Plymouth was probably inevitable. The compact, by not dignifying them, however,[!] left men's minds and spirits free to respond to deepening insight and the pressures of change.[2]

Follow? The Pilgrims unknowingly have written a legal document, which is a significant move away from the kind of society they wanted for themselves; but they were not precise enough to write a charter that could not be reinterpreted, and for that they deserve our praise.

Behind the words they set down in the compact lay certain age-old beliefs about the limits of individual freedom—very much narrower than we enjoy today—that continued to guide them in the government of the colony. Only gradually did these ancient ideas give way before the concept of full and equal rights for all, the essence of democracy. America today is a vision of freedom that coalesced out of the dreams and desires of a great diversity of peoples. For the Pilgrims, it is enough to say that they were among the first to nurture that vision, to enlarge its meaning, and to spread its influence over a good part of the country.[3]

It is not easy to surmise whether by this logic the first settlers in Virginia deserve to be praised as well. In their charter they state that their colony was founded to further "the true word and service of God," and that in their societal life, the Gospel should be "preached, planted, and used" openly and enthusiastically "according to the doctrine, rites, and religion now professed and established within our realm of England."[4]

The settlers in the Massachusetts Bay colony, on the other hand, apparently went too far overboard when they stated in their charter that "wholesome laws" are necessary since the "sins of men are like raging sea, which would overwhelm all if they have not banks."[5] That probably is a bit too Old Regime in mentality to be made into another secularist milestone.

The evidence is too conclusive, it seems, that the settlers of the Bay Colony were intent upon something fundamentally at odds with the secularist vision of a good society for comparably imaginative revisionism; which is why the Bay Colony has been made part of a different myth—the gloomy, narrow-minded, witch-hunting Puritans gathered round the pillory. (In Arthur Miller's *The Crucible*, the witch-hunters serve as prototypes of 1950's McCarthyites.) There were just too many Cotton Mathers on the record, men who informed us that there could be no "better or nobler work, and more worthy of a Christian . . . than to erect and support a reformed particular Church in its infancy"; and that the Puritans certainly "did not separate from the Church of England, nor from the ordinances of God there, but only from the corruptions and disorders of that Church."[6] Mather became explicit about how this Christian mission was to be carried out. He spoke with favor of John Cotton.

> Mr. Cotton effectually recommended it unto them that none should be electors, nor elected therein, except as were visible subjects of our Lord Jesus Christ, personally confederated in our churches. In these, and many other ways, he proposed unto them an endeavor after a theocracy.

Mather quotes Cotton: "Democracy I do not conceive that God did ever ordain as a fit government for either Church or commonwealth."[7]

Why then leave England, we might ask? Once again, as with the Pilgrims, the goal was not a less Christian society, but a purer Christian society—one free from what the Puritans felt were the corruptions of the established Church of England: "We came hither because we would have our posterity settled under the pure and full dispensations of the gospel; defended by rulers that should be ourselves."[8]

Not that they were suggesting that *everyone* was entitled to go off and form a society based on his own interpretation of the Scriptures. The Puritans held themselves uniquely qualified for this momentous task. *They* could, in community, without kings and lords, arrive at fit standards for a virtuous society, because of the depth of their inner Christian disciplines.

> The ministers and Christians, by whom New England was first planted, were a chosen company of men, picked out of, perhaps, all the counties of England, and this by no human contrivance, but by a strange work of God upon the spirits of men that were, no ways, acquainted with one another, inspiring them as one man, to secede into a wilderness, they knew not where.[9]

This is what the Bay Colony Puritans meant when they talked of their colony as the "city upon the hill"—a people who would show to the world the splendor of a society of God-fearing men organizing their lives in line with Scripture without the guidance of Old Regime authorities. As William Slaughter, another Bay Colony preacher, phrased it: "God hath sifted a nation, that he might send choice grain into this wilderness."[10]

Comparable sentiments abound in the sermons and chronicles of the colony.

Uriah Oakes: Religious freedom is the "first born of all Abominations."[11]

Increase Mather: He rebukes the "hideous clamours for liberty of conscience."[12]

John Norton: Liberty of worship is the liberty "to answer the dictates of the errors of Conscience in walking contrary to Rule. It is a liberty to blaspheme, a liberty to seduce others from the true God. A liberty to tell lies in the name of the Lord."[13]

And Nathaniel Ward: "All Familists, Antinomians, Anabaptists, and other Enthusiasts shall have free liberty to keep away from us."[14]

Similar understandings of the purposes of civilized society can be found in the other colonies. *The Fundamental Orders of Connecticut* (1639) for example, is usually treated in our history books as a glorious advance in the direction of liberal democracy, since the colonials who separated from Massachusetts to form their own colony argued that the foundation of political authority lay in "the free consent of the people." True enough. But the textbooks seldom go beyond that phrase to tell us what those people were expected to do with those liberties, which was

> to maintain and preserve the liberty and purity of the gospel of our Lord Jesus which we now profess, as also the discipline of the Churches, which according to the truth of said gospel is now practiced amongst us.[15]

One early Virginian began his history of the colony with Adam and Eve "to show how God had so managed the past that English colonization in the present was the fulfillment of his plan."[16]

Even William Penn, the archetypal freethinker we are told, described his Quaker colony as a "holy experiment."[17]

And Roger Williams . . . Roger Williams. We know the official line. His picture is always right there in the modern "social studies" texts, plodding on through the snow seeking a refuge from religious zealots, a land where men could worship and think and read as they saw fit. Perhaps there will be a picture next to him of Pete Seeger at a protest march, along with a For Class Discussion section: "The question of freedom of expression has had a long and bumpy history in America. Can you and your classmates see any similarities between your parents' reactions to certain books and movies and spokespersons for viewpoints different from their own and the Puritan magistrates who drove Roger Williams from Massachusetts?" Yes, Roger Williams.

Vernon Parrington has no doubts about the meaning of his crusade.

> A child of light, he came bringing not peace but the sword. A humane and liberal spirit, he was groping for a social order more generous than any theocracy—that should satisfy the aspirations of man for a catholic fellowship, greater than sect or church, village or nation, embracing all races and creeds, bringing together the sundred societies of man in a common spirit of good will.[18]

Parrington assures us Williams was a "Christian freethinker" who "sought to adjust his social program to the determining fact that human worth knows neither Jew nor Gentile, rank nor caste; and following the example of his Master he went forth into a hostile world seeking to make it over."[19]

It sounds as if Parrington were writing the inscription for a statue to be installed in the lobby of the League of Nations headquarters in Geneva. And such a description could not be farther from the truth.

It would be more accurate to picture Williams as a latter-day Pilgrim, fleeing from the religious orthodoxy he felt corrupt in Massachusetts for the purpose of establishing a new Plymouth in Rhode Island, where the Christian faith could be lived in a purer and more energetic form. He objected not to the infusion of Christian values into the life of the colony, but to the Massachusetts magistrates' claim that they were accurate interpreters of God's will. Society would be *more* Christian, Williams argued, when such magisterial claims are ignored, and, instead, Christian people, in their Christian communities, reach for and live by God's will unobstructed by the dictates of civil authority.

Now, unquestionably, this is a step away from the theocratic political structure of the Massachusetts Bay colony, but a step in the direction of outlawing prayer in the schools—a judicially demanded de-Christianizing—only to the extent that Madison Avenue is closer to Beirut than Fifth. We have no necessary or logical devolution to deal with. Williams desires a Christian society, but is convinced it can be more effectively realized without an established church. *But* he believes this because he takes for granted that the people likely to inhabit his Rhode Island will possess already formed Christian consciences, Christian inner disciplines, Burke's unbought graces. Good Christians, he argues, do not have to be told by a state authority how to be good Christians. Indeed, civil authority will be likely to distort the Christianizing impulse which will be put into effect by the Christian people in society. The government can be neutral about the religious identity of society, because the people will *not*. As long as the government does not interfere, a Christianity acceptable to Williams—one with denominational differences but orthodox on the fundamentals of the faith—will shape society.

To follow Williams' logic here it is necessary to keep in mind the differences between "state" and "society"—a difference sometimes blurred in political discussions. "State," remember, is the governmental apparatus organized *by* a society to serve certain basic and necessary, but nevertheless limited, functions. "Society" comprises all the other associations and organizations through which a people organizes its life—from the family, churches, religious groups, unions, professional and trade associations to clubs, fraternities, youth groups, etc. Williams is confident that the Christian presence in these subsidiary groups will be sufficient to shape society along Christian lines. Moreover, he is confident that the men elected by a Christian people will make policy at the state level corroborative of the Christian faith without any one Christian sect directing the legislative process through an official church-state relationship.

In his *Bloudy Tenent of Persecution* (1644), Williams' analysis of the ideal relationship between the churches and civil authorities, the point is made clear. Christians in government, as citizens, have no obligation to leave their convictions at home once they check in at the statehouse.

> The churches, as churches, have no power, though as members of the commonwealth they may have power, of erecting or altering forms of civil government, electing civil officers, inflicting civil punishments; . . . members of churches, who are public officers, also of the civil state, may suppress by force the violence of usurpers, as Jehoiada did Athaliah [for being soft on Baal, says the Bible], yet this they do not as members of the church, but as officers of the civil state.[20]

The point is confirmed by a careful reading of the charter for the new colony of Rhode Island hammered out by Williams' collaborator, John Clarke, while in England:

> And whereas . . . a most flourishing civil state may stand and best be maintained . . . with a full liberty in religious concernments; and that true piety *rightly grounded upon gospel principles* will give the best and greatest security to sovereignty, and will lay in the hearts of men the strongest obligations to true loyalty: Now know ye . . . that no person within the said colony at any time hereafter shall be in any wise molested, punished, disquieted, or call [ed] in question, for any differences of opinion in matters *of religion* [Emphasis added.][21]

The modern champions of freedom of expression read such documents with ideological blinders. After reading the above, for example, it is highly probable that the only words they will remember for their analyses of Williams' thought will be "full liberty" in the first paragraph and "differences of opinion" in the second. The rest, apparently, is to be understood as some kind of early American verbal panache.

But it is not. Williams' Rhode Island offers full liberty in *religious* concernments—not irreligious or antireligious—to those with a "true piety rightly grounded upon gospel principles." *Such* folk will not be "molested, punished," etc. for differences of opinion in "matters of religion." Put simply, Williams is doing no more than assuring the different Christian sects of colonial America a freedom to worship in the congregation of their choice if they take up residence in Rhode Island, although he did have some second thoughts about the Quakers. Their "inner light" seemed a less than reliable check upon will and appetite, too prone to self-indulgence. The modern liberals view the anti-Quaker writings of Williams as a product of his old age and approaching senility—as an aberration. Yet, taken in context, they would seem to be nothing of the sort. One suspects that Williams would turn green at a meeting of the Americans for Separation of Church and State or the ACLU; or perhaps he would start—Jehoiada-like—honing his sword.

Thomas Jefferson would very likely react comparably. His analysis of the proper role of organized religion in American life comes close to that of Williams. He too deplored the theocratic model of the Bay Colony: "They [later settlers] cast their eyes on these new countries as asylums of civil and religious freedom; but they found them free only for the reigning sect."[22]

So he wanted no state-church; of that there is no doubt. But the freedom he wanted was one he felt would make society more correctly moral. There is no trace of the moral relativism so often found in those who claim to wear Jefferson's mantle today.

> Reason and free inquiry are the only effectual agents against error. Give a loose to them, they will support the true religion, by bringing every false one to their tribunal. . . . It is error alone which needs the support of government. Truth can stand by itself. . . . Difference of opinion is advantageous in religion. The several *sects* [emphasis added—"sects," not atheist factions] perform the office of a *Censor morum* over each other. . . . If a sect arises whose tenets would subvert morals, good sense has fair play and reasons and laughs it out of doors without suffering the state to be troubled with it.[23]

It is not, then, a dissolution of the moral consensus that he seeks, a veneration of the moral autonomy of the individual. His concern is with the "churchgoers" of his time, as we might put it. He wants no established church so that they can practice their religion, their Christian religion. "Freedom of religion" is beneficial since it allows the Christian Jefferson knew "the comfortable liberty of giving his contributions to the particular pastor whose morals he would make his pattern." And it is not just preferable in human terms. "Whereas Almighty God hath created the mind free; that all attempts to influence it by temporal punishments or burthens . . . are a departure from the plan of the Holy author of our religion."[24]

Denominationalism

For a variety of reasons,* by the time of the Constitutional Convention, Roger Williams' approach to the relationship between church and state emerged triumphant over the older theocratic view. For some it was not a thorough conversion, however. That is to say, there were those in the late 1700s who desired to retain their established churches on the state level. They agreed that it would be unwise for the new national government to establish any one of the sects as an established church for the entire union, but they saw nothing wrong with allowing the separate states to go on with one sect or the other enjoying a privileged position. Indeed, in some states, in New England especially, established churches were maintained into the second quarter of the nineteenth century. The Constitution did *not* forbid such a practice. In fact, some have argued that the framers not only tolerated but expected and even wanted such a relationship to continue on the state level. But this might be carrying things a bit too far. There does appear to have been a new mood in the wind by the time of the Constitutional Convention.

One element in that mood, admittedly, was a religious indifference far more pronounced in the late eighteenth century than in Cotton Mather's time. The Enlightenment was having its effect in the New World. Benjamin Franklin had absorbed much of the prejudice. While close to his death he still could say:

As to Jesus of Nazareth . . . I have . . . some doubts as to his Di-

---

* Willmoore Kendall and George Carey's *Basic Symbols of the American Political Tradition* offers a penetrating analysis of the key documents in the evolution of the American perception of the relationship between religious authority and the political institutions established in the Constitution. It is a book that no reader concerned with acquiring a clear understanding of these issues can afford to ignore. Moreover, it is a good "read."

vinity, that it is a question I do not dogmatize upon, having never studied it, and I think it needless to busy myself with it now when I expect soon an opportunity of knowing the truth with less trouble. I see no harm, however, in its being believed, if that belief has the good consequence . . . of making his doctrines more respected and better observed.[25]

Of course, such dispositions were present too in Cotton Mather's time. Mather used to tell a story of a well-known Massachusetts resident who was being exhorted by his minister to live a life more in tune with the religious motives of the colony. He is said to have answered, "Sir, you are mistaken; you think you are preaching to the people at the Bay; our main end was to catch fish."[26]

Such feelings were more commonplace in Franklin's time, but to think Franklin's agnosticism the order of the day in the late eighteenth century in America is an error. The church membership figures according to a 1775 poll are as follows:

- 98.4 percent Protestant (with Congregationalists, Presbyterians and Anglicans the most numerous)
- 1.4 percent Roman Catholic
- ¾ percent Jews[27]

That does not leave room for many nonbelievers. We must not forget how culturally homogeneous were the Americans of the original thirteen states in the late eighteenth century. In fact 70 percent of them were English, 15 percent Scottish or Scotch-Irish.[28]

It is most unlikely that such a population would permit a First Amendment to be passed designed to make it more *difficult* to live as Christians. (Which a liberalized society festooned with porn palaces and junkies does. The secularizers, who argue that the availability of their favored pleasures does not interfere with a serious Christian or Jew practicing his religion as he sees fit, have no idea what "living a faith" means; no idea that religion is not just a one-hour Sabbath experience.)

But why then the no-establishment clause?

The answer is remarkably obvious, but, as with many obvious things, only after it has been seen once—like finding the six elves in the garden in the picture in the Sunday funnies.

The no-establishment clause was the Founding Fathers' attempt to avoid the near-certain sectarian strife that would result if any one of the Protestant churches in America was given the opportunity to become an established church on the national level the way the Congregationalists had on a state level in Massachusetts and the Episcopalians had in Virginia. The memories of the religious wars in Europe were still alive—especially the tremendous seventeenth-century upheaval in England, as Puritan battled Anglican for dominance. The Founding Fathers were determined to avoid the specter of Episcopalian and Presbyterian engaging similarly in America. They would close the door to that *ab initio*. The different sects were not to be permitted even the temptation of seeking establishment status on a national level. If they already enjoyed a privileged position on a state level, they would not be threatened with a disestablishment. But they were to be assured unequivocally that the country was not open to a national church.

The impression ought not be given, however, that such a constitutional provision had to be forced on America's Protestants. The something new in the wind included the growing acceptance of *denominationalism*.

As the name implies, denominationalism was the conviction among Protestants, especially American Protestants, that there was no need for the Protestant sects to demonstrate the universal validity of their established vision of the Christian faith and to attempt to secure status to complete that task. It was an indifferentism of a sort, but only in respect to the known and "respectable" variants of Protestantism in the thirteen colonies. Prof. Winthrop S. Hudson, a man who has done much work on the history of America's religious groups, phrases it well.

> The basic contention of the denominational theory of the Church is that the true Church is not to be identified exclusively with any single ecclesiastical structure. . . . No denomination claims that all other churches are false churches. Each denomination is regarded as constituting a different "mode" of expressing outward forms of worship and organization of that larger life of the Church in which they all share. The denominational theory of the Church was well adapted to the situation in which the Protestants of colonial America found themselves as they moved into the eighteenth century. . . . The great need was for the various churches to co-operate with one another, in freedom and mutual respect, in the great task of reducing the rest of society to Christian obedience. The Reformers, as a whole, were willing to recognize as true churches all churches that possessed an essentially evangelical faith.[29]

George Whitefield, a colonial revivalist preaching in Philadelphia, gives us an earlier version:

Father Abraham, whom have you in heaven? Any Episcopalians? No! Any Presbyterians? No! Any Independents or Methodists? No, no, no! Whom have you there? We don't know those names here. All who are here are Christians. . . . Oh, is this the case? Then God help us to forget party names and to become Christian in deed and truth.[30]

But, it bears repeating for emphasis, the tolerated diversity is of known Christian sects. John Burroughes, a Puritan leader in England who shared this new "liberalism," made the point: "Our divisions have been and still are between good men . . . there are as many godly Presbyterians as Independents."[31] Not the widest of poles.

In 1771, the Virginia House of Burgesses indicated the growing acceptance of denominationalism and the mutually corroborative fear of sectarian strife, when it voted against the "expediency of an American Episcopate."[32] A member, explaining his vote, said that a "religious dispute is the most fierce and destructive of all others to the peace and happiness of government. . . . I profess myself a sincere son of the established church, but I can embrace her doctrines without approving of her hierarchy."[33]

To such views, certainly, must be added the anti-Catholic animus of the time. Protestant leaders seemed to have become aware of how similar was their call for an established position for their sect to the Roman Catholic definition of a sacral political order. When the British Parliament in 1774 decided to allow freedom of religion for the Roman Catholics in Canada, as well as a continuation of the French policy of providing a state collection of tithes for the churches, there was a considerable uproar south of the Finger Lakes—Protestant fears of things to come.

The Pennsylvania Packet: "The city of Philadelphia may yet experience the carnage of St. Bartholomew's Day."[34]

William Henry Drayton, a South Carolina judge, warned of the encroaching "tyranny under which all Europe groaned for many ages."[35]

The legislature of Suffolk County, Massachusetts, formally resolved that the act is "dangerous in an extreme degree to the Protestant religion."[36]

The Continental Congress on October 21, 1774, proclaimed: "We think the Legislature of Great Britain is not authorized by the English Constitution to establish a religion, fraught with sanguinary and impious tenets . . . a religion that has deluged

[England] in blood, and dispersed bigotry, persecution, murder and rebellion through every part of the world."[37]

This is the atmosphere which must be kept in mind when one examines the Constitutional Convention and the Framers' words: "Congress shall make no law respecting an establishment of religion, or prohibiting the free exercise thereof. . . ." The Founding Fathers were representative of their society, and their words must not be interpreted within another framework, especially the framework of the modern academic enclaves which are often out of touch with the society of their own time.

So while it may be excessive to infer—as some have done—that the words "no law respecting an establishment of religion" were meant to grant to the individual states a monopoly power to establish whatever religion they desired on the state level (at the most, they were willing to tolerate this practice), it is an even greater error to argue—as does the modern Supreme Court on those rare occasions when it deigns to seriously consider the Framers' intent rather than act with a Holmesian flair—that the First Amendment, in effect, forbids laws and public policies that "make life easier" for the Christian churches in America. That is not what "no law respecting the establishment of religion" means.

The opposite of the modern secularizers' scheme was the Framers' intent. Sectarian strife was to be avoided; the churches in the individual states were to be guaranteed freedom of operation, by the national government if not by the state; they were to be guaranteed that their work in society as a Christian leaven would be unmolested by the new central government. Americans had passed, the Framers believed, from the stage where "wholesome laws," as the Puritans used to say, promulgated by an established church were required to insure the survival of a righteous people, to a nation of converted individuals who would voluntarily live as a virtuous people. Christianizing life henceforth would be *society's* responsibility and no longer the *state's*.

The people of the time—while the debates over ratification were being waged—understood the issue at hand. A Baptist preacher, John Leland, wrote to George Washington as spokesman for the "General Committee of the Baptists of Virginia":

> When the Constitution made its appearance in Virginia, we as a society feared that the liberty of conscience, dearer to us than property or life, was not sufficiently secured . . . fearing that we should

be accessory to some religious oppression should any one society [read: sect] in the Union predominate over the rest. . . .[38]

Denominationalism, in other words, had to be vouchsafed to satisfy these Baptists' fears. No one sect was to be given an advantage over the others. (The logic still applies, by the way. It is safe to say that the resistance to state aid to parochial schools would be considerably less if there were a working system of Protestant-run schools ready to receive tax breaks.)

The point is, simply, that the Framers were seeking a Constitution which would permit a Christian people to form a successful union, one which would impede in no way their staying Christian. It would not help *remind* them to stay Christian it is true; (that could prove to be a fatal flaw, since that omission is what has opened the door to the anti-Christian secularizers). But there was *no* pressure applied by the Framers to reduce the influence of the Christian churches on society.

Perhaps the Framers' approach to matters such as this can be illustrated by examining another institution chartered at roughly the same time by men of approximately the same social class, education, and outlook. Brown University drew up its charter in 1764. Its founding fathers—Baptists—tried to deal with the question of "freedom of religion" too. They also tried to disestablish religion. They promised that "all the members hereof shall forever enjoy full, free, absolute and uninterrupted liberty of conscience." Just the kind of phrase the liberal secularizers pounce on and carve in stone to serve their ends, correct? What could be more plain? But the Brown charter goes on to make explicit much of what was unsaid in the Constitution.

> And that the places of Professors, Tutors, and all other officers, the President alone excepted, shall be free and open for all *denominations of Protestants:* And that the youth of all religious denominations shall and may be freely admitted to the equal advantages, emoluments, and honors of the College. . . . And that the *sectarian* differences of opinion shall not make any part of the public and classical instruction. [Emphasis added.][39]

I submit: This last sentence is near to identical in intention to the Founding Fathers' "no establishment" clause. They are saying that a Christian people—a Protestant people—can live and work together without any one sect, in public, attempting to carry the day in religious matters; without any one sect becoming "triumphalistic," as the urge is sometimes phrased, especially in relation to Roman Catholics. What of Jews, Moslems, Hindus, Buddhists? Were they to be excluded from the public life of the new nation? The Framers had no reason to deal with the question; they had no reason to forsee it becoming a matter of consequence. The number of non-Christians in eighteenth-century America was miniscule—less than 1 percent. They could be granted the same First Amendment guarantees without any fear that they would influence social policy to the detriment of the Christian consensus.

It is on this point, if it needs be said, that the Nativist brand of anti-Catholicism was launched. Catholics, who make the claim that their church is the "one, true Church," were looked on with disfavor and fear once their numbers increased in the waves of nineteenth-century immigration. American Protestants were convinced that Catholics would not "play by the rules" of denominationalism, that they would establish a state-church if they became a voting majority. And the doubts linger to this day, even though Vatican II's *Declaration of Religious Liberty* seems to have abandoned the demand for established status. (There are some Catholics who argue that the claim has not been relinquished, only reshaped.)

Perhaps one day Roman Catholics and American Protestants will have to deal with this question in a manner more serious than John Kennedy did, with his verbal sleight of hand in meeting with the Protestant ministers in Dallas while campaigning for the Presidency. But the point just now is that both Protestants and Catholics can take comfort from the fact that the Founding Fathers never intended that Christianity be forced from a central position in the life of the American people. The First Amendment has been fraudulently conscripted into that effort by twentieth-century secular humanists, probably fully aware of the level of deception involved. By wrapping their antireligion biases in the Constitution and the words of the Founding Fathers, and playing on the American respect for law (which, you will recall, was not as much a virtue in the same circles when the issue was resistance to the war in Vietnam), what might have been a determined and vigorous opposition to the de-Christianizing of the country was derailed. Imagine for a moment the reaction in the typical American city or town thirty years ago if Americans were told that—for some reason never known before—their Constitution demanded that they allow the kind of porn that sells now in the stationery stores next to the Donald Duck comics, the strutting vulgarity of the movie marquees, and the millions of aborted babies, while forbidding their children to pray, as they did for decades, at the start of the school day

It would be well for Americans to remember how different we have become—how much less Christian; how much religion has been driven from the center of our lives by the secularists. Rereading Al Smith's defense of his Roman Catholicism during the 1928 campaign for the Presidency—he was answering a *Harper's* article which alleged his religious ties to Rome would give him a divided loyalty—seems now like reading something scratched on a dusty parchment from a long-lost civilization. Smith's answer to the charge that he would bring his religious beliefs into the public arena? There was nothing to worry about, he assured his audience, the voters he was trying to woo. Sure, he had learned his morality in Catholic schools; sure, he took those teachings seriously, and they would *of course*, influence his actions as President. But,

> I am unable to understand how anything that I was taught to believe as a Catholic could possibly be in conflict with what is good citizenship. The essence of my faith is built upon the Commandments of God. The law of the land is built upon the Commandments of God. There can be no conflict between them.
>
> Instead of quarreling among ourselves over dogmatic principles, it would be infinitely better if we joined together in inculcating obedience to these Commandments in the hearts and minds of the youth of the country as the surest and best road to happiness on this earth and to peace in the world to come. This is the common ideal of all religions. What we need is more religion for our young people, not less; and the way to get more religion is to stop the bickering among our sects which can only have for its effect the creation of doubt in the minds of our youth as to whether or not it is necessary to pay attention to religion at all.

II

Hamilton v. Jefferson

There is an old saying: "Everyone is three people: the person he thinks he is, the person other people perceive him to be, and the person he really is." Whether there is much truth overall to the thought, the quip accurately describes the ideological quarrel between Thomas Jefferson and Alexander Hamilton. Proponents of modern causes make use of their words to champion changes that neither man would be likely to approve; and Jefferson and Hamilton themselves did consider the ground between them to be wider than it really was. Or, at any rate, that ground narrows as we look back on it from the vantage point of our modern moment in history. Certainly the political and social presumptions shared by Hamilton and Jefferson were more numerous and substantial than those shared by spokesmen at opposite ends of the spectrum in modern political debates. If Jeffersonian democracy is the antithesis of Hamiltonian, then there is need for a stronger word than that to describe the relationship between, say, McGovernite and Reaganite, or Minuteman and Weatherman.

Does this mean that the oft-expressed view that Hamilton and Jefferson represented conflicting and irreconcilable perceptions of the American republic is in error? To the extent that this view concentrates on the differences between their thought over *how* government ought to be constructed, at the expense of their shared understanding of *what kind* of society that government was to help build and preserve—yes. But let us take one step at a time.

First of all, it should be readily admitted that conventional wisdom pictures the positions of both men as poles apart, and that by and large, Jefferson comes out the better in the comparisons. Hamilton, we have been told, was the pro-British cynic, a would-be monarchist—archetypal Fascist even—the enemy of popular democracy, which he considered dangerously subject to the irresponsible whims of the masses, the masses he is said to have called "The Great Beast."* Jefferson, on the other hand, is championed as the man of the people, a Father of Democracy (of Jeffersonian democracy, to be exact), a good man with faith in human nature, uncynical, confident in the natural goodness of the common folk, and therefore willing to trust them with the responsibility for running their own government without the help of Old Regime kings and nobles and their priests, thank you.

Or, as Samuel Eliot Morison put it in his widely read *Oxford History of the American People:* "In their approach to life and its problems, these two typified Goethe's dichotomy: the spirit that creates and the spirit that denies, the hope that man is perfectible and the belief that he is irremediably stupid and evil."[1] This, mind you, not from some New Left revisionist, but from the kind of middle-of-the-road mantlepiece history that people buy for their grandchildren to provide a solid and stable source of information about our country.

Such descriptions of Hamilton's thought actually appeared early in our history. Jefferson himself, in one of his less temperate moments, asserted flatly that Hamilton was "not only a monarchist, but for a monarchy bottomed on corruption."[2]

Martin Van Buren was more analytical, and accurate, when he noted that Hamilton "produced a deep and settled conviction in the public mind, that a design had been conceived to change the government from its simple and republican form, to one, if not monarchical, at least too energetic for the temper of the American people."[3]

In the twentieth-century, spokesmen for political reform designed to check the increasing wealth and influence of the beneficiaries of American capitalism picked up the tempo, using Hamilton as a symbol of early wheeler-dealers in high places in government seeking to line their pockets through legislation favorable to big business. Vernon Parrington was just one of

---

*Actually, the source of the "Great Beast" quote is a third-hand account of an after-dinner conversation of Hamilton's.

many: "But no ethical gilding could quite conceal a certain ruthlessness of purpose [in Hamilton]; in practice justice became synonymous with expediency, and expediency was curiously like sheer Tory will to power." And in case the threat of Toryism did not elicit sufficient cause for alarm, Parrington (writing in the late 1920s with Fascism already established in Italy and Nazi ideology on its way in Germany) added: "His philosophy conducted logically to the leviathan state, highly centralized, coercive, efficient."[4]

Yet Parrington was not entirely condemnatory. He himself was eager in his time for the kind of reforms Franklin D. Roosevelt carried out in the New Deal, reforms conceived with what one would have to call a Hamiltonian understanding of the powers of the central government. The problem then with Hamilton, Parrington argues, was not that he called for an energetic application of the powers of the central government to the economy. It was how those powers were applied. Hamilton's "mind and his understanding of the economic forces that control American society" were correct, Parrington states. It was just that a "traditional Tory psychology" distorted his vision. It led him to the point where "Hamilton detested republicanism only a little less than democracy."[5] "For the common people, about whom Jefferson concerned himself with what seemed to Hamilton sheer demagoguery, he felt only contempt." Hamilton's roots clung to the wrong soil for enlightened thought. "The thinkers to whom he owed most seem to have been Hume, from whom he may have derived his cynical psychology, and Hobbes whose absolute state was so congenial to his temperament."[6]

Not all Progressive Era reformers were as harsh. Herbert Croly, for example, one of the most articulate and interesting early proponents of a managed economy, in his much-applauded *The Promise of American Life*, gave some reverse spin to the issue. Croly tells us that Hamilton was actually the first American thinker to understand clearly the full responsibilities of a modern government. He was "a sound thinker, the constructive statesman, the candid and honorable, if erring, gentleman" who sponsored a "vigorous, positive, constructive national policy . . . that implied a faith in the powers of an efficient government to advance the national interest."[7]

Croly's problem is obvious, of course. Jefferson, the champion of the little man, of popular democracy, called for a weak central government to free the people from the monied interests of his time. Hamilton, the protector of those monied interests (so the story goes), deemed a strong central government the most effective tool to further his cause. When Croly in the early twentieth-century came to view Hamilton's strong central government as the best hope for the lower classes, when he became convinced that the moneyman's method was needed to serve the little folk, the new industrial masses, the moneyman's reputation had to be rescued.

The Common Ground

How accurate are these and the other analyses of a similar character we have heard over the years? On the surface, quite accurate. It is true, after all, that Jefferson was the propounder of an early states'-rights position, in opposition to Hamilton's efforts to strengthen and make effective the new government established at the Constitutional Convention. In fact, their feud took shape precisely over the question of whether the Constitution should be ratified. Jefferson refused to support the Constitution until the Bill of Rights was included to limit the power of the newly created national government, which Hamilton wanted to enhance. Jefferson was an outspoken opponent of Hamilton's plan to establish a Bank of the United States. He opposed Hamilton's proposal that the central government assume the war debts incurred by the states during the Revolution, especially after learning of the plan to repay war bonds at face value, including those purchased from the original holders by big money speculators. Jefferson encouraged support for the government established in France after the overthrow of the Bourbon dynasty in its war against Hamilton's preferred England because of his ideological sympathies with its Jacobin fervor. And it is true that Jefferson wrote and spoke during the last years of the eighteenth and early nineteenth century specifically for the purpose of supplanting Hamilton's Federalist party with his party. All this is true.

In short, Jefferson's public life was devoted largely to a defense of his belief that a healthy society could be maintained without the need for an elite—whether hereditary aristocracy or Eastern monied interests—to hold the reins on popular opinion.

Likewise, it is correct that Hamilton believed republican sympathies of this sort dangerously naive. He did believe democracies unacceptably susceptible to demagoguery, and that checks against popular enthusiasms had to be instituted in the law of the land. Moreover, if an American version of the English House of Lords was required to accomplish that goal, Hamilton would not have batted an eyelash.

Nevertheless, as we proceed with an analysis of their conflicting political theories, it should become clear that Jefferson *concedes* Hamilton's critical point. He treats as legitimate the Hamiltonian fears for the fate of popular government. To be specific, he admits that democracy—in certain forms—is likely to degenerate into a most offensive state. Indeed, he assures those of a Hamiltonian bent that in a republican system—as he envisions it—the sort of citizenry Hamilton called a "Great Beast" (if indeed he did use just those words) would *not* come to hold directive control over society. Jefferson does not dismiss Hamilton's concern for the fate of the newly established republic if the uneducated urban masses and backwater roughnecks were to end up in a position where they could formulate public policy. Far from it. His pitch to those beset with such Hamiltonian anxiety aims at convincing them that a republic can be built without such people even *existing* in substantial numbers.

It is the Hamiltonian pessimism, then, that he deplores, not the determination to safeguard society against radical change. In fact, Jefferson's call for states' rights should be seen as conservative at the source. He was working to prevent ambitious Eastern financiers, Hamilton's people, from reconstructing, through their Federalist proposals, the way of life that obtained in the individual states after independence had been secured from England. Life in his Virginia, in other words, was more than satisfactory for Jefferson. He was no longer the revolutionary in search of a new political system. Not that he was opposed to change. He was for it, but for the kind of change that would be likely to develop within the structure of the established social order—a social order shaped by the moral beliefs of his fellow Virginians, a social order with private property rights firmly secured by custom and law. And he remained confident that this society would be *preserved* through a properly constructed republic, not overthrown.

Notice too, as we review Jefferson's words, that his case for freedom of expression does not at all resemble the one argued by many modern advocates of "free speech": the indifferentness of a "different strokes for different folks" view of life, where anything goes mainly because it is impossible to articulate the reasons why not.

Jefferson does not champion freedom of expression for its own sake, in other words. He does not encourage a wide diversity of opinions as an end in itself. He is not a relativist. All opinions are not of equal value. There is a God in his scheme of things, and criteria for good and evil established by Him in His creation—a natural law. (Although it is doubtful, to say the least, that moderns who demand the right to proselytize their beliefs under the banner of Jeffersonian "freedom of expression" would be willing to extend that right to dissenters if they were to achieve power. Certainly the Marxists would not. Maybe we have set up a straw man of sorts here.)

Faith in the Common Man?

Admittedly, at first glance, it does appear that Jefferson's words call for the kind of absolutist understanding of the notion of freedom of expression that one would find in an ACLU brief. Proposals for "moral guardians" offended him, even when proposed by a mind as revered as Plato's. *The Republic*, he tells us, filled him with "disgust," and he wondered why "the world should have so long consented to give reputation to such nonsense."[8]

He could find no reason for philosopher kings or other instruments of social control over and against the process of political debate in the newly formed republic. Philosopher kings were no more likely to uncover truth than Bourbon monarchs, and far less likely to do so than a free exchange of ideas in a democratic society, since "morality, compassion, generosity, are innate elements of the human constitution." No ruling elite is entitled to demand conformity to a preestablished moral or political order since "no one has a right to obstruct another exercising his faculties innocently for the relief of sensibilities made a part of his nature,"[9] kings and nobles and churchmen included. Jefferson chides: "Sometimes it is said that man cannot be trusted with the government of himself. Can he, then, be trusted with the government of others? Or have we found angels in the form of kings to govern him."[10] Obviously not, thinks Jefferson. "I do believe that if the Almighty has not decreed that man shall never be free (and it is a blasphemy to believe it), that the secret will be found in the making himself the depository of the powers respecting himself . . . and delegating only what is beyond his competence. . . ."[11]

When one considers Jefferson's position here there is a certain irony to the way some American Christians of a fundamentalist disposition have taken him to task for his Deist beliefs. Now, without question, Deist he was. His religious understandings left no room for miraculous, divine interventions in the life of the planet, including the divine intervention in the person of Christ.

But the Deist Watchmaker God as pictured by Jefferson does somehow (let us not get into the process here; it is an important question, but not for our purposes) incorporate into His universe standards of right and wrong. And He does grant to mankind the capacity to discern them. Jefferson's logic, consequently, does not at all lead to an "anything goes" society. Jefferson is on the side of the religious fundamentalists on this one. There is no sound reason to assume that Jefferson would be with the liberalizers on the questions of, say, pornography or "gay" rights or abortion. For him, the problem with the kings and Old Regime clergy was not their attempt to "legislate morality," as the saying goes, but their presumption that they were better equipped for that task than the average man, whose God-given "innate elements" of morality ought not be obstructed when used "innocently."

He becomes explicit. The people can be trusted to arrive at standards of justice and truth democratically. They will not allow a dissipation of the moral consensus upon which life in society depends. "Men may be trusted to govern themselves without a master. . . . Could the contrary of this be proved, I should conclude, either that there is no God, or that he is a malevolent being."[12] A Times Squaring of society is no danger then, not because there is nothing to fear from swingers doing their thing, but because democratic man, democratically, will not let moral rot work its way into the pores of society. It will not happen, he promises, not in his America.

Corruption and decay are not impossibilities, though. Societies have fallen in history. But "the mass of the citizens is the safest depository of their own rights . . . and the evils flowing from the duperies of the people, are less injurious than those from the egos of their agents."[13] Monarchy can deteriorate. So can republics, but not as easily. Their citizens will be *more* vigilant, not less concerned with maintaining public virtue.

An opinion then is neither correct nor constructive *merely* as a consequence of being expressed. For Jefferson, different drummers can have the wrong beat. But the collective opinion of the American people is more likely to find the correct cadence than the old aristocracy: "I know of no safe depository of the ultimate powers of society but the people themselves; and if we think them not enlightened enough to exercise their control with a wholesome discretion, the remedy is not to take it from them but to inform their discretion by education. . . ." And much to the point (and very Burkean to boot), "if a nation expects to be ignorant and free in a state of civilization, it expects what never was and never will be."[14] (*Who* will do the educating—who will act as moral guardians, and in pursuit of what norms, when Jefferson is opposed to elites—is a question Jefferson does not satisfactorily answer. We will return to this point shortly.)

The edges grow sharper. Jefferson does not call for freedom of expression for all men at all times in history. Only a certain breed of man is fit to be democratic man in his eyes. He was speaking of the citizens of the American states he knew, a people he felt to be able to preserve the laws of God without the need for any spiritual overlords; a people he knew to be God-fearing, church-going Christians in search of righteousness; a people capable of retaining a "state of civilization" while free. Other peoples did not make him as confident. They would be the ones more in need of having their "discretion" informed "by education." As long as that education was not carried out by pre-Enlightenment ruling classes, that is. While in Europe during his term as ambassador to France, he drove that point home when writing to a friend, George Wythe:

> If anybody thinks that kings, nobles, or priests are good conservators of the public happiness, send him here. It is the best school in the universe to cure him of that folly. [Here, where] a people . . . surrounded by so many blessings from nature are loaded with misery by kings, nobles, and priests, and by them alone.[15]

But, he assures us, the legitimate fears that a democracy might self-destruct into something less than a "state of civilization" do not apply to North America. The American people were worthy to participate in what was to be history's great experiment. They were in the process of disproving the Old Regime pessimism and its Hamiltonian American variations. They were capable of self-government. In his Inaugural Address of 1801, he stated the theme:

> I know indeed, that some honest men fear that a republican gov-

ernment can not be strong [by this, of course, Jefferson means able to preserve itself against anarchical forces], that this Government is not strong enough; but would the honest patriot, in the full tide of successful experiment, abandon a government which has so far kept us free and firm on the theoretic and visionary fear that this Government, the world's best hope, may by possibility want energy to preserve itself? I trust not.[16]

On another occasion: "But with all the imperfections of our present government, it is without comparison the best existing or that ever did exist."[17]

But Why?

At this point a modern American reader is likely to find himself with mixed emotions. Everyone likes to be flattered, and Jefferson certainly is flattering our forefathers and, by implication, us. Nearly two hundred years later, the American government-by-discussion he praised goes on, and remains comparatively sound. So he is calling us too the "world's best hope."

Yet there is a nagging suspicion that something is wrong, isn't there? Something incomplete, at any rate. Why, we ask, *why* were the American people Jefferson knew in his Virginia "like that" so exceptionally capable of faithfully articulating a healthy moral and political order, of discerning the will of the Creator?

If Jefferson champions political freedom in America because of his trust in his fellow Americans, what was it that equipped them for political decision-making so much better than kings and bishops and the like? Where did all that wisdom come from?

If Jefferson would find repugnant—as he would—life in a democratic society that was corrupt and riddled with "duperies," a society lacking a "state of civilization," why was such a devolution unlikely in Virginia? Remember, in Jefferson's words, a state "ignorant and free . . . never was and never will be." And ought not be. Such a society would be in need of the educating process required to "inform their discretion" (presumably conducted by moral guardians following Jeffersonian guidelines). Why were Americans beyond this point in their cultural development? What happened to them?

Jefferson does not say. Neither do the other highly praised men of the Enlightenment—the *philosophes*. And, curiously, they are seldom challenged for the lapse by their intellectual descendants in the modern world. They are permitted to treat as a *given* the felt moral consensus of the people of Europe and their American cousins; they are allowed to presume the presence in society of Rousseau's naturally good men, without examining or explaining the reasons for their existence. Are naturally good men like Topsy? If not, where *did* they come from? Why in Europe? Why not with the headhunters and Aztec practitioners of human sacrifice?

What Jefferson and the Enlightenment *philosophes* fail to seriously consider is the role played by the authoritarian regimes in Europe's history, from the medieval Age of Faith through the era of the powerful kings, in shaping the moral and political consensus they describe in the people of Europe. Instead, they proceed in their political analysis as if these self-disciplines are an *inborn* quality of some sort.

The fact is, however, that it took centuries of authoritarian rule—with the Christian churches enjoying a privileged position in the political order—before the moral precepts of the Christian faith became internalized in the people of Europe and their American cousins. Only after these centuries of forced unity was coercion no longer needed to insure "good Christian" behavior and a concern for one's fellow man. Only then did the rigorous, and often brutal, enforced disciplines of a Charlemagne, say, become unnecessary to guarantee the kind of social consciences a Jefferson or a Diderot relied upon in their libertarian schemes.

By the eighteenth century, it is true, the God-fearing attitudes and pious humanism of the Christian faith so filled the folklore, poetry, drama, and song of Europe and the colonies that intelligent men could easily imagine such values natural and *inborn*, instinctive, forgetting that their ancestors worshipped quite different gods and lived by quite different codes of honor. Thor's and Odin's, for example. Quite simply, it took centuries of moral persuasion to turn out a culture filled with what the *philosophes* thought were "naturally good" men.

Edmund Burke called these Christian beams in the infrastructure of European civilization the "unbought graces" of Europe's Christian past. His point was that men acquire the capacity for self-rule, when and if they do, the way they acquire the skills needed to play the piano or write a poem, not the way they do freckles or buck teeth. The inner restraints are taught and culturally transmitted, not inborn.

Why was Jefferson so intolerant then (yes, intolerant is the right word) of the Old Regime authorities when they would seem to be perfect examples of the societal agencies he called for in order "to inform the masses discretion by education" so as to prepare them for self-rule? Why does he talk instead as if freedom of expression would make men virtuous by itself, when, in fact, he should have understood that virtuous men are what make freedom of expression a desirable political goal?

The answer would seem to be obvious. He shared the anti-Catholic animus of the men who led the French Revolution. He would brook no ambivalence here. Mankind's full emancipation required the dissolution of the remains of the Christian view of man as taught by medieval church authorities. No tinge of legitimacy could be granted to the Old Regime institutions as the eighteenth-century Age of Revolution reached its climax. Whatever socially beneficial role the church played in Europe's development had to be treated as coincidental and minimal in comparison with the full flowering in store in a world molded by the *philosophes*.

It is hard to imagine what other calculations could lead a man to react as cavalierly as did Jefferson to the Reign of Terror, including the thought of the guillotine in operation. A protégé of his had written to him from France in horror over the atrocities being perpetrated there in the name of Jefferson's vision of a republican form of government. Jefferson replied:

> Many guilty persons fell without the forms of trial . . . and with them some innocent. These I deplore as much as anybody, and shall deplore some of them to the day of my death. But I deplore them as I should have done had they fallen in battle. It is necessary to use the arm of the people, a machine not quite so blind as balls and bombs but blind to a certain degree. . . . The liberty of the whole earth was depending on the issue of the contest and was ever such a prize won with so little innocent blood. . . . Were there but an Adam and Eve left in every country, and left free, it would be better . . . rather than should it have failed, I would have seen half the earth devastated.[18]

Quite a price to pay for the blessings of rule by Robespierre rather than that of a Christian king.

Faith in Which Common Man?

It was stated at the outset of this chapter that Hamilton and Jefferson were not as far apart as they are usually pictured. From

what has been said so far about Jefferson, that would not seem
to be the case. How much could Jefferson, defender of Robespierre, have in common with Hamilton (who whether he called
the American masses a "Great Beast" or not, certainly considered Robespierre and his cohorts less than fully human)? Not
much, one would think.

But there is more to the story. Deeper reading of Jefferson
reveals that he did believe that *certain* checks on raw human will
were required to preserve civilization. As long as they were not
those offered by the older European elites and their American
counterparts, obviously.

Jefferson felt there were more effective ways to control the
Great Beast that Hamilton feared. In fact, rather than searching
for a way to discipline and guide the Great Beast, Jefferson offers
the Hamiltonians a way to construct a society without the presence of such an animal, and with none of the undesirable urban
masses of the Hamiltonian nightmare. Jefferson shared that
nightmare.

> I think our governments will remain virtuous for many centuries;
> as long as they are chiefly agricultural. . . . When they get piled
> upon one another in large cities, as in Europe, they shall become
> corrupt as in Europe.[19]

And, by clear implication, unfit for self-rule.

We must be precise here. In Jefferson's eyes, men are not,
after all, born fit for self-rule. (Would it be unfair to say that he
pressed such a line only when his foremost objective was the
overthrow of the old government, and that he dropped it once
the task became the construction of a workable social order?) It
was the social experience of living in eighteenth-century Virginia
that fashioned a people capable of sustaining a republican form
of government; America's self-sufficient small farmers—because
they were small farmers—were equipped to handle a degree of
self-rule. The learned virtues acquired managing their land-
holdings enabled them to accept responsibilities beyond those
within the scope of the urban masses in Europe or
America—beyond Hamilton's Great Beast.

> Those who labor the earth are the chosen people of God, if ever He
> had a chosen people. . . . Corruption of morals in the mass of cul-
> tivators is a phenomenon of which no age nor nation has furnished
> an example. It is the mark set on those, who, not looking up to
> heaven, to their soil and industry, as does the husbandman, for their

subsistence, depend for it on casualties and caprice of customers. Dependence begets subservience and venality, suffocates the germ of Virtue, and prepares fit tools for the design of ambition.[20]

Or easy victims for demagogues, as Hamilton would say.

The rigors of farm life, the regular hours, careful husbanding of resources, attention to detail, marketing—most especially the wisdom that comes from managing one's affairs in conformity to the divinely ordained rhythms of nature—all lead to a kind of man resembling not at all Hamilton's feared mass man. And Jefferson promises that a society can be organized with such people in the overwhelming majority.

In fact, Jefferson continues, the industrialization and urbanizing favored by Hamilton and his Eastern monied constituency are destined to enlarge and further degrade the Great Beast of their nightmares. He is giving them a better method to realize their end of minimizing the influence of the mob.

> While we have land to labour then, let us never wish to see our cities occupied at a workbench . . . for the general operations of manufacture, let our workshops remain in Europe. . . . The mobs of great cities add just so much to the support of pure government, as sores do to the struggle of the human body. It is the manners and spirit of a people which preserve a republic in vigour. A degeneracy in these is a canker which soon eats to the heart of its laws and constitution.[21]

Thus we find out that the great American champion of the "natural goodness of man" theory did not intend anything resembling the theories of the free thinkers and moral relativists who favor such a phrase nowadays. Jefferson's version of republican virtue is reached when a man rises above his base instincts (not when he submits and champions every other man's right to do the same in style.) He elaborated on the thought in a letter to his daughter from France. "Of all the cankers of human happiness none corrodes with so silent, yet so baneful an influence, as indolence. No laborious person was ever yet hysterical. It is while we are young that the habit of industry is formed."[22] And that habit, if widespread, would ennoble society far better than the directives of Hamilton's governing classes. So convinced was Jefferson of this, that he seriously proposed a plan that seems quite radical in retrospect. It was a plan reminiscent of the twentieth-century call for "distributism" associated with G. K. Chesterton and Hilaire Belloc. If ever the land needed for the homesteads that build moral character became genuinely scarce in America, Jefferson flatly states that those with more land than they could work would have to relinquish their property rights.

> Wherever there is in any country, uncultivated land and unemployed poor, it is clear that the laws of property have been so far extended as to violate natural right. The earth is given as a common stock for man to labor and live on. . . . If we do not, the fundamental right to labor the earth returns to the unemployed. It is too soon yet in our country to say that every man who cannot find employment but who can find uncultivated land shall be at liberty to cultivate it, paying a moderate rent. But it is not too soon to provide by every possible means that as few as possible shall be without a little portion of land. The small landholders are the most precious part of a state.[23]

Versus Hamilton

Certainly, then, there is no thoughtless leveling instinct at work in Jefferson's writings. Why then have we stated that his works compare unfavorably with Hamilton's?

Well, for one thing there is little question that Hamilton emerges more the realist. In fact, it could be just this lack of sentimentality that has earned Hamilton some popular disfavor. He can rub the wrong way those who relish the role of sacrificing humanitarian.

But Hamilton was a monarchist down deep, wasn't he? And surely monarchy is not most people's idea of cold rationality at work in politics. He was. And he made no bones about it. But his understanding of monarchy was not quite like the caricature of that political system held by many modern Americans. He shared the once widely held belief that democracy could not long endure. Perhaps time will prove that pessimism wrong. The jury is still out. But if this pessimism was bizarre and sinister, so was Plato's and Aristotle's and that of almost all the most praised minds of pre-Enlightenment Europe. He shared Plato's belief that some are born better-equipped than others to make the intelligent choices for a society, and that a good government will be the one where these "men of gold," as Plato phrased it, hold authority over their more impressionable neighbors of baser metals. With Aristotle, he argued that the poor would be susceptible to the unprincipled flattery of demagogues. Far better to live under a wise and just king, who will preside faithfully over laws written in defense of liberty and high-minded social norms, than under a jealous and impassioned majority running roughshod over the property and civil rights of the minority. Republican government was a method that might—but, then again, might not—lead to a just society in the Hamiltonian view. It was not mankind's highest political achievement by the very nature of its process. Something had to hold sway over possibly turbulent public opinion, over a "giddy and fluctuating populace," for a just society to endure. "Mobocracies," he believed, were too often the consequence of democratic regimes, governments whose "very character was tyranny."[24]

There is too much at stake, he insists: "If everything floats on the variable and vague opinions of the governing party, there can be no such thing as rights, property or liberty."[25] Having read the accounts of the bloodshed in France in the name of liberty, equality, and fraternity, those words held no magic for him. At least corrupt and tyrannical kings stood some chance of being checked by public opinion, tradition, and religious authority (upon which their position depends). What is there in a democracy to check the inflamed passions of a degenerate public opinion?

Hamilton was not about to accept the view that public opinion would *always*, by some inner logic, be virtuous and high-minded and self-correcting. The voice of the people was not his voice of God. Too often it tended to "be duped by flattery, and to be seduced by artful and designing men," men unscrupulous enough to make an art of "working on the passions and prejudices of less discerning classes of citizens." These were the "demagogues" who knew too well how to offer "what will *please*, not what will benefit the people."

It is by no means difficult to name a twentieth-century mass movement or two that would verify this insight; groups and leaders who "instead of taking a lead in measures that counteract a prevailing prejudice, however [they] may be convinced of their utility . . . either flatters it, or temporizes." This is "the disease which infects all our constitutions—an excess of popularity."[26]

Hamilton's concern then is with preserving and extending the political and property rights already established in American society, against the kind of challenge tearing France apart in the name of "the people." There are laws which the ascendant masses as well as kings and lords must revere. Western civilization is not to be confirmed or rejected by a show of hands.

This is what is called the law of nature, which being coeval with mankind, and dictated by God himself, is, of course, superior in obligations to any other. It is binding over all the globe, in all countries, and at all times. No human laws are of any validity, if contrary to this; and such of them as are valid, derive all their authority, mediately, and immediately, from the original.[27]

Hamilton could be quoting St. Paul. Republics too must remember that

> the sacred rights of mankind are not to be rummaged for among old parchments or musty records. They are written, as with a sunbeam, in the whole volume of human nature, by the hand of the Divinity itself; and can never be erased or obscured by mortal power.[28]

Republics can claim no additional moral authority *solely* on the basis of the greater mass participation in the process of government that they allow. *The Federalist*:

> Has it been found that bodies of men act with more rectitude or greater disinterestedness than individuals? The contrary of this has been inferred by all accurate observers of the conduct of mankind; and the inference is founded upon obvious reasons. Regard to reputation has a less active influence when the infamy of a bad action is to be divided among a number than when it is to fall singly upon one. A spirit of faction which is apt to mingle its poison in the deliberations of all bodies of men, will often hurry the persons of whom they are composed into improprieties and excesses for which they would blush in a private capacity.[29]

And what of all the naturally good men Hamilton had heard about, the words echoing across the ocean from the Paris salons?

> Take mankind in general, they are vicious, their passions may be operated upon. . . . One great error is that we suppose mankind more honest than they are. Our prevailing passions are ambition and interest; and it will ever be the duty of a wise government to avail itself of the passions, in order to make them subservient to the public good.[30]

For Kings for Freedom's Sake

Ironic as it seems (from our modern point of view), it is this concern of Hamilton for liberty that leads to his preference for monarchy. Where we moderns tend to make an axiomatic link between "freedom and justice" and "democracy," Hamilton sees nothing of the sort. He champions the belief that government ought to have the "consent of the governed." He states flatly that "the origin of all civil government, justly established, must be a voluntary compact between the rulers and the ruled." Furthermore, he argues, quoting Blackstone, the accepted interpreter of the English common law, "the first and primary end of human laws, is to maintain and regulate these *absolute rights* of individuals."[31] But it is *monarchy*, not democracy, he believes, that can best achieve such lofty goals.

The point is that, for Englishmen like Blackstone as well as for Hamilton, the English monarchy was a symbol and guarantor of a political system that had established in law and history the most highly developed network of individual liberties ever known. For them there was no question but that an Englishman's rights were better protected than a Frenchman's under Jacobin rule. Both would agree with Thomas Babington Macaulay, that "an acre in Middlesex is better than a principality in Utopia." Especially a Utopia lined with the shadows of guillotines.

And, to Hamilton, those seemed the choices: the French revolutionary or the English model of development. If someone could demonstrate otherwise, he would listen.

> I desire above all things . . . to see the equality of political rights, exclusive of hereditary distinction, firmly established by a positive demonstration of its being *consistent with the order and happiness of society* [My emphasis].[32]

(It must be remembered that Hamilton had no inherited rank in society. He had no self-interest here.)

But until the time when liberty, equality, and fraternity did not seem likely to lead to Robespierres, he preferred the older English model.

It was not that Hamilton thought—as we are now sometimes told all monarchists do—that kings were superiorly endowed beings. It was the monarch's self-interest that was to be *used* in Hamilton's scheme—used to protect the system and its delicate network of individual liberties and civilizing norms. The trick was to establish in a titled position a person who would enjoy great privileges and power, thus making him immune to radicalizing influences; to entwine his personal privileges with the system so totally that he would give everything, including his life if necessary, to protect the established order.

> The English model was the only good one on this subject. The Hereditary interest of the King was so interwoven with that of the

Nation, and his personal emoluments so great, that he was placed above the danger of being corrupted from abroad—and at the same time was both sufficiently independent and sufficiently controlled, to answer the purpose of the institution at home.[33]

An aristocracy too should be formed "so circumstanced that they have no interest in change."[34]

Speaking as Publius

Naturally this openly stated preference of Hamilton for the English monarchical system led many to question his support for the American Constitution. Some wondered if his writings as Publius in *The Federalist* and his advocacy of ratification of the Constitution, as a member of the Federalist party, should be taken at face value, or as a ruse behind which he plotted for the eventual overthrow of the Republic. Some went so far as to assert that his true long range interest lay in a formal reunion with Great Britain and the king.

Hamilton felt the heat generated by these charges and met them with candor.

No man's ideas are more remote from the plan [the Constitution] than my own are known to be; but is it possible to deliberate between anarchy and convulsion on one side, and the chance of good to be expected from the plan on the other?[35]

If the delegates to the Constitutional Convention could not be brought around to Hamilton's schemes for the new republic, if they would not accept his proposals for more effective checks on popular opinion,* then Hamilton saw it his responsibility as a patriot to make the best of the situation. He wanted stability for the fledgling republic and believed that the Constitution—if properly understood—could realize that goal. His quarrel was with the judgment, not the dream, of those who favored popular government. He stated flatly that he "was affectionately attached to the republican theory" as an *aspiration* for mankind. He wanted it to be true that men were fit for self-rule: "This is the real language of my heart." But he would not allow his heart

---

*Some of which were: a) installing the President for life; b) Senators elected for life or good behavior, elected by electors who were able to meet restrictive property qualifications; c) a veto power over the states held by the executive. One critic somewhat acerbically remarked that it was the "British Constitution as George III had tried hard to make it."

to overrule his mind, for "in candor . . . I am far from being without doubts."[36]

Through *The Federalist*, in his collaboration with James Madison and John Jay, he worked both to encourage ratification of the Constitution as it stood as a viable alternative to domestic anarchy and third-rate status for the new nation in its dealings with foreign powers, and to promote a healthy understanding of the dangers of plebiscitary democracy.

The Role of the Rich and the Well-Born

It was not over the ratification of the Constitution, however, that the differences of opinion between Jefferson and Hamilton became most visible. Once the Bill of Rights was included within the Constitution to limit the power of the central government, Jefferson too supported ratification.

It was later, while Hamilton served as Secretary of the Treasury during Washington's term in office, that the big guns were brought out.

This is neither the time nor the place to analyze in detail the background of the specific issues that fired their dispute. And it isn't necessary. Jefferson charged that Hamilton was working to earn the support of the monied classes by securing for them financial advantages in the new republic. Hamilton *agreed*.

Hamilton admitted that the economic survival of the new nation required a strong cooperative relationship between the established financial vectors of society and the new national government: "Our new money," said Hamilton, is "depreciating almost as fast as the old [under the Articles of Confederation]. The reason is that the moneyed men have not an immediate interest to uphold its credit. They may even, in many ways, find it their interest to undermine it." Secure financial footing had to be secured, and the "only certain manner to obtain a permanent paper credit is to engage the moneyed interests immediately in it . . . giving them the whole or part of the profits."[37]

Once one gets over the initial impression that Hamilton is advocating some kind of backwater courthouse payoff for the local gentry in return for their support in the last election, the logic becomes most persuasive. Socialists and Communists would have an alternative to Hamilton's suggestion, but what course was available for those who shrink from outright expropriation of private wealth?

Jefferson's perhaps. A country populated by small farmers would not be in need of large doses of credit to insure its survival. But the thriving and growing land of shippers and manufacturers—able to provide work for an ever increasing population—would. And that credit would be impossible to secure if investment reservoirs within the country, to say nothing of foreign investors, were hostile to the government or suspicious of its stability. So bring them into the thick of things, Hamilton argues. Show them how they can make money helping the national economy expand. Tie up their bankrolls in the economy. Force them—out of *self-interest*—to be energetic supporters of the country's well-being.

Of course there is more at stake for Hamilton than providing economic support for the infant economy. Hamilton's interest lies in using the wealthy as a stabilizing force against "the imprudence of democracy," as an intuitively conservative force. He intends to convert this potentially hostile investment segment of society into a powerful and influential group of patrons of the established order "who will find it their interest to support a government intended to preserve the permanent happiness of the community as a whole."[38] The rich and well-born, then, are going to be *used*, as he proposed kings and aristocrats be used. They will labor against radical alterations of the system in order to protect their positions of privilege—because the "system" insures their economic well-being. But in doing so they will also be laboring to preserve the social order, which benefits society as a whole. It is not—it must be stressed again—that Hamilton imagines the rich and well-born a *natural* aristocracy. They are not philosopher kings born virtuous. He is as starkly unsentimental about them as about the masses.

> All communities divide themselves into the few and the many. The first are the rich and well born, the other the mass of the people. . . . The people are turbulent and changing; they seldom judge or determine right. Give therefore, to the first class a distinct, permanent share in the government. They will check the unsteadiness of the second; and as they cannot receive any advantage by a change, they therefore will ever maintain good government. Nothing but a permanent body can check the imprudence of democracy.[39]

So while the monied classes' hearts will be with their bankrolls, as long as society puts that bankroll in support of a system *society* wants preserved for *society's* sake, the rich will end up as powerful and influential patriots. Society will have them right where it wants them. Blackstone argued similarly when he defended the notion of property qualifications for voters:

> The true reason of requiring any qualification, with regard to property in voters, is to exclude such persons as *are in so mean a situation*, that they are esteemed to have no will of their own. If these persons had votes, they would be tempted to dispose of them, under some undue influence or other. This will give a great, or artful, or a wealthy man, a larger share in elections than is consistent with personal liberty.[40]

Or, if you prefer, George Washington: "The proposition that the people are the best keepers of their own liberties is not true."[41]

The Unasked Question

It is necessary at this point to deal with an objection—a most valid one, which is often raised by those opposed to the Hamiltonian train of thought. It is an objection that spotlights a chink in the Hamiltonian armor.

It is true: Hamilton's logic is directed at the preservation of the established order. It is true: He *assumes* his society to be a just society. He venerates the status quo. His political theory is constructed to slow down the process of change, to put a damper on movements for political reform. He assumes reformers dangerous. He assumes society as he knows it to be so desirable that he is willing to grant the monied interests of his time (and their descendants) financial advantages to gain their support for things as they are. He assumes that Americans will be so pleased with their society that they will not mind the presence of such an elite; he assumes they will be willing to pay that price to preserve the "system."

All this is true. It is as if Hamilton placed a ceiling on his public comments, marking off an area he would not explore, an Index of Prohibited Thoughts, in effect. Specifically, he takes for granted that English and American historical development has led to certain valid conclusions about life and the purposes of political and social organization. The task for leaders, in his eyes, is to find the best vehicle for infusing these verities into the political process and safeguarding them afterwards.

He opposes Jefferson mainly because he does not agree that republican government can handle this responsibility. It is not the process of popular government he abhors as much as the likely effect.

But, he does not go on to explain *why* a government—be it monarchy, aristocracy, or republic—should be eager to preserve the established order in the first place. If Jefferson is naive for presuming that a democratic debate carried out by small, independent farmers would lead to desirable conclusions, Hamilton can be criticized for not explaining why the way of life he loved and wanted to protect from radical popular enthusiasms was worth maintaining.

Admittedly such criticism is, in a sense, unfair: an attack on the book Hamilton didn't write, so to speak, rather than the one he did. Hamilton is not an ivory-tower theorist pushing for the ultimate philosophical answers to the questions of government. He is a politician, a statesman, writing and speaking for the purpose of building a stable government for a quite specific place on the globe. He is under no obligation to demonstrate the universality of his conclusions. He is looking for a system of government that would work *in America*, in a society which he can presume high-minded men will agree is worth preserving.

Still, he, like Jefferson, leaves untouched an important question. Not all *status quos* deserve to be preserved. A political order is not lovable merely because it is of long duration. A tradition does not become venerable simply as a result of its longevity. Duration does not always equal virtue. No matter how long the Bolshevik regime remains ensconced in Moscow, it will not become a fit object for a loving preservation for those with a Hamiltonian view of man.

Why, then, should the eighteenth-century society Hamilton knew and loved be protected from the agents of radical change? He does not say. He points to the Reign of Terror to show what radicalism can lead to. But that is not enough. Hamilton is even more open to Thomas Paine's verbal jab than Edmund Burke. He too can be said to be a man who "pitied the plumage, but forgot the dying bird" when he wrote with disgust of the Reign of Terror.

One searches Hamilton in vain for the parry. He dismisses men such as Paine as malcontents who would prefer the specter of the guillotine to an imperfect established order, as if that observation in itself is sufficient indictment.

And on certain levels it is—on all levels, in fact, up to that aforementioned ceiling. One is left wondering if Hamilton was unable—or just unwilling—to push through to the upper levels of political discourse; to explain *why* the European and

American civilization he knew was so noble and worthy of the conservative efforts of good men. Perhaps such analyses would sound too much like a defense of the *res publica Christiana* even for Hamilton, who, remember, was a revolutionary himself in 1776.

Let us not be cute. Hamilton is as remiss as Jefferson in paying due homage to the accomplishments of the church-dominated ages in Europe's history. Where Jefferson fails to ask how his naturally good men "got that way," Hamilton fails to describe the characteristics—the enshrined values—of the social order he wants protected from the fury of the Jacobins. How did *it* "get that way?"

We ought not brush aside this failing in Hamilton's arguments. Recommending an elite, without first defining the value system which that elite is to be entrusted to protect, is weak and ultimately dangerous political theory. (This is certainly true in our time, if not in Hamilton's, when terms such as "Western civilization" implied more than an ethnocentric presumption.) *Shutzstaffels* and Politburos are elites of sorts. A society's goal should be the maintenance of justice and public virtue. Its government structure should be determined by an evaluation of what will work best to achieve that goal. A society of high-minded and self-disciplined citizens can flourish with large doses of civil liberty. A society in crisis, polarized, facing civil war or self-dissipation, simply cannot.*

Still, it is likely that Hamilton's analyses will better stand the test of time than Jefferson's. America in the 1980s could provide the proving ground. As the decade comes to a close, few thoughtful Americans echo the 1960s call for "liberation" of the "natural man" from society's "illegitimate" and "repressive" rules and regulations. The drug-fed, sexually irresponsible, sloppy, self-indulgent horror show has been too unnerving for any more of that weary moral indifference once fondly called the "greening" of America.

One cannot be sure, obviously, but the suspicion is strong that a stroll through a modern Times Square or Sunset Strip would lead Jefferson himself to rethink his belief that society needed no norms superior in authority to the free exchange of ideas.

---

*For example, it could easily be argued that the traditional values which Hamilton cherished will be protected best in our time by the masses and their middle-class morality, and that an elite of the academic liberals would build a society hostile to those values.

Admittedly, it could be argued that a nation of Jefferson's husbandmen would not have allowed such social decay to take root. But one wonders. What is it that working the soil would do to ennoble the conscience? (Ask New Yorkers about some of the farm-boy sailors on leave in New York's Times Square cesspools.) Is the nurturing and harvesting of crops enough? Are all farmers virtuous people, or was it "something else" about Jefferson's Virginia that made his neighbors so admirable in his eyes? It must have been. If not, why had not those social refinements which Jefferson revered arisen in every society where the population was forced to squeeze their sustenance from the land? In Africa? In Polynesia? The Indies? Colonial America was not the most agricultural of all eighteenth-century societies.

Something—it seems clear—is needed above and beyond a life in tune to seedtime and harvest to build what Jefferson would call civilization, a society fit for self-rule. High-minded norms, pieties, traditions, principles, ennobling beliefs are required—ideals to which the masses can aspire, and will aspire, if the ideals are preserved, protected, and extended by some version of Hamilton's elite. Hamilton understood what was needed for a worthy civilization to endure, even if he could not, or would not, tell us why America deserved that honor. It could become modern America's historical task—like it or not—to add those chapters to Hamilton's work.

III

The Changing Court

American conservatives have taken some delight in recent years in ribbing the liberals who, after years of calling for increased power in the Presidency all during the Kennedy and Johnson years, suddenly discovered the dangers of an "imperial Presidency," to quote Arthur Schlesinger. The liberals assure us their conversion was precipitated by the shock treatment of Watergate, Vietnam, and Spiro Agnew, but one cannot help but suspect that it was more the successes of the Nixon years that brought about the turn of heart. Whatever else the man did, he was on the way toward welding a political coalition that would have derailed many of the most favored causes of the American Left and stranded its leadership out on the rim of American political life. Which accounts for the intensity and perseverance of the effort to get him on Watergate.* While there is much truth to the charge made by some American conservatives—that the man was not really of the Right—he nevertheless represented the political ascendancy of groups in America usually considered right wing. If conservatives did not always love him, leftists certainly hated him, and usually with good reason.

But there is another liberal flip-flop as illuminating as the one turned on the Presidency. Their view on the role of the Supreme Court has changed dramatically too, but in a conversion that has been given far less attention. There has been criticism of the

*There is no way to avoid the conclusion that history students fifty years from now will have fits trying to discover exactly what it was about these campaign "dirty tricks" that made impeachment imperative.

Supreme Court's assumption of unprecedented legislative power certainly, and from many quarters, but the stress seldom has been placed on how different was the older liberal view, on the fact that the American Left not that long ago held high the banner of judicial restraint.

Why? Perhaps because conservative intellectuals sense that they might throw light on an issue—a conservative flip-flop—embarrassing to their side as well. For the fact is that the judges and commentators considered conservative in the first half of the twentieth century viewed judicial power quite differently from the critics of the Warren Court and its legacy.

Of course this conservative reversal occurred after the passage of many more years than the liberals'; and thus is less subject to the charge of inconsistency. Furthermore it is not at all self-evident that modern conservatives ought to be considered part of a continuum stretching back to those who were called conservative in 1910.

Still, modern rightists who have made near-dogmatic their opposition to the judicial activism of the Warren Court should find themselves with second thoughts if they have never before taken the opportunity to examine the nature of earlier opposition to a powerful Supreme Court. (Remember, it was FDR who tried to "pack" the Court.) And modern liberals who take it for granted that a dominant Court is the surest protector of minorities, civil rights, and a woman's right to an abortion, will have to find a way to explain to themselves how the Court could have stood in the way of the social reforms of the Progressive Era and the New Deal. (Oliver Wendell Holmes' barb that the Constitution had not institutionalized Herbert Spencer's *Social Statics* was turned toward the Supreme Court of his time, at what he considered its slavish devotion to the Framer's conception of private property rights.)

One is left with the strong suspicion, in other words, that views on the role of the Supreme Court—past and present—are more a result of the conclusions the Court has reached than an impartial evaluation of whether a Court with the power to direct public policy is good for the nation: that it is *what* the Court orders that determines the line of opposition, not judicial power in and of itself. And, in fact, there have been defenders of judicial activism who expressed some reservations in public when it appeared likely that Richard Nixon was about to remake the

Court in his own image and likeness. But Watergate apparently ended that threat to the republic. The Court, once again, with Nixon on St. Helena (or Elba?), especially after the abortion decisions, seems in the good graces of its defenders. It is interesting to speculate on what it would take to force the conservative enemies of the Court to reconsider too—to speak in a manner of judicial review consistent with the positions so many conservatives take on the need for checks against plebiscitary democracy. Would more Reagan appointees do it?

Perhaps the Court's track record over the last quarter of century will be too hard to forget for any right-wing revisionism in this area. James J. Kilpatrick, one of the most intelligent and lively critics of the Court, is representative of the depths of the anti-Court sentiment on the Right. He speaks of a "judicial usurpation":

> When the Warren years began, the power of the states to operate racially separate schools, so long as the schools were substantially equal, was "well settled" as a matter of law. The question had been "many times decided," and decisions had formed a gloss on the Fourteenth Amendment. It was equally clear that nothing in the Fourteenth Amendment prohibited the states from fixing their own boundaries for legislative districts. . . .
>
> When the Warren years began, there was little doubt that "obscenity" could be reasonably well-defined, and punished, under both state and federal law. The right of public schools to conduct voluntary religious observances, such as class prayers and baccalaureate sermons, was not challenged. . . . During the Warren years, the ends of justice, and the needs of society . . . disappeared into a rarefied gas of vaporized rhetoric. Newly fabricated rules on self-incrimination, on confessions, on jury trials, on rights to counsel, on post-conviction remedies, suddenly have been imposed on police and prosecutors. In North Carolina, a brute criminal goes free: He had twice raped a girl, shot her and her escort with a rifle, and left them to die; but the rifle, obtained without a proper warrant, was inadmissible. In California, a bank robber gets off; it was unconstitutional for police to obtain a sample of his handwriting. . . . Eddie Harrison, who *three* times confessed to murder could not be sent to prison; none of the three confessions could pass the purity test.[1]

Add to his list the decision (*Roe v. Wade*) prohibiting state restrictions on abortions and court-ordered busing, and we get a working summary of the modern conservative case against the Court. (Although Kilpatrick himself, in a mood that puzzles and disappoints many of his conservative brethren, is pro-abortion.)

Prof. Lino T. Graglia, another critic favored by conservatives, is no less unequivocal. He calls the Court's new role a "fraud," arguing that "the Court has . . . done by deception what it felt it could not do honesty." The Justices

> have been forced to explain and justify their actions with opinions that can make no claim to intellectual coherence or respectability, and they have engaged in practices—perversions of legislation, misstatements of fact, and patently fallacious reasoning that would, if they were engaged in by any other government officials, be considered scandalous and lead to demands for impeachment. . . . In the American system, a victory at the polls remains a victory only so long as it is not disapproved by the courts—a function performed in some other systems by the military.[2]

Angry words? But not without reason, all things considered. But even if conservatives in such moods are unlikely to concede that there might have been a time when they would have welcomed an activist Court (or that there could be such a time in the future),* let us examine the course of the Supreme Court's rise to power. The conservatives of today are right on the historical equation: the Framers of the Constitution, the Founding Fathers, and the American tradition up until the Warren years provide no support to the claims of the judicial activists. If someday conservatives wish this were not the case, they will have to face the issue at that time. (Let us hope, for scholarly reasons alone, that they do something more than make the "flip-flop.")

Three things must be considered: (a) the role assigned the Supreme Court in the original "scheme of things"—at the Constitutional Convention and in *The Federalist*; (b) the extent of any "new" power assumed by Chief Justice Marshall under the rubric of "judicial review"; and (c) the reasons for the modern judicial activists' willingness to ignore both history and legal precedent to create a Supreme Court with powers denied the Court by the Founding Fathers, never contemplated by Justice Marshall, and deemed a threat to freedom by the American consensus up until quite recently as history measures time.

In the Beginning

Perhaps it will be an attack on a straw man to take the time to demonstrate that the Founding Fathers never intended the

---

*By no means do I claim that there can be no such case. After all, the "conservative" Supreme Court justices who voted down the social reforms of the Progressive Era and New Deal were acting as strict constructionists. Activist strict constructionists, if you will.

Supreme Court to exercise as much authority as the modern Court. The judicial activists of today rely more for their mandate on later theorists and historical developments than on the authority of the Constitutional Fathers.

Occasionally, however, the case is made that there was considerable, and respectable, sentiment in the debates over the ratification of the Constitution for a Court with the power to control the legislature; that even if the Convention voted against the idea, it is not foreign to American political thought. Alexander Hamilton, interestingly, the thinker often favored by modern rightists and deplored by liberals for his distrust of democracy, is considered the "pro-Court" Founding Father.

And it is true that Hamilton, in *The Federalist*, argues for a Court with considerable power over the legislative branch, but for reasons, one would think, liberals would not want to be associated with. His clearest call for what would later be called "judicial review" comes in No. 78.

> No legislative act . . . contrary to the Constitution, can be valid. To deny this, would be to affirm that the deputy is greater than the principal, that the servant is above his master. . . .
>
> The interpretation of the laws is the proper and peculiar province of the courts. A Constitution is, in fact, and must be regarded by the judge, as a fundamental law. It therefore belongs to them to ascertain its meaning, as well as the meaning of any particular act proceeding from the legislative body. . . .
>
> . . . the courts were designed to be an intermediate body between the people and the legislature, in order, among other things, to keep the latter within the limits assigned to that authority.[3]

The wording is indeed reminiscent of that used by defenders of the Warren Court; of that there is no question. But what can be overlooked is the fact that Hamilton's view on the role of the Supreme Court is part of a package—his overall political theory. To be direct, Hamilton wants a powerful Court for the same reasons he pushed for a chief executive appointed for life, or even better, an American monarch. He is seeking another check on his "Great Beast," the masses he considered likely to "be duped by flattery and to be seduced by artful and designing men."[4] That is what he means by "among other things" in the above quote. He is hoping to use the Court as an aristocracy of sorts, as a guardian elite for the traditional values of his American upper class, and as a check on Jacobinical impulses. Hardly the service defenders of a strong judiciary want performed today. On the contrary, their usual stress is on the Court as a democratizing force, an agent of social equality and civil liberties.

To be sure, there are similarities between Hamilton's position and, say, Thurgood Marshall's or Ramsey Clark's. It is true. The moderns too see the Court as the servant of an aristocracy, although they would never phrase it quite that way. The modern Court is understood by its defenders to be a representative of the high-minded values of the American educated class, the voice of a conscience-elite which shares the reformist ardor associated with the social science departments of the leading American universities and journals of opinion. The modern judicial activists have their "Great Beast" too—the middle Americans, the Silent Majority, the masses apparently not quite ready to be entrusted with democratic control of society in those areas where they have not yet absorbed the enlightened attitudes of the Brahmins.

But there is no reason for the opponents of the modern Supreme Court to concede too much here. In addition to having a different motive from modern liberals, Hamilton does not grant the same degree of authority to the Court. He never concedes to the Court an "umpire's" role. The modern judicial supremacists can quote Hamilton to give some historical respectability to their own views, but only by doing so out of context. Hamilton goes on in *The Federalist*, beyond the oft-quoted No. 78, to define more fully what part he intended for the Court to play. No. 81: ". . . the courts on the pretence of a repugnancy, may [not] substitute their own pleasure to the constitutional intentions of the legislature." Justices are not "to construe the laws according to the *spirit* of the Constitution."[5] There were to be no flights of the imagination. Justices were to act as a check on the legislative and executive branches, but within a quite specific and narrow mandate.

There is nothing self-contradictory or mysterious about his stance. Academic commentators on the Constitution have made the point repeatedly through the years. The genius of the Constitution, according to the authors of *The Federalist*, can be found in the system of checks and balances carefully built into its structure. Because of it, the political freedoms won from the British could be preserved without sacrificing an effective central government. The choice was not the tyranny of King George or the chaos of the Articles of Confederation. The central government could be entrusted with the power to rule the nation, without the fear of a loss of liberty, because the separate branches of government—legislative, executive, and judicial—would have the power to effectively thwart overly ambitious men in the other branches. Most of us learned the formulas in grade school: checks and balances.

What Hamilton calls for is no more than a Court sufficiently equipped to play this role: judicial *adequacy*, not judicial supremacy. But why then would he write of the Court as he did ("the interpretation of the laws is the proper and peculiar province of the courts etc.")? Because he could not *conceive* of a Court acting as if it possessed the kind of authority the Court claims today. A Court proceeding as if it possessed ultimate authority, in his eyes, would be put in its place by the other branches so fast the gavels would smoke. Indeed he was convinced the Court would know its limitations *more* than the other branches. The judiciary was the least likely branch to get uppity. The power of impeachment especially was too clear a threat. It "would give to that body," the Congress, a hold "upon the members of the judicial department. This is alone a complete security. There can never be danger that the judges, by a series of deliberate usurpations on the authority of the legislature, would hazard the united resentment of the body intrusted with it."[6] Consequently

> the judiciary, from the nature of its functions, will always be the least dangerous to the political rights of the Constitution; because it will be least in capacity to annoy or injure them. The executive not only disperses the honors, but holds the sword of the community. The legislature not only commands the purse, but prescinds the rules by which the duties and rights of every citizen are to be regulated. The judiciary, on the contrary, has no influence over either the sword or the purse, no direction either of the strength or the wealth of society; and can take no active resolution whatever.[7]

Clearly, we do not have here an outlook favorably disposed to the role played by the Court today.

If it needs be said, the other Constitutional Fathers were even less likely to grant anything like judicial supremacy. It was Hamilton who was the suspected monarchist, the shadowy figure so different, we are told, from the other delegates to the Convention. Logic alone tells us the others would be less inclined to assign to Supreme Court justices appointed for life the power to thwart the popular will as represented in the legislative and executive branches. And what logic does not reveal, the record does. Proposals to increase judicial authority were resoundingly defeated.

It must be kept in mind that, in spite of the differences between the Hamiltonian and Jeffersonian wings in early America,
there was no substantial interest in "reversing" the Revolution.
The Founding Fathers saw themselves as the vanguard of representative democracy; men who would prove to the world that
government by discussion did not end forever with the fall of
the Roman Republic; that free men, organized politically without
kings and lords, would not inevitably fall into political anarchy
and moral turpitude. On this there was agreement. The Revolution was fought to allow the elected representatives of the
community to rule without a guardian class—be they kings,
bishops, or Supreme Court justices appointed for life. The Revolution was viewed by its supporters—and not even Hamilton
was a Tory—as one of the final links in a chain going back
through English history to the Glorious Revolution and beyond
to the Magna Carta, a link in the development of parliamentary,
or *legislative*, supremacy. Blackstone spoke of the "omnipotent
parliament."

The question at issue in the debates of the time centered on
how unfettered the legislature should be in practice. Hamilton's
supporters argued for considerable checks; Jefferson's for less.
But all were looking for a government representative of the people—based on the "just consent of the governed," in the Declaration of Independence's words. There was no room in this
tradition for philosopher kings or the Court with the power to
nullify, or upgrade, the determinations of popular government.
Slow it down, keep it within clearly marked Constitutional
guidelines, tame the political passions of the moment—all these,
yes, especially in Hamiltonian eyes. But no more.

George Mason, for example, concedes that in a clear-cut case
of legislative violation of the Constitution, the Court may act.
(Obviously. Why else have a Court?) But the violation had to
be patent and demonstrable: "But with regard to every law however unjust or oppressive or pernicious, which did not come
plainly under this description [plainly in violation of Constitutional guidelines], they would be under the necessity as Judges
to give it a free course."[8]

James Wilson: "Laws may be unjust, may be unwise, may
be dangerous, may be destructive; and yet be not so unconstitutional as to justify the Judges in refusing to give them effect."[9]

But what then was to save the republic from a corrupt legislature? Certainly not an arbitrary and authoritarian Court,

which would be at least as likely to become corrupt as a legislative body. The system of checks and balances was to work by allowing no one branch the upper hand. There were to be no umpires, no elite above the workings of the republican system. Thomas Jefferson, although not at the convention, expressed the viewpoint:

> Our judges are as honest as other men, and not more so. They have, with others, the same passions for party, for power, and the privilege of their corps. Their maxim is *"boni judicis est ampliare jurisdictionem,"* and their power the more dangerous as they are in office for life, and not responsible, as other functionaries are, to the elective process.[10]

Put otherwise, the Framers were willing to pay the price of a certain lack of decisiveness in order to prevent abuses of power. Better, they believed, to live with an unresolved problem until a clear-cut consensus formed in society in favor of reform than to risk the tyranny of an unchecked faction in control of the government. There was little danger, they were convinced, of any one branch being able to obstruct the popular will for an indefinite period of time. At worst, desirable changes would be delayed. And that, it bears repeating, was a price they were more than willing to pay to protect popular government. In fact, an extended period of time to consider and reconsider the proposed change was in the nation's best interest. The slower the process the less the likelihood of error.

Elbridge Gerry: "It was quite foreign from the nature of the office to make them Judges of public measures. . . . It was making Statesmen of the Judges."[11]

Charles Pinckney: ". . . opposed the interference of the Judges in the Legislative process."[12]

Rufus King: ". . . the judges must interpret the Laws, they ought not to be legislators."[13]

Roger Sherman: ". . . disapproved of Judges meddling in politics and parties."[14]

James Iredell: "Having smarted under the omnipotent power of the British parliament . . . we should have been guilty of . . . the greatest folly had we established a despotic power among ourselves."[15]

And Thomas Jefferson. Now, admittedly, he cannot be assumed to represent the perspective of the Constitutional Framers. Once again, he was not even at the convention. And his states'-rights views did make him perhaps extraordinarily suspicious of federal power in every form. Yet the record indicates that he was in line with the majority on this issue. A justice's job?

> On every question of construction, carry ourselves back to the time when the Constitution was adopted, recollect the spirit manifested in the debates, and instead of trying what meaning may be squeezed out of the text, or invented against it, conform to the probable one in which it was passed.[16]

This view remained the self-evident understanding of the Court's function until well into the twentieth century. More judicial power was simply an unacceptable proposition for a republican form of government. Against those who argued the contrary, Jefferson dug deep for some of the hot mustard:

> According to the doctrines [of those who favored a powerful judiciary] the States are provinces of the Empire, and a late pamphlet [written by the pro-Court faction] gives to that Court the infallibility of the Pope. Caesar then has only to send out his pro-consuls and with the sanction of a Pope all is settled; but the battle of Bunker Hill was not fought to set up a Pope.[17]

Enter Justice Marshall

"Ah yes," judicial activists will say, "but do not you realize, my fine fellow, that our Constitutional heritage did not end in 1788? Every schoolchild knows about John Marshall and judicial review; every schoolbook treats his contribution to our governmental operations; it is as much a part of our heritage as Bunker Hill."

Well, it is true that Chief Justice Marshall by the early 1800s was forced to deal in the concrete with the ambiguity surrounding the Court's power, and in doing so strengthened the Court. He was faced with what he was convinced was a legislative transgression of constitutional limits and acted to reverse it. He declared a law passed by the Congress unconstitutional. But the question is: did he define the Court's powers of "judicial review" in a manner comparable to that exercised in the heyday of the Warren Court?

The landmark decision, the reader will recall, was *Marbury v. Madison* (1803). The background details of the case are not as important for our purposes as Marshall's logic, but a brief summary is in order to make clear how different was the situation

Marshall faced with the Judiciary Act of 1789 from that when the Warren Court ordered the integration of southern schools, or when the Burger Court overthrew state laws prohibiting abortion on demand.

Marbury had been appointed a justice of the peace in the District of Columbia by John Adams in the last days of his administration (just one of many appointments made by Adams to insure Federalist control of the Courts before "mad Tom" Jefferson and his radicals took the helm). Jefferson, upon taking office, ordered his Secretary of State, James Madison, not to deliver the commission. Marbury consequently petitioned the Supreme Court for a writ of mandamus to force his commission. Marshall refused, arguing that such a writ was not within the Supreme Court's jurisdiction as defined by the Constitution, even though the power to issue it had been conferred upon the Court in Sec. 13 of the Judiciary Act of 1789. The Judiciary Act, Marshall held, could not confer what the Constitution denied. Only an amendment could grant new powers to the Court if such powers were deemed necessary. Hence the Judiciary Act was unconstitutional; and it was the Supreme Court's right to make that determination.

> The question whether an act repugnant to the Constitution can become the law of the land, is a question deeply interesting to the United States; but, happily not of an intricacy proportioned to its interest. . . .
>
> The Constitution is either a superior paramount law, unchangeable by ordinary means, or it is on a level with ordinary legislative acts, and, like other acts, is alterable when the legislature shall please to alter it. If the former part of the alternative be true, then a legislative act contrary to the Constitution is not law; if the latter part be true, then written constitutions are absurd attempts, on the part of the people, to limit power in its own nature illimitable.
>
> Certainly all those who have framed written constitutions contemplate them as forging the fundamental and paramount law of the nation, and consequently the theory of every such government must be that an act of the legislature repugnant to the Constitution is void.[18]

Marshall's reasoning appears parallel to the modern Court's defenders; but it is not, not on all fours. First of all, Marshall is not demanding *new* social policy. He is acting as a *nay-sayer* only, demanding that a specific and demonstrable violation of the Constitution *as written*, as seen by the Framers, be declared null and void. He is acting to guarantee *their* understanding of the law, not his. Throughout his career he argued this point, and most precisely: the Court could exercise its power of judicial review when, and only when, faced with an obvious legislative transgression.

The Court, in other words, is entitled to limit—to check—a Congress which goes beyond its constitutional authority; but it is not entitled to generate social changes that the majority of the moment on the Court happens to feel are desirable for the country. There must be a *"bold* and *plain* usurpation to which the Constitution gave no countenance" before the Court can invoke "the judicial power of annulment" (emphasis added).[19] A "bold and plain" usurpation, not a "failure to act progressively," or a "lack of social concern for the downtrodden," or a "lack of familiarity with Gunnar Myrdal's work." The courts, when they act, must remember that "judicial power is never exercised for the purpose of giving effect to the will of the judge; always for the purpose of giving effect to the will of the legislature."[20]

By this is it meant that Marshall would be willing to sit back and allow what he felt were obvious social evils to endure merely because the legislative bodies refused to act? Yes.

> The Constitution . . . was not intended to furnish the correctives for every abuse of power which may be committed by the State governments. The interest, wisdom, and justice of the representative body and its relation with its constituents furnish the only security . . . against unwise legislation.[21]

The Liberals: Status Quo Ante

But surely arguing about Marshall in the above manner involves setting up a bit of a straw man too, does it not? True. Not as much as with the Founding Fathers, however. The judicial activists of our time often talk as if Marshall were one of their own, without reservation. But, admittedly, they do not rest their case upon him. There are other forces of judicial wisdom they favor, twentieth-century masters of the law who, they tell us, understood the new role the Courts must play in the industrial age: Oliver Wendell Holmes, for example, Roscoe Pound, Louis D. Brandeis, and the other pioneers of the school of "sociological jurisprudence." It matters little actually, for those who favor the role the modern Supreme Court has played, whether Hamilton and Marshall, in the final analysis, are truly on all fours with them. There is a new pantheon. What Marshall would not allow, Holmes does; and that is sufficient. Yet this is where the plot thickens.

We all are familiar with the basic thrust of the proponents of the new sociological jurisprudence or legal positivist school of thought. Holmes and Pound and the others are held in high esteem by moderns, who consider themselves liberal, because they laid the intellectual groundwork for those who now argue that Supreme Court justices ought not be bound by the "dead letter of the law"; that the Constitution is a "living document" that must be interpreted in the light of new societal needs and discoveries in the social sciences rather than frozen as it stood in the eyes of the Framers; that it matters little whether the Framers of the Fourteenth Amendment, for example, wanted to end segregated schools—we can use their words inventively to end them anyway, to effect new and progressive insights. Chief Justice Charles Evans Hughes:

> If by the statement that what the Constitution meant at the time of its adoption it means today, it is intended to say that the great clauses of the Constitution must be confined to the interpretation which the framers, with the conditions and outlook of their time would have placed upon them, the statement carries its own refutation. It was to guard against such a narrow conception that Chief Justice Marshall uttered a memorable warning—"We must never forget that it is a *Constitution* we are expounding" . . . a constitution intended to endure for ages to come, and consequently to be adopted to the various crises of human affairs.[22]

For the general public in a speech at Elmira, N.Y., Hughes spoke in more direct language (compounding his mistaken interpretation of John Marshall's thought): "The Constitution is what the Supreme Court says it is."

Felix Frankfurter made the same point from a different angle. For him, not only did modern problems require new interpretations of constitutional language; judges also had to be freed to apply "canons of decency and fairness which express the notions of justice of English speaking people."[23]

Oliver Wendell Holmes, of course, was the champion of the new thinking. He argued that justices ought to be imaginative enough to demonstrate why the law ought *not* be applied as the Framers intended if a pressing social need required solutions that would have been unacceptable in the past. The constitutional spirit is "perverted when it is held to prevent the natural outcome of a dominant opinion, unless it can be said that a rational and fair man necessarily would admit that the statute proposed would infringe fundamental principles as they have been understood by the traditions of our people and our law."[24] And on another occasion:

> I think the proper course is to recognize that a state legislature can do whatever it sees fit to do unless it is restrained by some express prohibition to the Constitution of the United States or of the state, and the courts should be careful not to extend such prohibitions beyond their obvious meaning by reading into them conceptions of public policy that the particular court may happen to entertain.[25]

Naturally, one must keep in mind the historical context when considering the nature of the modern support for the judicial positivism of Holmes and the others. In *Lochner v. New York*, for example, Holmes delivers a dissenting opinion against a majority, which held unconstitutional a law regulating working hours in New York bakeries since it violated constitutionally guaranteed contractual and property rights—that portion of the Constitution that assured that "no State . . . shall deprive any person of life, liberty, or property, without the due process of law." Similar laws were being struck down, laws attempting to regulate wages, working conditions, and child and woman labor. The Court was overthrowing laws it felt went beyond Constitutional limits as understood by the Framers. Wages and working conditions were being declared none of the government's business, the concern only of the owner, and the worker free to enter or not into contract to work for him. A man's factory or steel mill was his castle.

Holmes receives the praise of the modern liberal, then, because he was seeking to convince the legal establishment of his time to be imaginative in their interpretation of the Fourteenth Amendment, to use it to bring relief to the sweatshop poor of urban America, to be as creative as was the Warren Court later in history when its majority ordered school integration in spite of the fact that the framers of the Fourteenth Amendment presided over the establishment of segregated schools in Washington, D.C., *after* having ratified the amendment. Who cares if the framers would not have wanted the federal government to interfere with the salary negotiations of their time? What is good for America *now* should be the question—that is the primary concern of an enlightened justice.

But, whoa, the harness is torn and the team scrambling. True, both Holmes and the modern activists desire a Court freed from precedent, but for *opposed* reasons. They both seek humanitarian—liberal—social reforms. But Holmes and the judicial positivists of the first half of our century wanted to shake loose from precedent in order to secure *legislative* dominance; the legislatures of the time were the branches of government most likely to enact the reforms considered necessary. Would it not be quite simple, then, to argue that their understanding of the function of the Supreme Court is more supportive of those who do not want the Court interfering nowadays in legislative decisions—decisions on integration, busing, abortion restrictions, censorship, school prayer, etc.?

What would Holmes say about the Warren Court? Considering his liberal instincts and social activism, can anyone seriously think he would be shaking his finger at Thurgood Marshall, telling him that "a state legislature can do whatever it sees fit?" Not likely—which is the point, precisely. Whose ox is being gored? Judicial theory is invented to support political preferences, in Holmes' time, in ours.

And, yes, those moderns who deplore the Court's "usurpation" nowadays have to keep in mind that the Court in the first half of this century was exerting itself against what some would think the first historical stirrings in America of "creeping socialism." Like the liberals, the conservatives owe it to themselves to ponder whether their objections are to a Court with clout, or to a Court with clout acting against their interests and convictions. Is strict constructionism really the issue?

The Warren Court

The Supreme Court is the great liberalizing force in America, overthrowing traditional norms and local liberties—we have become so accustomed to the charge that it now seems cliché. The Court is the favored instrument of social levellers, bleeding hearts soft on criminals, the liberals. Such thoughts are so much a part of the political vernacular that it could be a jolt to recall that it was only twenty-five or thirty years ago, in the years just before the Warren Court first flapped its wings to take flight, that American liberals were actually celebrating their victory over the Court's obstruction of democratic growth. A political science text, widely used in the early 1950s, an anthology of American political theory, makes the point. Its editor taught his readers to be proud of the accomplishment. Never again would "nine old men," representatives of the conservative American propertied classes, stand in the way of progressive social legislation as they did with the New Deal. FDR did not succeed in "packing the Court," but the Court learned enough from the close call to pull back its horns. Sociological jurisprudence, after its earlier setbacks, had carried the day, and America was a better place because of it.

> The power of judicial review has been greatly modified . . . and the Court has made a substantial withdrawal from the doctrine of *Marbury v. Madison*, in fact, if not in theory. The Court is not yet of a single mind regarding its proper role in the future, but it is hard to see how it can return to its earlier view. The indications are that a fundamental change in the position of the Supreme Court in the American governmental system is in the process of taking place; . . . it will represent another example of the triumph of the democratic over the aristocratic principle in America, with the Court accepting the curtailment of its powers as the price of survival in a democratic age.[26]

All that just a few short years before Earl Warren was in full flight, with the academic liberals in a tight pattern to his rear—a quite remarkable transformation. (Comparable to the author of the popular high-school social studies textbook, who wrote to all the New York newspapers in 1976, apologizing to his students and ex-students and readers for having pictured the United Nations as mankind's best hope, the culmination of all of the history of the West, in fact. He had just seen on television a pistol-packing Yasir Arafat receive a standing ovation from the galleries of the august body.)

But why? What happened? The liberals knew of Jim Crow laws in the early 1950s. Why the sudden conversion?

If a rightwinger were to give the answer, he would be dismissed as paranoid. Presumably Archibald Cox, one of the heroes of the Watergate saga, will be immune to that charge.

> By the 1950s the political atmosphere had changed. The legislative process, even at its best, became resistant to libertarian, humanitarian, and egalitarian impulses. At worst, the legislatures became repressive, in the libertarian view, because of the Cold War, increased crime, the fear of social disorder.[27]

In other words, a complaisant Court was desirable only when the "common man" elected representatives who agreed with the secular, internationalist, and behaviorist biases that prevailed within liberal academic circles. And Cox is proud of this manifest resiliency of the American establishment in its dealings with the simple folk.

Hence in a twinkling, with a snap of the fingers, the nine old men on the Court were transformed in liberal mythology into the ultimate tribunal, the defenders of liberty and the downtrodden, protectors of democracy, enemies of bigotry and privilege. For those uneasy with the new liturgy, respectable publications—*The New York Times Magazine*, for example—comforted with the assurance that there was no heresy, in spite of appearances. Earl Warren had not really overstepped his bounds. Not really. He was appropriately flexible, that's all—a man who understood hobgoblins and little minds. "Warren was quite unworried that legislative history, dug from a library, might not support his reading." He wisely "brush[ed] off pedantic impediments to the results he felt were right." He was not your obsolete "look-it-up-in-the-library" legal scholar. With an admirable "pragmatic dependence on the present day results" to guide his hand, and an "off-hand dismissal of legal and historical research," which pointed out his break with legal precedent, he proceeded to right America's wrongs.[28]

There were some objectors, of course, especially on the Right, but not enough to be heard over the chorus of hosannas in high places, at least until the Nixon appointments gave second thoughts to some. Justice Black was one, however, who saw some dark clouds even before Nixon. "What if all this [judicial power] is turned on us? If real reason goes out of fashion, can we be sure it will not happen? . . . Have we not, after all, asked for it?"[29] He brooded especially over the possibility of judges someday allowing a resumption of capital punishment.

A Hobgoblin?

But why place this stress on the way opinions have shifted on the role of the Court—why in practical terms? What does it matter, really, if those involved in the debates over judicial power persist in arguing as if the central issue were the system, the appropriate allocation of judicial power? What does it matter if Americans seem oblivious to the degree of the conservative-liberal flip-flops that have occurred? So what if they happen again? Would it be better if we all were wedded to one understanding of the Court's role, no matter what, like the ACLU leaders whose absolutist vision of the First Amendment convinces them to defend Nazi marches at the expense of the large numbers of Jews in the organization who leave when they do?

Hardly. The point is not that methodological rigidity is required for the maintenance of a healthy society. *What* a society stands for is more important than the techniques it uses to develop itself in history. The system is of consequence, but it does not save; it is not the ultimate question, and political debate that pretends otherwise serves only to blind us to the need for societal standards above and beyond the preference for centralized or decentralized structures of government. Only a fool or a villain, for example, would speak in libertarian tones after being shipwrecked with ninety-nine other survivors on a desert island if fifty-one felons being transported to Devil's Island were among the total one hundred. Likewise, a man who preaches respect for central authority and law and order after a gangster syndicate has taken control of the statehouse. Authority must be valid to be worthy of respect. A people must be virtuous to survive political liberty. And no system, no mechanics of government, can define "valid" and "virtuous" for us. Something else is required for these insights—a moral consensus, religion.

Not that our systems are of no importance. Once we know what *kind* of people we wish to be, it is both wise and necessary to make the political analyses required to find the best way to particularize our norms. But without a clear vision of our identity as a people, political debate becomes futile and self-deceptive. We ignore the moral rejuvenation required to preserve our national well-being, and assign our best minds instead to that search for "systems so perfect that no one will need to be good."

Only for those who make the mistake of being concerned more with the methods of government than ends, is it illogical to defend parental rights to determine the textbooks used in schools in West Virginia, while at the same time being a critic of "thought control" in Communist China. Or, from another angle, to call for freedom of expression for campus radicals in America while favoring Stalinism in Russia and Cuba, as does Angela Davis. The problem is that the Marxists, by and large, appear to know this—know that their goal of a Marxist world is to be sought through whatever methods are available and functional. While Americans under the spell of secular liberalism find themselves preoccupied with the ongoing debate over "big government," and open to the suggestion, for example, that a government with the power to deny an Angela Davis a teaching position at a state university will be a government with the power to one day take everyone else's freedom of expression too—a government that could go from applying pressure on Communists one year to Billy Graham the next. A society's primary concern should be with maintaining a national character, with preventing the fragmentation which would make such inconsistencies plausible to the imagination, rather than searching for an approach to government that would somehow neutralize changes in leadership as drastic as one that would militate against Christians one year and admitted Communists the next.

IV

John C. Calhoun—Patriot?

Sectionalism, states' rights, interposition, nullification, secession, minority rights, concurrent majorities—the issues seem always to have been with us and likely to be a key ingredient in the political controversies of our future. Jefferson and Madison drawing up the Virginia and Kentucky Resolutions to give states the power to nullify the Alien and Sedition Acts. New England shipping states threatening to secede at the Hartford Convention of 1814, rather than live with a federally ordered embargo and ongoing war with their favored trading partner, Great Britain. The Webster-Hayne and Lincoln-Douglas debates. The Civil War. Barry Goldwater musing—probably only half in jest—over the advantages of cutting New York from the mainland and letting it float out to sea. Norman Mailer and Jimmy Breslin concurring in a serious manner (well, as serious as they could) during their campaign for the mayoralty in New York in the late 1960s. The residents of the Pacific Northwest rearing up in the 1970s in opposition to the continued use of "their" rivers to turn the generators that keep Los Angeles and Las Vegas bathed in neon. Midwest and Sunbelt legislators indignant over the prospect of sending more of their tax dollars to New York to bail out the Big Apple's government apparatus, so swollen by their standards. It goes on and on.

And there is no question but that it is a genuine problem for any society that grows beyond the intimacy of a Greek city-state.

Must a society that accepts majority rule accept too that 50 percent plus one of the population can pretty much have their way with the remaining 49 percent plus? If not, what are the limitations? How are they to be constructed in law?

It is generally conceded that the most adept and vigorous scholarly argument in defense of local liberties, and regionalism in general, came from the pen of John C. Calhoun: his theories of nullification and concurrent majorities, as developed in *Disquisition on Government*, and *Discourse on the Constitution and Government of the United States*. Throughout his career in Washington, in fact until his death in 1850 (as a congressman from South Carolina, Vice President, senator, and secretary of state), Calhoun worked to provide a sound philosophical justification for the southern states' right to refuse to bend to the will of a national majority determined to end slavery, one having, as well, the political muscle to effect it. Did he succeed? Clearly not in the political arena, although it took a Civil War to prove wrong his supporters in the South.

But what of the theoretical and philosophical level? Did he build a sound political theory, which now lies in wait for future American minorities to use against the tide of standardizing big government? The temptation seems to be to say, yes, especially at the present moment on the American Right. At the height of the furor following the Supreme Court's order to integrate southern schools, a rather impressive array of southern writers-in-opposition, accepting the label neo-Calhounite, employed his words to press their case. It does not take much imagination to picture how such groups could gain greater support at some future date—and Calhoun's writings greater attention—as the ambitions of the social engineers at HHS grow with each passing day.

In fact, one could quite easily picture certain more liberal areas of the country—parts of San Francisco and New York City, for example, where a counterculture permissiveness and an attraction for welfarism have taken hold—turning to something like Calhoun's reasoning (by some other name) to defend their enclaves from the reformist ardors of "straight" Middle America. We might, in other words, hear talk of interposition and nullification once again in America, but this time from both sides of the political fence—and simultaneously—as Sunbelters, and straight ethnics, and Biblebelters, and gays, drug aficionados, New Leftists, and long-established welfare clients seek to make it as easy as possible to have nothing to do with each other.

Admittedly, such a prospect can have an appeal at first glance, but it deserves little thoughtful support. Calhoun, in the final analysis, ought to be attractive only to those willing to preside over a national decline. Too strong a charge? Before dealing with it, let us first take an honest look at his thought, and the reasons—legitimate and otherwise—for its appeal, past and potential.

Changing Sides

Once again, the American flip-flop. Calhoun, arch-symbol of states' rights, and Daniel Webster, nationalist *par excellence*, were at opposite poles in the early years of the nineteenth century. Calhoun was the nationalist; Webster the states' righter—the economic interests of their respective regions apparently determining the political philosophy they preached. The New England states at the time were shipping states. Tariffs, to say nothing of outright embargoes, threatened the European trade upon which their economic well-being depended. Webster, consequently, reminded his fellow Americans that the "Government of the United States is a delegated, limited Government,"[1] with no constitutional power to destroy New England's trade, much less conscript New Englanders to fight a war against their economic self-interest. When the federal government continued to conscript during the War of 1812, he warned:

> The operation of measures thus unconstitutional and illegal ought to be prevented by a resort to other [more drastic] measures. . . . It will be the solemn duty of the state governments to protect their own authority over their own militia and to interpose between their citizens and arbitrary power.[2]

Calhoun, on the other hand, at the time confident that protective tariffs would provide an umbrella under which manufacturing could grow in the South, became an enthusiastic supporter of Henry Clay's American System of tariffs and the federally financed internal improvements—the roads, canals, bridges—which would encourage national industrial development. He would brook no sectional obstruction of the nation's rendezvous with destiny.

But by the 1830s? In New England, manufacturing had grown under the protective tariffs opposed by earlier New Englanders. In the South, though, for a variety of reasons, it failed to take hold. South Carolina remained a cotton-planter state. Thus the stage was set for John C. Calhoun and Daniel Webster as history remembers them: Calhoun the states' righter, defender of slavery, opposed to the tariffs that would benefit northern manufacturers and hurt the cotton interests (by raising the price of their imports and lowering the volume of their cotton exports, as the European powers retaliated); Webster, the great unionist, the defender of the national government's right to institute tariffs for the purpose of encouraging the home industries (conveniently located in his area of the country) and beneficial to the majority of Americans—except for some backward and obstreperous southern slave owners, who clearly had no right to stand in the way of the majority's economic advancement.

Is this a charge of hypocrisy against Calhoun and Webster? Only to the extent that these inconsistencies are evident in so much of American history. What went on in Calhoun's (or Webster's) mind as he switched his position, one cannot tell. Did he feel his conversion genuine, unique, the result of a sudden flash of insight (what the Greeks called *metanoia*), unlikely to be repeated in his life? Would he have stayed a defender of concurrent majorities if he had lived to see the shoe on the other foot; lived to see a situation where the national majority included his home state, while Northern factions were demanding the right to be freed from that majority's authority? Would he have defended antislavery minorities as concurrent majorities in a successfully independent Confederate States of America? Or would he have flopped back to become the centralist Calhoun of his earlier years in these last two instances, fully conscious of the inconsistency? In other words, might Calhoun (and all the other American thinkers who have made the same kinds of reversals) have admitted over a bourbon and branch with an old crony that "hell, we'll find a way, no matter what, to use the Constitution to get what's best for our people. If a man's sharp enough he can find whatever he needs in that sacred parchment." Did he approach the expression of his political theory the way a gangster syndicate's lawyer approaches the law, seeking to secure his client's interests by working the letter of the law, looking for whatever loopholes will carry the day? We will never know, unless, that is, some early version of unedited Watergate tapes shows up to give us insight into the man's mind when his polemicist's guard was down (if, in fact, there was a greater candor about these things in his private conversations).

Certainly one would think Calhoun too profound a thinker never to have brooded over the way his, and his people's, political stance had reversed. He has been called by many—friend and foe alike—this country's only original and truly profound political theorist, the one whose writings will live beyond the topical issues they analyzed and prove universal enough to be of interest to political analysts who are not American. It is difficult to disagree. Calhoun deals with the fundamental questions of government; his analysis is crisp and well-wrought, his logic persuasive, even when in error; his style, if cold at times, has a flair that retains a surprising freshness over a hundred years after publication date. Even a modern northern NAACP attorney would have to admit his work makes Webster's, say, seem bloated and drifting in comparison, all gas and little bite.

Natural Rights—an Objection

Calhoun's *Disquisition on Government* early on offers a treatment of the nature of government itself, an analysis that can strike the unsuspecting reader as a venture into ivory-tower philosophizing. He seeks an alternative to the claims of those who hold for the social-contract theory of government. But he is in no ivory tower. His concern is with those who were arguing that a government, to be legitimate, must be committed to the establishment of political liberty and equality; with those who had pledged themselves to the emancipation of the South's black slaves. He is seeking to cover all the bases, in other words; trying to establish, first of all, that slavery is not an evil by definition; and only then, that the North has no legal right to force an emancipation even if the "peculiar institution" were of a questionable moral nature.

It is, obviously, on this point that much of the modern opposition to Calhoun's thought is built. Since his political theory was constructed to guarantee the continuation of slavery, some see it as flawed from the outset. But it is not that simple. His character can be criticized because of his proslavery sentiments; to the extent that all pro-slavery Southerners of the time can be criticized. But to dismiss his entire political theory, firmer ground is required. Calhoun claimed to be dealing with universals, offering a political theory meant to do more than protect slavery; that slavery was just one of many southern liberties he was protecting from a power-hungry majority. Democracy, after all, leaves more room for crime to flourish than a Nazi dictatorship; and criminals tend to favor laws that provide civil liberties for the accused. But this, in itself, does not invalidate the claims of those who argue for mass suffrage and civil liberties. A gangland lawyer, for the worst of reasons, might very well build a sound theory of the relationship between law enforcement officers and the accused.

Likewise the theory of concurrent majorities can be used to protect the interests of groups other than slave owners. It is possible, at least theoretically, to imagine a scenario in the late 1800s with a minority of anti-slavery states using Calhoun's words to keep slavery out of their areas against the wishes of a national pro-slavery majority. Possible, if not plausible. (The better question is whether Calhoun would be on their side.)

The point is, if it needs be said, that Calhoun's thought can be praised, however much one is opposed to nineteenth-century slavery. His critical analysis of Locke's and Rousseau's contractual theory of the origins of government stands irrespective of his attachment to slavery. He provides moderns, looking for some balance, with a way to parry the thrusts of the liberal social levellers who have argued so successfully for so long now, especially in academic circles, that a society is illegitimate if it makes claims on the individual conscience or maintains a hierarchy among the once absolutely free and equal humans who lived in the "state of nature" before the social contracts were made. (So much of modern liberalism hinges on the existence of this "state of nature" of Locke's and Rousseau's.)

Calhoun makes the point, and convincingly, in a manner that deserves not to be forgotten (for scholarly reasons alone), that men, rather than being born "equal" and with a long list of "natural" rights, are born with a patrimony of duties and responsibilities to society. Are "all men created equal," he asks?

> Taking the proposition literally there is not a word of truth in it. It begins with "all men are born," which is utterly untrue. Men are not born. Infants are born . . . incapable of freedom, being destitute alike of the capacity of thinking and acting, without which there can be no freedom.[3]

He correctly observes our ability to speak; to read; our capacity to work intelligently with concepts such as rights, liberties, freedom, honor, decency, sacrifice, loyalty are *taught* to us by society. Without the heritage a society preserves and hands down to us, we would be savages, men who do not share in the blessings of life in society. (One is reminded, ironically, of the self-proclaimed bohemian intellectuals who "drop out" to glory in their independence from society, moving to rural areas or counterculture urban enclaves—with their shelves of books and records, paintings, fine wines, and a concoction of radios and stereos and other electronic gadgetry they can neither build nor repair, and their eyeglasses, diet pills, etc.)

Then what of the "golden age" of Locke and Rousseau? The time in history before man lived under government authority, as free as the breeze?

> The very supposition that he lived apart and separated from all others . . . free and equal [is false]. . . . Man cannot exist in such a state; . . . he is by nature social, and society is necessary not only to the proper development of all his faculties, moral and intellectual, but to the very existence of his race.[4]

Our society, then—if his logic holds—is not something we are free to undo and remake at will; it is not something *made* by man, at least not the way an automobile or computer is made. Its design is not the prerogative of the present generation of adults. We are part of it, as well as molders of its contours. We never "joined" in any way as legalistic or mechanical as the social-contract theorists would have us think.

> There never was a state as the so called state of nature, and never can be, [and] it follows that men instead of being born in it, are born in the social and political state; and of course, instead of being born free and equal, are born subject, not only to parental authority, but to the laws and institutions of the country where born, and under whose protection they draw their first breath.[5]

Liberty is not something we enjoy, then, when we separate ourselves from social authority, claims of libertarians notwithstanding. Society *gives* us our liberty by providing for our sustenance until we are physically able to enjoy it; teaches us what it means (those societies that do—some teach us an eternal obeisance to the sultan or witchdoctor instead); and maintains the police agencies that prevent the strong and cruel and cunning from depriving us of it at will. Without society, the only liberties we would enjoy would be the liberty to be ignorant, to starve to death as infants, to be enslaved as adults. Man is made in the image and likeness of God, but man is man only in society. Outside the *polis* (or what the Romans called the *civilis*), as Aristotle taught, man's capacity to reason would actually make him an animal more dangerous than the others, one able to plot its depredations in a manner more effective than the wild beasts' instinctive search for prey. Ironically, the Enlightenment's social contract could be formed only by those fortunate enough to have been raised as members of a highly developed *civilis*, by already civilized men, residents of the kind of *civilis* whose authority the Enlightenment thinkers worked so hard to disparage.

The "state of nature" of the Enlightenment thinkers, Calhoun continues, would be a "universal state of conflict between individual and individual, accompanied by the connected passions of suspicion, jealousy, anger, and revenge—followed by insolence, fraud, and cruelty—if not prevented by some controlling power. . . . This controlling power, whether vested or by whomsoever exercised, is GOVERNMENT."[6]

Hence liberty is the accomplishment of civilization, the proud achievement of centuries of societal development in the West. (Whether it has been achieved any place else today is problematic, but in Calhoun's time it was the *sole* possession of the West.) To call liberty a "natural right," enjoyed in direct proportion to the decline of society's authority over us, then, is a grave error in historical perception; but, more important, it is an assault on the legitimacy of the social ties which allow for civilization's—and liberty's—continuation.

Now, without question, Calhoun is making this point in order to defend slavery. If men are not born with a natural right to liberty, then slavery is not wrong *by definition*. Some other reason must be found to establish the dignity and brotherhood of man. Religion seems the most viable alternative, as the history of Christianity in the West has shown. Still, whatever his intentions, Calhoun punctures the balloon of the social-contract theorists. One would not deny a doctor the use of his scalpel because some thug uses it for a murder weapon. Harried college presidents, urban judges afraid to levy a stiff sentence, distraught parents, among others, would profit from a study of his words when faced with challenges to their authority wrapped in banners marked "liberty" and "individual rights" and "freedom from society's dictates."

> It is a great and dangerous error to suppose that all people are equally entitled to liberty. It is a reward to be earned, not a blessing to be gratuitously lavished on all alike;—a reward reserved for the intelligent, the patriotic, the virtuous and deserving; and not a boon to be bestowed on a people too ignorant, degraded and vicious, to be capable either of appreciating or of enjoying it. . . .

A community may possess all the necessary moral qualifications in so high a degree as to be capable of self-government under the most adverse circumstances; while, on the other hand, another may be so sunk in ignorance and vice as to be incapable of forming a conception of liberty or of living . . . under any other than an absolute and despotic government.[7]

But how does all this jibe with our topic—with what is best remembered about Calhoun: his staunch defense of the South's "liberty" to maintain slavery in the face of a developing northern and western consensus against it? Could not Northerners have used his words to deny the South that "liberty"? Could not Northerners have argued that the South had become a community "sunk in ignorance and vice," one "incapable of forming a conception of liberty" when they dug in their heels to preserve slavery? It is difficult to see why not. Which brings us to the reason why visions of concurrent majorities arose in the mind of a man who had earlier seen great wisdom in Henry Clay's American System.

Liberty *per se* is not *really* an attractive political condition, in spite of the liberal tradition, which has been teaching Americans and Europeans otherwise for over two hundred years. No one who ponders the issue can say with conviction that "I may disagree with what you have to say, but will defend to the death your right to say it" (whether or not Voltaire ever said the words).

Such verbal pomposity is reminiscent of the strutting morons who taunt the tigers in the cages at the zoo. We are "for" liberty when, and only when, we have confidence that our fellow citizens, by and large, will use their liberty for ends with which we feel comfortable; when we have a trust in their basic civility. It is possible to picture a man "defending to the death" another's right to expression when the discussion centers on proposals that he opposes, but only if those proposals are within certain acceptable boundaries—when they suggest policies for which he can serve as a member of the *loyal* opposition. A meeting called to plot the best way to burn his house to the ground will strike different nerve endings.

In the recent and widely discussed question of whether to allow Nazi and Ku Klux Klan marches and rallies, for example, even the libertarian types tended to agree that these groups should lose some of the cherished freedom of expression if they ever get to the point where they are a political force to be reckoned with. Only as long as they are harmless is the suggestion to *tolerate* them. "Tolerate" of course implies that we allow something to continue when we are within our rights to end it.

The counterculture types, too, who pride themselves on their limitless permissiveness—"different strokes for different folks, etc."—come under this qualification. When they tell us they thrive in an atmosphere where anything goes, what they really mean is "anything" that fits under the umbrella of their own counterculture orthodoxy. Cherish they might, a neighborhood with lots of gays, drug users, sexual pioneers, religious cultists, health-food faddists, underground left-wing radicals, communes, etc.; but an influx, it is safe to say, of neo-Fascists seeking an urban base or Black Muslims willing to use a little muscle to clean up their neighborhood would be something else again.

As soon, then, as a society becomes polarized, fragmented into conflicting and competing blocs—groups which cannot view each other as loyal opposition and with ostensibly irreconcilable differences—its members tend to develop nuances of their understanding of what is meant by liberty. The dominant majority, seeking to retain the advantages of its dominance, is likely to speak in disparaging terms of the minority's "liberty" to its (now evil) view. (Calhoun, again, would not have been amenable to a South Carolina abolitionist group claiming to be a concurrent majority in relationship to the proslavery majority within the state.) And the minority, sensing its tenuous position, begins to express the more absolutist libertarian view. Pockets of resistance must be formed against the majority: concurrent majorities.

The Calhoun remembered in history is in this last position. The Poobah of the Enlightenment understanding of liberty becomes the great defender of local communities in the face of a hostile northern majority. Neither blacks in the South nor northern whites—who, we must conclude *do not* "possess the necessary moral qualifications"—are to be allowed directive control of society. Southern civilization is to be preserved against its enemies by authoritarianism within Carolina; by the call for a respect for "concurrent majorities" in the national arena.

The national government is now to be instructed that its abolitionist desires are futile and self-defeating since

> the main spring to progress is the desire of individuals to better their condition. . . . Now, as individuals differ greatly from each other, in intelligence, sagacity, energy, perseverance, skill, habits of in-

dustry and economy, physical power, position and opportunity, the necessary effect of leaving all free to exert themselves to better their condition must be a corresponding inequality. . . . The only means by which this result can be prevented are either to impose such restrictions on the exertions of those who may possess them in a high degree [ambitious slaves?], as will place them on a level with those who do not; or to deprive them of the fruits of their exertion.[8]

The northern majority is reminded by Calhoun of the history of well-meaning reformist governments seeking to remake society in the name of social justice; shown that government "has itself a strong tendency [except on the state level?] to disorder and abuse of its powers, as all experience and almost every page of history testify"; and told that the special wisdom of the Anglo-American political development is the understanding that a government's tendency towards the abuse of its power "is prevented, by whatever name called, by [a] CONSTITUTION."[9]

And the Founding Fathers wrote a Constitution, he argues, meant to assure the individual states that their local liberties would be preserved against the newly established federal government. An "equilibrium between the two sections [North and South] afforded ample means to each to protect itself against the aggression of the other," using Constitutional machinery. With the passing of time, however, this equilibrium "has been destroyed." "One section has the exclusive power of controlling the Government" by virtue of a "numerical majority."[10] The North is moving increasingly closer to the day when it will be able to force an end to Slavery and the plantation system and impose its drab industrial order on the South.

> A single section, governed by the will of the numerical majority, has now in fact, the control of the Government and the entire powers of the system. What was once a constitutional Federal Republic is now converted, in reality, into one as absolute as that of the autocrat of Russia. . . .
> As, then, the North has the absolute control over the Government, it is manifest that on all questions between it and the South, where there is diversity of interests, the interests of the latter will be sacrificed to the former, however oppressive the effects may be.[11]

And the right to vote will be to no avail.

> The right of suffrage, of itself, can do no more than give complete control to those who elect, over the conduct of those they have elected. . . . The dominant majority . . . would have the same tendency to oppression and abuse of power which, without the right of suffrage, irresponsible rulers have.

Consequently, rather than sanction the effects of majority rule, the need is "to prevent any one interest or combination of interests from using the powers of government to aggrandize itself at the expense of the others."[12] Society must find a way to take into account the fact that "the numerical majority, instead of being the people, is only a portion of them,—such a government, instead of being a true and perfect model of the people's government . . . is but the government of a part,—the major over the minor portion."[13]

His theory of "concurrent majorities" is that "way"; a new—or more penetrating, some would say—analysis of the nature of the Constitutional bond.

The Original "Deal"

Calhoun's theory of nullification and concurrent majorities hinges upon the accuracy of his understanding of the exact nature of the relationship between the original thirteen states and the federal government given birth upon the ratification of the Constitution. He maintained that the Constitution was a compact between thirteen separate, sovereign states, "distinct communities—each with its separate charter and government, and in no way connected with each other, except as dependent members of a common [British] empire."[14] Consequently,

> ours is a system of government, compounded by the separate governments of the several States composing the Union and of one common government of all its members. The former preceeded the latter, and was created by their agency, . . . by the people of each, acting separately and in their sovereign character.[15]

These separate states, he admits, united themselves through the Constitution, *but* "without merging their respective sovereignties into one common sovereignty." Their new Constitution established a "common government" but only "for certain specific objects which, regarding the mutual interest and security of each and all, they supposed could be more certainly, safely, and effectually promoted by it than by their several separate governments." He suggests the point is made clear if we, instead of using the term "United States," say "the States united, which inversion alone, without further explanation, removes the ambiguity."[16]

If, then, the central government established by the states

oversteps its bounds and assumes powers beyond those delegated to it by the states . . . well, the deal is off. The states become free to ignore the resulting unconstitutional legislation. Moreover, it is for the states, separately and without qualification, to judge when such unconstitutional measures have been enacted in Washington. No proportionate right to declare the states in error inheres in the federal government. The Supreme Court has no power to settle the dispute as an arbiter, as Daniel Webster would have it. The central government cannot be seen as equal disputant in these matters, Calhoun insists.

> The error is in the assumption that the General Government is a party to the constitutional compact. The States . . . formed the compact, acting as sovereign and independent communities. The General Government is but its creature.[17]

Calhoun proceeds to develop the system that he hopes will provide the individual states an orderly method to override legislation they deem contrary to the Constitutional bond. He tells us he seeks a "limitation which shall . . . effectively prevent any interest or combination of interests from obtaining the exclusive control of the government." His theory of concurrent majorities:

> There is but one mode in which this can be effected; and that is by taking the sense of each interest or portion of the community, which may be unequally and injuriously affected by the action of the government, separately through its own majority . . . to require the consent of each interest either to put or to keep the government in action. This, too, can be accomplished only in one way; . . . by dividing and distributing the powers of government, give to each division or interest, through its appropriate organ, either a concurrent voice in making and executing the laws or a veto on their execution.[18]

The exact mechanics he constructs ingeniously. An individual state, when faced with legislation of executive decisions, may decide "whether an act of the federal government or any of its departments be or be not in conformity to the provisions of the constitutional compact; and, if decided to be inconsistent, of pronouncing it to be unauthorized by the Constitution and therefore null, void, and of no effect."[19]

Upon such a declaration of nullification by any one state, the federal government is to be obliged to seek an amendment to the Constitution, to specifically receive from the states the powers originally sought in the legislation. The law is held null and void until the states grant it this authority. Thus, two-thirds of the states will have to propose the amendment, and three-quarters ratify it, before the law blocked by the nullification proclamation of one state can go into effect. Any minority substantial enough to block the amendment fills the bill as a concurrent majority, entitled to protect its interests against the raw power of the numerical majority.

Does this mean that Calhoun would accept the abolition of slavery as long as the anti-slavery states brought it about through a specific amendment, which they might have been able to do as the number of free states admitted to the union from the Western territories increased? (The fear of this, by the way, is what made Calhoun so implacably opposed to the prohibition of slavery in the West.) Not exactly. There are exceptions to even the best laid schemes. No matter how large the anti-slavery majority, it could not abolish slavery without the consent of the slave-holding states. The Constitution would never have been ratified in the first instance, Calhoun points out, if the slave-holding states had not been assured that their interests would be vouchsafed. Slavery, in fact, he argues, was the only form of property specifically mentioned in the Constitution—the three-fifths Compromise—"the only property . . . that entered into its formulation as a political element both in the adjustment of the relative weight in the Government, . . . the only one that is put under the express guaranty of the Constitution."[20] If such a basic right were to be ignored by an anti-slavery coalition of states, the fundamental spirit of the Constitution would be sufficiently violated for the slave states to secede from the union at will. (This deft footwork, to this reader at least, gives substance to the claims of those who view Calhoun as a clever apologist for the slave states rather than a political philosopher.)

The Vis Medicatrix of the System

In response to those who protested that such a states'-rights arrangement would prevent the central government from carrying out its mandate and eventually destroy the nation, Calhoun argued:

> By giving to each interest or portion the power of self-protection, all strife and struggle between them for ascendancy is prevented. . . . Each sees and feels that it can best promote its own prosperity by conciliating the goodwill and promoting the prosperity of the oth-

ers. . . . And hence, instead of faction, strife, and struggle for party ascendancy, there would be patriotism, nationality, harmony, and a struggle for supremacy in promoting the common good of the whole.

"When something must be done," he assures, "and when it can be done only by the united consent of all, the necessity of the case will force to a compromise, be the cause of that necessity what it may."[21]

Far from promoting a destructive sectionalism, then, he feels his system will actually encourage a stronger sense of national unity, as each state comes to understand that its interests lie in the survival of the national union, which not only does not threaten local liberties, but encourages and insures them. Each state will seek to perfect a nationhood advantageous to all; each will know beforehand that it can prosper only as a member of the union, not in competition with the other states for dominance.

Thus the power which, in its simple and absolute form, was the creator, becomes in its modified form the preserver of the system . . . the vis medicatrix of the system . . . its great repairing, healing, and conservative power,—intended to remedy its disorders. . . . The stronger . . . are prevented from encroaching on and finally absorbing the weaker.[22]

Daniel Webster in Opposition

The prospect of a federal government unable to pursue policies clearly in opposition to the interests of a substantial minority of the population can be attractive to many vectors of society. It is the notion enshrined in our time by such terms as "minority rights" and "civil liberties"; it is what the philosophers attempt to insure when they warn of mob rule, "the tyranny of the majority." Well, why not, now that slavery is no longer a threat, set up the machinery that Calhoun suggested to provide an effective check on federal power? Why not let the federal government act only in those areas where it can secure the approval of three-quarters of the states?

The most celebrated contemporary response to Calhoun came from Daniel Webster. Webster challenged the obvious practical disadvantages: (1) the threat of a hamstrung national government, as ineffective and indecisive as the Articles of Confederation it was instituted to replace; and (2) a weakened, and eventually impoverished, America unable to compete with the major European powers or develop the western frontier. But he also dealt with Calhoun's philosophical propositions. He rejected Calhoun's notion that the union was a compact between still sovereign states, something like an early version of NATO.

The union was not revocable, Webster insisted; it was not an association a state joined for certain advantages, and which it could leave when those advantages no longer obtained in as clear cut a manner. For Webster the political bond was permanent; the American people had become a fledgling nation-state in 1789, committed to forming an even "more perfect union." Individual states could no more move to disband this political unity than Gascony could leave France or Sussex leave England. An act of secession in the United States would have the same identity as one in any European nation: treason, an act of rebellion.

> This government . . . is the independent offspring of the popular will. It is not the creature of the state legislatures; nay, more, if the whole truth must be told, the people brought it into existence, established it, and have hitherto supported it, for the very purpose, amongst others, of imposing certain salutary restraints on state sovereignties.[23]

Furthermore,

> The truth is, and no ingenuity of argument, no subtlety of distinction, can evade it, that, as to certain purposes, the people of the United States are one people.[24]

And the Congress, as representative of "one people," is empowered to make laws binding on the separate states, subject only to constitutional guidelines. If it is alleged to have overstepped its bounds, he argues, the Constitution provides the machinery—the system of checks and balances and, ultimately, the Supreme Court—to settle the dispute. No individual state on its own can proclaim a law null and void in opposition to these procedures. The "Constitution itself decides [to the contrary] . . . by declaring that '*the judicial power shall extend to all cases arising under the Constitution and laws of the United States.*' "[25]

There is no state superiority over, or immunity from, these decisions.

> It is the people's Constitution, the people's government, made for the people, made by the people, and answerable to the people. The

people of the United States have declared that this Constitution shall be the supreme law. . . . So far as the people have given power to the general government, so far the grant is unquestionably good, and the government holds of the people and not of the State governments.[26]

So wherever sovereignty lay before the Revolution and during the days of the Articles of Confederation, it is now in Washington, Webster insists. A state may refuse to accept that jurisdiction, but not legally, not within constitutionally permitted guidelines. A state, if it feels it imperative, may "throw off any government it finds oppressive"—as the Declaration of Independence proclaims to the world—"and seek to erect a better one in its stead."[27] That is an American as apple pie. But it must accept the consequence of what it has done; accept that it has initiated an act of political rebellion. And, as with all rebellions, it must expect those who still believe their government to be legitimate and worthy of support to oppose the rebellion with as much dedication and force as the rebels are willing to employ in fulfilling it.

There are noble and ignoble rebellions, but no legal ones, no easy ones—none that should expect to receive the blessings of the established government. King George, from the American point of view, was not villainous for opposing the rebels; he was an enemy for opposing them in defense of a wrongful cause. A rebellion is praiseworthy, when it is, because it seeks noble goals, not by virtue of its very rebelliousness, its contrariness. A state proclaiming the authority to ignore or "nullify" a federal law upon the threat of secession is in a state of rebellion, Webster holds, nothing less; it cannot picture itself in some more respectable status under the banner of a concurrent majority. The Congress of the United States, the elected representatives of the majority of the American people, properly checked and limited by the Constitution, correctly interpreted by the Supreme Court, are not to be prevented from carrying out the national will by sectional or partisan minorities. "Liberty and Union, now and forever, one and inseparable," as Webster phrased it with characteristic flair in the epigram learned by generations of (mostly northern) schoolchildren.

Calhoun: Prophet of Despair

But is Webster right, as we look back on his words with the advantages of hindsight and without an impending civil war to help us make up our minds? Is it not true that his arguments have been elevated more by the North's victory in the Civil War than by the force of their own logic? In all honesty, is not Calhoun on firmer ground in his analysis of the states in the days just before the ratification of the Constitution? The delegates to the convention were from separate states, sent by individual state legislatures—state legislatures that had decided to consider a new constitution because the national government under the Articles of Confederation did not have enough power to act as a sovereign—thereby indicating the sovereign status (desirable or not) of the individual states. And the Constitution was ratified not by Americans, but by state conventions called by the state legislatures. There was no national referendum. The Constitution was ratified state by state.

Is not Webster, to be blunt, wrong, no matter how grand and rafter-ringing the oratory he employs in protest, when he argues that the Constitution was the expression of an already formed national will? The record is clear. Americans at the time of the Convention, by and large, thought of themselves as New Yorkers, Virginians, Carolinians, etc. It was the era of regional loyalties, as the failure of the Articles of Confederation amply demonstrates.

Why not, then, in our time, allow for the development of a political system that would return to the state governments jurisdiction over as much public policy as possible? Have we not learned by now that the government closest to the people, most under their control, is government most likely to reflect the popular will? The Left tells us of the need for "community control"; that "patriotism" and "nationalism" are but superstitions of a passing dark age; that "people are just people"; that our loyalties ought to be to "mankind," to a "spaceship earth," where national ties will become even more obsolete as some of us come to see that we have more in common with the denizens of Marrakesh than Orange County, California.

The Right, in turn, speaks of the dangers of "big brotherism," creeping socialism, HHS busybodies, the loss of individualism resulting from excessive power concentrations in Washington, D.C. Why not then allow states to develop a truly distinct character of their own? Why not allow the different American tribes to establish homelands? A rugged individualist Southwest? A swinging California, maybe, a land of porn and neon, perpetually bathed in a haze of marijuana smoke? Little Scandinavias, welfare-state enclaves around New York and Massachusetts? Why not permit states' rights to mean more than the power to choose the color of license plates and high-school graduation requirements? If you do not like the tribe that dominates your state, move to one where your tribe reigns. Out of fifty there should be one or two acceptable to everyone—one where each American will truly feel free. Diversity. Independence. States' rights. It seems just what the doctor ordered. Certainly many conservative pundits would welcome the scenario, one would think. And leftwingers might be on the verge. Some New York liberals, who used to tremble at the thought of being severed from the federal purse strings, now have bought the argument heretofore associated with the Conservative party in that state: that federal aid is only tax money returned, after the expenses for the trip down to Washington and back have been subtracted from the original amount. Well, why not?

Because, as we alleged, talk of concurrent majorities and nullification (as opposed to more limited claims for states' rights and strict constructionism) can be entertained by the serious-minded only when they have given up on the survival of their national union. The fact that Calhoun suggested the southern states secede if his system of concurrent majorities was not able to prevent the abolition of slavery is an indication of the depths of his alienation from the national union. From his point of view, the northern majority had become a separate nation, with views for which he could not serve as loyal opposition. He no longer wanted to be part of forming "a more perfect union" with the "them" developing in the North in opposition to "us" Southerners. Before that sense of alienation reached crisis proportions, he dreamed the great dreams of nationhood, of a nation expanding and prospering under Clay's American System; but afterwards his goal was to protect "his" people, the way the leader of any less powerful nation deals with a hostile neighboring country: by cunning (concurrent majorities, nullification) for as long as it works; by the threat of heroic armed resistance, foredoomed to failure or not (secession), if it fails.

Let us for the moment ignore the question of whether the North was obnoxious enough to deserve great contempt from Southerners of Calhoun's stripe. Even if it was; even if it was becoming as oppressive as King George's England in 1776, the point is that we must remember that we are talking about a theory constructed by Calhoun to break down the union, dissolve the American nation-state, and we cannot employ it today without seeking the same ends. Good rebellion or bad, it was rebellion he was promoting. Regionalism to the point Calhoun suggested is no vis medicatrix of national unity. It is despair.

Look: the Security Council of the United Nations has the kind of limited authority he wanted—at least it is closer to his model than the American nation-state that emerged after the Civil War—and its impotence has not engendered great endearment around the world or a lingering affection for the survival of the world body (except, perhaps, from the sleek Third World solons with the cat-that-got-the-mouse grins who keep three-quarters of Manhattan's East side restaurants in business). It is no vis medicatrix.

One must always ask himself why Calhoun showed no inclination toward favoring concurrent majorities within South Carolina, an area as large as a good many European nation-states. The answer is that he cared about South Carolina; it was a political union he still wanted to nurture rather than break into fragments that could achieve none of the fruits of a cooperative political bond. The political machinery needed to bring about the necessary compromises could be constructed in South Carolina, you see, among *his* people (just as he once thought it could in all of America); whereas, he believed, it could not with *them* in the North. He is not seeking to achieve the ends of good government as defined by the great minds of the Western political tradition, all his talk of the vis medicatrix to the contrary. (Whether he was fully conscious of this disingenuousness, once again, we leave an open question.) He is seeking to hinder the development of a national community, not encourage it; seeking to disassociate his people from another with whom he no longer shares a brotherhood; seeking to disassociate from them without the pains of rebellion, if possible—in an act of secession, if not. And those attracted to his thought nowadays, if they are honest with themselves, will admit they are in the same boat. Perhaps they are not yet ready to talk of secession. Yet it is an alienation from our co-citizens—blacks against whites, hippies against Sun-belters, hardhats against environmentalists, etc., etc.—which draws us to his words; it is the feeling that the residents of the United States are no longer our fellow-Americans, and that we no longer really want "them" to be.

Calhoun conceded:

If the whole community had the same interests so that the interests of each and every portion would be so affected by the action of government, that the laws which oppressed or impoverished one portion would necessarily oppress and impoverish all others,—or the reverse,—then the right of suffrage of itself, would be all sufficient to counteract the tendency of the government to oppression and abuse of its powers; and, of itself, a perfect constitutional government.[28]

Calhoun is, of course, being sarcastic here, implying that clear-headed men will agree that such a national consensus cannot be formed; that laws acceptable to both North and South—either favorable, or unfavorable only to the extent that the aggrieved side can continue as the loyal opposition—cannot be written.

And maybe they could not in his time. Maybe a civil war had to be fought to keep the country together. It is entirely possible. But those are the only choices: the maintenance of a national government capable of ameliorating sectional and ideological strife through some version of division of powers and checks and balances—the sweet burden of political life, nation-building, forming a more perfect union—or rebellion, dissolution, and probably, civil war. There is no middle ground of concurrent majorities whereby we pretend to be a people while allowing a tribalism to flourish, which makes the national development impossible.

One would think that even the most die-hard apologists for the Confederacy, and Calhounites, would concede the point that the Founding Fathers certainly intended nothing like a system of concurrent majorities to be a part of the union they established. And that neither did Calhoun until the slave question reached center stage; until he became convinced the division between North and South was irreconcilable. (And once again, it must be stressed, conceding this point need not imply any preference for the North's position in the crisis years; it implies only that Calhoun's writings are dedicated to a national dissolution. To recommend him, one must be a "rebel" in the strictest sense of the word.)

Curiously, then, it could be said that Webster, although wrong in his analysis of the relationship between the states before the Constitution was ratified, was nevertheless "correct." And that Calhoun, although the better historian, and therefore more logical in his analysis, makes a case for states' rights that cannot hold. It is true, the thirteen states were not yet a nation in 1789. They *were* "states united" for the purposes clearly described in their Constitution. The national will Webster describes had not yet formed (*he* apparently did not feel it in 1814). The "American people" could not have formed the union. There was no such animal.

Yet Webster is "correct." We are dealing with something here that retains an element of mystery: nationhood. We know the world today is made up of nations. But we also know that there was an earlier time when that was not the case. In Europe, to say nothing of African and Asian lands, only five or six hundred years ago people did not identify themselves as Frenchman or Germans or Italians, etc. They considered themselves part of something larger—Christendom; or something much smaller—subjects of some feudal lord. Yet now we have men willing to give their lives for Namibia and Palestine, Basque and Breton independence, Croatia, Bangladesh.

Nationhood is so much a part of our world that we take it for granted, as if it always was and always will be. Well, it wasn't always and perhaps will not always be. But for as long as there has been an America, political survival on this planet has taken the shape of nationhood. We know no alternative. If there had been no American nation, the people living in the land mass we now call the United States would have been made part of some other nation's political development—the prolongation of the British Empire probably; perhaps a Spanish or Hispanic union moving up from the south; a Russian empire moving west from Alaskan or Californian strongholds. Thirteen separate ex-colonies just could not have survived in the modern world.

The reason for the development of nations has taxed some of the best minds in modern intellectual history. There is no need just now to review the theories that attempt to describe the way once separate and distinct people were welded into Frenchmen, Englishmen, Germans, Spaniards, Americans. Walter Bagehot, the late 19th Century English economist and political scientist, speaks of how nations are first forced to live as a political unity by dominant personalities (William the Conqueror, Bismarck, Ferdinand and Isabella, Garibaldi and Cavour, etc.), and how, only later, a collective identity—nationalism—develops, which makes the association seem natural and spontaneous. He is undoubtedly correct. The point now is only that, for whatever the reason, this is how the world has been turning since at least the late 1600s. People live in nation-states, or under the control of assertive nation-states as part of their Empire. Not even a John C. Calhoun could make the people of the ex-British colonies in America exempt from this historical fate.

The people of the United States, in other words, were going to become a nation. The Founding Fathers understood this. They knew they were not acting as the representatives of a fully formed national will in 1789. But they knew a national will had to be formed—a "more perfect union" secured. That or disaster. They might have winked if they had lived to hear Webster's puffed oratory. But they would have applauded him at the same time—unless of course they became wrapped up in the same alienation and despair that deadened Calhoun's nationalist fervor, which is quite possible in certain cases.

Ironically it might be Southerners, who continue to display a greater fondness for patriotic display (think of the half-time show at an Alabama game compared to one at Harvard) and who appear less enamored of the supranationalist sympathies of certain sections of the Northeast, who know this as well as anyone. Where would an America of today be if it had been divided into concurrent majorities in an age of powerful international corporations, Arab oil cartels, global war, and other nations mobilized by dictatorships of the Left and Right? No place, one would think, where John C. Calhoun would feel comfortable.

V

Henry David Thoreau—Idealist?

One hesitates to be critical of Henry David Thoreau. In a very real way he has become a patron saint of sorts for Americans—Americans of all political persuasions. No one, apparently, from Bircher to Weatherman, seems willing to challenge at the core his exposition of the rights of the individual conscience. Law and order rightists and totalitarian leftists alike have learned either directly from him or from summaries of his thought popularized by disciples. Or they have intuited on their own, and learned later of Thoreau's agreement, that the man was right; that the individual conscience may correctly reserve for itself the right to dissent from, and, at least, peacefully noncooperate with a government pursuing policies it considers immoral. What American has not at one time or another used his "following the beat of a different drummer" to justify some individual nonconformity to custom or law? Everyone seems to feel that the day could come when he too will want to dissent and adopt at the minimum Thoreau's posture of nonviolent noncooperation toward his government: the Right, if the day comes when the Marxists begin to take hold of directive power in the country; the Left, when it is necessary to make life difficult for the capitalist lackeys in the establishment.

So by now it is a hackneyed observation: Thoreau is the philosophical progenitor of Gandhi, Martin Luther King, peace protectors on the White House lawn, hunger strikers, labor leaders jailed for violating anti-strike injunctions, ecology demonstrators chained to the gates of nuclear power plants, southern governors standing in the doorway of about-to-be integrated schools, angry parents illegally keeping their children home from school to avoid busing programs, anti-abortion demonstrators singing hymns while blocking hospital deliveries, generals speaking out against Commanders-in-Chief gone soft on Communism. Thoreau is as American as apple pie, apparently, the writer almost all Americans come across at one time or another in their high-school or college days. To be of a different mind places one in the company of the Germans who were "just following orders" during World War II. You might not like it when the other guy uses him, but for sure, you have got to keep him ready for yourself.

Strange to have earned such universal acceptance? Not really. It should be kept in mind that although Thoreau has had many popularizers, he was a popularizer himself. His basic insight is not really new. His genius, such as it was, lay in his ability to express in the vernacular, and in a manner applicable to American politics, an idea that can be traced back to St. Thomas Aquinas and medieval Catholicism, to Socrates, and beyond to the Old Testament: that is, that man's first loyalty is to his Maker; to Truth; to Justice; that unjust laws are to be opposed; in the extreme, tyrants may be overthrown, even killed, in order to avoid greater evils. And needless to say, this is a tradition which most Americans and Europeans would claim as their own. In fact, probably, only those who have adopted the near-deification of the state associated with nineteenth-century German historicism would be able to offer a coherent scholarly alternative (a school of thought, it is true, often denied a fair hearing because of its association with the Hitler years).

Nevertheless, there are questions that should be raised about Thoreau. One need neither desert the older tradition of resistance to unjust laws, nor subscribe to German historicism, to observe that there is something quirky about Thoreau's particular affection for civil disobedience, as well as that of some of his most visible modern disciples. Praised he may be by both modern leftists and rightists, but only perceptively by the Left. Thoreau's brand of civil disobedience—as contrasted to Socrates' and St. Thomas'—is clearly a manifestation of a political and cultural outlook that, since the Enlightenment, has been considered leftist in its least defensible and most jejune form.

To be specific, Thoreau does not seek to reawaken in his fellow men, through a dramatic act of disobedience, an appreciation of the highest ideals of their civilization. He seeks rather to invalidate the claims of political and religious authority—of any, of all, political and religious authority. He is, to be direct, an irresponsible, and ultimately shallow thinker, one who would be unable to distinguish, by his own guidelines, between the anti-social actions of Harriet Tubman and Charles Manson. This is not to say that Thoreau would not react differently to such extremes; only that he offers mankind in his most serious writing no gauge other than subjective and emotional responses. And, more important, Thoreau does not appear to have been bothered by the omission. The refusal to abide by society's rules, in and of itself, was the object of his highest praise. Society is presumed to be in error in his writing—always. The rebel is the saint; all martyrs are Christs. Which just isn't so.

Too Good for the World

There is further reason why one hesitates to attack Thoreau. Not only does one run the risk of striking at a sacred American idol, but also, if the criticism follows a careful reading of Thoreau's works, of striking out at an old friend, a gentle and eccentric cousin who never made much of a success of himself in the world, but a prince nevertheless. It is no accident that Thoreau remains a favorite in schoolbook anthologies. On first reading, most people, especially when they are young, *like* the man. He possesses a mystique. There is no denying that. The loner, the dreamer, leaving the humdrum world of village merchants and front-porch gossips; building his cabin in the wilderness; raising his own food; communing both with nature and a handful of the classics; and finally, refusing to pay his poll tax and going to jail because of that refusal, in protest over slavery and the Mexican War. He is one of history's great men of principle for many high-minded folk, one of the giants who stand against the tide of a majority that has lost its idealism, risking everything, asking nothing but the right to not cooperate in evil. The Thoreau myth.

In addition, he writes with the poet's touch. Few readers forget the delightful hours they spend with him, hoeing the dark brown soil of the bean patch in the morning sun, paddling through the mist-adorned surface of Walden in pursuit of northern perch, spying on the epic warfare between the red and black ants, angling through a hole in the ice with a birch pole to retrieve a sunken axe.

The reader can find it hard to escape the conclusion that such a refined soul could not have been the guilty party in his conflict with the government of his time; that he must have been too good, too gentle for the authorities; a prophet scorned by little, self-centered men. We are left with no suspicion that it might have been something else indeed. But might it have been? Could jealousy, or a mean-spirited hate for that matter, have had more to do with his alienation and withdrawal from society and proud obstruction of the law?

Let us admit, at the outset, at least, that such things are possible. Many, who would not have before, agree by now that much of the "Luv" and effusive humanitarianism of the late 1960s—all that Age of Aquarius outpouring of "open" and "free" sex, the interracial coupling, the deep concern over the ravaging of Vietnamese villages—were the outward signs of a middle- and upper-class self-abnegation; an attempt by young Americans to strike out at the lives and values of their parents; a need to wound those close to them through a preening display of affection for opinions and people and practices repugnant to "middle-class morality." In real life it was more often hate than love that prompted recreations of the theme of *Guess Who's Coming to Dinner?*

Was Thoreau in such a disingenuous position? Was he genuinely distressed by the plight of southern slaves and Mexicans under siege by American armed forces? Or were these groups the tools he employed—exploited, if you will—to strike at the legitimacy of a society he despised long before he ever thought for more than a second or two about a slave or a Mexican, and which he would have despised even if slavery had never been introduced and Mexico never attacked?

Well, one cannot tell for sure or pretend otherwise unless he is a practitioner of the dubious science of psychohistory. Still, there are indications enough in Thoreau's writings to make clear that his idea of civil disobeidence just does not belong within the older and honored tradition of resistance to unjust laws; that there was more of the element of spoiled college protestor in him than noble martyr; that he was far from being a nineteenth-century Socrates.

The Older Tradition

It is not that Thoreau was unfamiliar with the older tradition. He knew it quite well, which is not surprising. He was familiar with the classics, a member of the educated elite of the time: Harvard College, Class of 1837. His family was not wealthy, but early in life he secured the patronage of Ralph Waldo Emerson and the Massachusetts Transcendentalist group which clustered about him. He even lived as a member of the Emerson household from 1841 to 1843, and again from 1847 to 1848. It was Emerson who used his influence to secure Thoreau a place at Harvard.

In fact, a reader can quite easily make the mistake of assuming that Thoreau is writing simply to restate in an American context the older tradition, acting as a teacher to his less educated fellow citizens of Massachusetts. One might even think him *less* demanding on the established order than a St. Thomas, say—less willing to encourage violent political upheaval. Moving to Walden, after all, is not exactly armed insurrection.

> It is *not* a man's duty, as a matter of course, to devote himself to the eradication of any, even the *most enormous* wrong [emphasis added]; he may still properly have other concerns to engage him; but it is his duty, at least, to wash his hands of it, and, if he gives it no thought longer, not to give it practically his support. If I devote myself to other pursuits and contemplations, I must first see, at least, that I do not pursue them sitting upon another man's shoulders.[1]

The thought seems straightforward enough, and not controversial. A citizen who is also a moral man, if nothing else, ought not cooperate with the implementation of laws he considers directed toward evil ends. He must make witness against such laws; oppose his government in the hope of converting his leaders and fellow citizens, if possible; if not, to not assist in the wrongful activity himself. It is not sufficient to say that the king wills it or the majority rules. In the context of America in the 1840s:

> I do not hesitate to say, that those who call themselves Abolitionists should at once effectually withdraw their support, both in person and property, from the government of Massachusetts and not wait until they constitute a majority of one, before they suffer the right to prevail through them. I think that it is enough if they have God on their side, without waiting for that other one. Moreover, any man more right than his neighbor constitutes a majority of one already.[2]

In other words, for starters, do as Thoreau did—refuse to pay the taxes likely to go for the support of immoral politics: black slavery in the South, war with Mexico, especially. Moral men ought to be able to see the evil of these things. Yet they do not act. Why, he asks?

> All men recognize the right of revolution; that is, the right to refuse allegiance to and to resist, the government, when its tyranny or its inefficiency are great and unendurable. But almost all say that such is not the case now. But such was the case they think, in the Revolution of '75.[3]

Naturally, Thoreau refuses to buy that argument. Only the morally callous or intellectually dishonest can look at the America of his time, he says, and argue that the conditions for resistance do not obtain. When

> a sixth of the population of a nation which has undertaken to be the refuge of liberty are slaves, and a whole country [Mexico] is unjustly overrun and conquered by a foreign army [the American] and subjected to military law, I think that it is not too soon for honest men to rebel and revolutionize.[4]

Hence he calls on his fellow citizens to join with him at once. Not with the force of arms, but morally. It would be preferable, he agrees, because so much more effective, to first secure the backing of the majority, but if such a consensus cannot be achieved, the good man must act on his own.

> Some are petitioning the state to dissolve the Union, to disregard the requisitions of the President. Why do they not dissolve it themselves—the union between themselves and the state—and refuse to pay their quota into its treasury?[5]

Simple enough tactics. And if just a few good men start the ball rolling, they will not long have to stand alone. A conscience elite will be formed sufficient for the objective: widespread civil disobedience. "A minority is powerless when it conforms to the majority; it is not even a minority then; but it is irresistible when it clogs by its whole weight."[6] Soon the government will face the inevitable. "If the alternative is to keep all just men in prison, or give up war and slavery, the State will not hesitate what to choose."[7] (Quite an assumption, by the way. A state ruled by certain oriental Sultans or Genghis Khan, rather than men shaped by the prescriptions of the Christian West, would "not hesitate" to put the civilly disobedient to the sword.) Shamed, shown the errors of their ways, the rulers will bend to moral force.

Thoreau ponders why so few Massachusetts residents, especially those who profess an abhorrence of slavery, are willing to take his recommended step.

> What is the price-current of an honest man and patriot today? They hesitate, and they regret, and sometimes they petition; but they do nothing in earnest and with effect. They will wait, well disposed, for others to remedy the evil, that they may no longer have it to regret.[8]

Objections?

Nothing scandalous? Seminal American thinker? Gentle idealist? Yes, his words could be posed as a paraphrase of Edmund Burke's famous "all that is needed for the triumph of evil is for good men to do nothing." This is not exactly radical company.

There is more to Thoreau, however. Perhaps unwittingly in his essays he bares more of his soul, uncovers murkier motives. Why, for example, should the individual not consider himself bound by his government's laws?

> I hereby accept the motto—'That government is best which governs least'; and I should like to see it acted up to more rapidly and systematically. Carried out it finally amounts to this, which also I believe,—'That government is best which governs not at all'; and when men are prepared for it, that will be the kind of government which they will have.[9]

Nothing murky yet? True. It is not a confession of anarchism. "Only when men are prepared for it" does he argue that a government "which governs not at all" is possible. One could hold this too to be a way of phrasing Burke's rule that "inner checks upon will and appetite" will make checks "from without," from government, unnecessary—that a virtuous people can be free. If Thoreau said no more on the topic than this, we might think so.

To put Thoreau in perspective we must first make clear what Burke meant by "inner checks." Burke does not speak of inner checks formulated by an individual conscience acting in a vacuum, upon subjective dictates, to the beat of some "different drummer." By "inner checks" he means the norms, values, the pieties of the Christian West absorbed by the individual and made his own, made natural and spontaneous—a voluntary rather than forced acceptance of the highest standards of civility his society has to offer (in Burke's case England). An individual given an ordered introduction from childhood to the noblest accomplishments of the West—through parental love, high-minded fairy tales, folklore, mythology, uplifting sermons, well-directed schools, fine music and literature, and the social pressures of a righteous community—stands a good chance of possessing as an adult, says Burke, the virtues enshrined in these cultural expressions. And the greater the number of citizens thus blessed with a system of inner disciplines, the less authoritarian their government need be. (The reverse, of course, is true too, which was Burke's primary message to his contemporaries—a degree of authoritarian government remains necessary until such a virtuous citizenry is realized.)

Does Thoreau mean anything comparable? Not at all. In fact, the inherited wisdom of the Christian West was more likely, for him, to be an impediment to the noble individual in his search for truth.

> I have lived some thirty years on this planet, and I have yet to hear the first syllable of value or even earnest advice from my seniors. They have told me nothing, and probably cannot tell me anything.[10]

Strange words? Out of character for America's gentle hermit-martyr, wounded by the coarse self-interest of his fellow men? Not when considered in the fullness of his work. Such prideful airs are most characteristic, forgotten, or overlooked, though they may be in the official literature. (And undoubtedly many neither forget nor overlook them. They revel is that part of Thoreau, perhaps privately. They identify with it in their own rejection of modern, "bourgeois" Middle America) Thoreau separates himself from society because of a contempt for his fellow men; he breaks society's laws because he considers himself above them, immune, not bound by the legislative self-realization of his people. "I simply wish to refuse allegiance to the State, to withdraw and stand aloof from it,"[11] he tells us.*

---

*One could at this point begin a detailed analysis of the meaning of the term "state" in contrast to "society" or "community." There is a significant difference within scholarly circles. It would, for instance, be quite possible to argue that an individual may withdraw his allegiance to his state while continuing to respect his society's right to articulate its standards of right on a local or nongovernmental level. But there is no reason for us to concern ourselves with these matters when dealing with Thoreau. Thoreau does not make the distinctions. It happened to be the federal government's policies—not those of Massachusetts or Concord—he opposed and declared not binding. But he would have been as willing to dismiss local authorities if they enacted legislation he considered unacceptable.

And Socrates

It is often ignored—or misunderstood—but nevertheless, the intended moral of Socrates' death was not the superior claims of the individual conscience; he was not demonstrating the tyranny implicit in a society's demands upon individual behavior or thought. Socrates, remember, could have escaped. A quite foolproof jailbreak had been engineered by an ardent disciple, Crito. Everything had been set up—the pay-offs, the get-away route, a secure hideout in Thessaly. And surely we would think any individual dealing with institutionalized evil would have gone over the wall in a flash, like POWs breaking through the fence in the old war movies.

Yet Socrates *refused*. His mission was to show respect for the Law of his beloved Athens even while breaking an individual law: the Law of his people, not that of the subjective distant drummer. He understood the legacy afforded him through the Athenian *communitas*; knew that Law provided the civilizing structure within which the literature, poetry, philosophy—the very language he spoke—all that made him civilized, was nurtured. He dared summon his society to a higher level of truth by breaking specific laws he deemed immoral; he would not "just follow orders." But he reprimanded his disciples who argued for an escape attempt; insisted that he must take his punishment; expressed a reverence for the Law's integral role in his people's societal development, regardless of specific aberrations that he would not accept. He would have verbally cut to ribbons any pompous ass who blithely announced that he never heard a "syllable of value," or a piece of "earnest advice" from his "seniors" who "cannot tell me anything."

A sense of duty called Socrates to correct his society's errors, but a sense of duty to his people as well as to Truth in the abstract. He accepts his punishment, not gladly of course, but willingly, in order to provide the dramatic witness he hopes will lead his countrymen from their errors. He remains proudly an Athenian, a patriot, the suffering servant. There are no indications in the dialogues that he considers himself somehow above the community that reared him, taught him to speak, to read, to appreciate lofty thoughts, that civilized him. He remains keenly aware of this debt, unlike a spoiled child conscious of little beyond his own inflated ego; unlike Thoreau.

The greater part of what my neighbors call good I believe in my soul to be bad, and if I respect anything, it is very likely to be my good behavior. . . . One generation abandons the enterprises of another like stranded vessels.[12]

Stranded vessels? Need we say it? Would it be too obvious? Shakespeare, Newton, Dante, da Vinci? Rembrandt, Mozart, Beethoven, the wheel? The West? Yes, but Thoreau has seen through all this.

> The civilized man is a slave of Matter. Art paves the earth, lest he soil the soles of his feet; it builds walls that he may not see the Heavens; year in, year out, the sun rises in vain for him; the rain falls and the wind blows, but they do not reach him. . . . Our Indian is more of a man than the inhabitant of a city.[13]

But is this not simply the sort of writing we have learned to expect from those who tend toward a little poetic exaggeration for the sake of emphasis? Surely, Thoreau is only trying to warn us of Faustian impulses by reminding us of the power and beauty and majesty of the natural world. Unfortunately, this is not the case. If one returns to *Walden* and his lesser essays with a discerning eye; if one reads him without the preconception that we are dealing with a wonderfully poetic lumberjack—an Eric Hoffer of the northern woods, some melancholy John Denver, determined to point out the friendly little furry friends and frolicsome magpies to an urban population that has lost its sense of wonder for the world of nature—the hubris, the insufferable scorn, and the un-Christian contempt Thoreau expresses for his fellow man become unmistakable. The man is too beautiful for *everybody*, except the Indians and black slaves and Mexicans—that part of mankind he knows only from a distance and in caricature. Like some of the intense, all-you-need-is-love, one-world folk-singers with the string of broken homes and neglected children, he seemed to be able to love everyone except the people near to him; the people for whom a profession of love includes duties, responsibilities, sacrifice, and a spirit of self-denial.

Thoreau on the country folk around Concord:

> Talk of the divinity in man! Look at the teamster on the highway, wending to market by day or night; does any divinity stir within him? His highest duty to fodder and water his horses. . . . How godlike, how immortal is he? See how he cowers and sneaks.[14]

But perhaps, you say, he would show more of his reputed humanitarianism—that concern for blacks and Mexicans and Indians for which he was famous—if he were observing people beyond the confines of a smug and narrow village. I mean, after all, those woodchucks . . . How about New York, then? He worked there for a while.

> Who can see these cities and say that there is any life in them? I walked through New York yesterday . . . and met no real and living person. . . .
> The city is a thousand times meaner than I could have imagined. The pigs in the street are the most respectable part of the population.[15]

One is led to the conclusion that really having to live with black slaves or Indians would have led Thoreau to despise them too, except for the ease with which these unfortunates could be used to chastise his own neighbors and corroborate his feeling of moral superiority.

He could achieve that goal by looking backwards into history too. Certain of the long-deceased were worthy of his company: "Some of the Puritan stock are said to have come over and settled in New England. They were a class that did something else than celebrate their forefathers day and eat parched corn in remembrance of that time."[16]

Walking the streets after his night of suffering in jail for refusing to pay the poll tax, Thoreau became especially aware of the rarefied status of his mind and soul.

> I saw yet more distinctly the State in which I lived. I saw to what extent the people among whom I lived could be trusted as good neighbors and friends; that their friendship was for the summer weather only; that they did not greatly propose to do right; that they were a distinct race from me by their prejudices and superstitions, as the Chinaman and Malays are.[17]

Why then not simply leave society, we might ask; go into the wilds and never return? Move to a more virtuous land? Become an Arapaho? Why not, if he wanted to "withdraw and stand aloof effectively" simply go and do it? But, you say, is not that exactly what he did when he moved to Walden? Not even remotely.

For one thing, it should be remembered that Thoreau stayed at Walden only two years. His Walden experience was closer to a camping trip than an exile. The famous cabin was within walking distance of Concord and along a trail not infrequently traveled.

His stay in the wilds, not to mince words, was largely insincere. It reminds one of a rich college boy moving to a family-subsidized Greenwich Village or Paris loft for a year or two after graduation, pretending to be one of George Orwell's "down and outers" in unkempt hair and sandals and unironed shirts, knowing full well that a job in Daddy's firm awaits once his proletarian fling has ended—or a helpful grant-in-aid from home if he prefers (to help with the rough spots if the fling lingers on), as well as the eventual inheritance when old Dad kicks off. He seeks to have his cake and eat it too. He pretends to be above society, aloof, beyond the superficial and materialistic needs of his fellow men; yet he never really *leaves* them. He wants to be a nonconformist, but a very, very visible one; to appear to be free from society, while actually depending upon it for survival.

The point is that if Thoreau *really* wanted to be free from society's rules, he could have been. All he had to do was *really* go into the woods; to the Western frontier, which was not very far west in 1840. But instead of becoming a mountain man, genuinely living on his own, independent of society's system of needs, he becomes—and revels in his becoming in his writings—something closer to a cunning hobo who has mastered the secrets of stealing pies from unwatched windowsills; one who survives by taking from society without contributing to it or abiding by its norms. Does anyone remember the way he would write, "Every day or two I strolled to the village to hear some of the gossip which is incessantly going on there"[18]—and no doubt to enjoy the scandalized stares from those staid and unimaginative villagers shocked by the strange loner from Walden.

From his very first days in the cabin, the man is dependent. He lists for us the things fellow wilderness adventurers should be prepared to bring with them in their self-exile: rice, molasses, rye meal, port, salt, clothing. He does not mention the doctors available for any illnesses, the soldiers who made the Walden area safe from hostile Indians and frontier brigands (his stay would have been decidedly less pleasant along the Mississippi at the time), to say nothing of the teachers and preachers and writers who had prepared his mind for an appreciation of the dramatic ramifications of his act of social protest. "At the present day and in this country," he confides to his readers, men similarly disposed to leave society can survive since

as I find by my own experience, a few implements, a knife, an axe, a spade, a wheelbarrow, etc., and for the studious, lamplight, stationery, access to a few books . . . can be obtained at a trifling cost.[19]

Get it? You can be free from society's mandates, because the society you condemn has advanced to the point where the necessities of life, which you like Thoreau probably are unable to provide for yourself, can be purchased at a nominal cost. *Voila!* You no longer have to be a member of society, a contributor, one who reciprocates by providing for the needs of others in order to obtain these things. You just have to stay close enough to town when you go into your conscience-exile, and have some inherited money or generous friends (and they do not have to be too generous since the necessities have become so inexpensive) to score off every now and then. Thoreau, one of America's first great hustlers:

> [For] civilized people . . . the life of the individual is to a great extent absorbed, in order to preserve and perfect that of the race. But I wish to show at what a sacrifice the advantage is at present obtained, and to suggest that we may possibly live as to secure all the advantage without suffering any of the disadvantage.[20]

How did P.T. Barnum say it? Or was it W.C. Fields? Or is it more the proud bohemians of our century that he reminds us of—the altruists who refuse to sell their soul to mammon, to corporate America, who become instead social workers and poverty-project overseers, and spend the rest of their lives organizing a union to raise their salaries to the same level as that of accountants and advertising agents?

Sacrifice without pain; heroism without a price: "It is not necessary that a man should earn his living by the sweat of his brow, unless he sweats easier than I do."[21]

It is intriguing to observe the measured calm with which Thoreau builds his case: not only for the right to disobey, but also to avoid punishment. He actually seems sincere. It is reminiscent of listening to a polished network radio announcer in dulcet tone explaining the merits of a new miracle salve to cure baldness. (Might Thoreau have been sincere? If that is the case, an analysis should focus on the shallowness of his thought rather than on disingenuousness. But it has to be one or the other.)

Thoreau on the duty to obey authority:

> There will never be a really free and enlightened State until the State comes to recognize the individual as a higher and independent power, from which all its power and authority are derived, and

treats him accordingly. I please myself with imagining a State at least which can afford to be just to all men, and to treat the individual with respect as a neighbor; which would not think it inconsistent with its own repose if a few were to live aloof from it, not meddling with it, nor embraced by it, who fulfilled all the duties of neighbors and fellow men.[22]

Instead, he asks, of demanding obedience to law and conformity to cultural patterns, "Why does it [the State] not encourage its citizens to be on the alert to point out its faults and do better than it would have them? Why does it always crucify Christ, and excommunicate Copernicus and Luther, and pronounce Washington and Franklin rebels?"[23]

Where to begin with such a jumble of thoughts? Indeed, is a systematic analysis of Thoreau fair? Are these poetic expressions, meant to be felt rather than studied? They may very well be, whatever Thoreau's intentions. Nonetheless questions demand to be asked. Thoreau does not stand before his audience as an artist seeking to cultivate moods and sentiment. He is calling for quite specific responses to quite specific wrongs in his society.

But on what basis? Is it true that the individual is a "higher and independent power" from which "all power and authority are derived"? A man separated from his community at birth would become something out of a H. Rider Haggard caveman story, unable to even think out the concept of "authority"—or spell it for that matter, or express it, certainly, in a sentence as well-turned as one of Thoreau's.

Can a man "live aloof" from his society (except when he has to get his tools etc.) and still fulfill "all the duties" to his "neighbors and fellow man"? Certainly a man can be completely aloof from society—as were the mountain men of Thoreau's time—and a man can live *in* society as a member, sharing in the benefits and responsibilities of the commonwealth. But he cannot "sort of" be in society, cleverly appropriating just enough to maintain a lifestyle that permits him to survive without giving anything in return—not honorably.

True, Thoreau contributed his books. But this is beside the point. Thoreau does not hinge his case upon his success as a writer. He *denies* the individual's responsibility to contribute to society, rather than asking us to widen our perception of what constitutes a contribution. Unless a government is organized exactly to Thoreau's liking (which, necessarily, would put it in opposition to the rest of society who were "a distinct race" from him), he will grant it no legitimacy. All of society must step to the best of *his* drummer, to warrant his loyalty. The America of his time he considered a "most hypocritical and diabolical government,"[24] and states flatly that

> the only government that I recognize—and it matters.not how few are at the head of it, or how small its army—is that power that establishes justice in the land, never that which establishes injustice. . . . [America's is a] government that pretends to be Christian and crucifies a million Christs every day.[25]

It is not difficult to imagine how a black slave in the antebellum South could think such thoughts. A slave very well might be able to say in good conscience that he owed American society no more than a hatred for his captivity and degradation. For such a man there might be little good in America to balance with those evils. (For other slaves it might be different, considering the extent to which they had absorbed the heritage of the West and were grateful.) From a man who had enjoyed the full benefits of American society, however, more temperate thought can be demanded. Thoreau would not have been able to construe a coherent case against slavery, not even take the first steps, if it had not been for the Christian precepts taught him from his youth. Remember, some form of slavery, most far worse than the American South's, continued throughout the world in the 1840s. Christian Europe was one of the few places where it had been ended; and America, where those same Christian influences were felt, was one of the few places where an abolition was seriously being proposed. A perception of the evils of slavery just is not one of the natural rights a man is born with in the state of nature.

And is it "always" the Christs and Copernicuses that society condemns? And—do we have to say it—*never* the Charles Mansons and Jack the Rippers and Marquis de Sades? Are not Socrates and Christ and Copernicus remembered (and taught to men like Thoreau) precisely because they are the exceptions, the great teachers who raise mankind's levels of truth and wisdom? Certainly Christ and Socrates would not say that it is *always* the Socrates and Christs who are condemned. Socrates did not start from scratch; neither did Christ. They built upon, corrected, and perfected a heritage that they held to be basically sound.

The First Existentialist

It would not be stretching a point to call Thoreau history's first existentialist, even though the term is of twentieth-century origin. The same intellectual and religious despair, and resulting nihilism, that motivates a Sartre or a Genêt lies at the heart of Thoreau's discontent; the same conviction that the great lessons of the past, as well as the social order and religious truths which give purpose to the lives of the Christian people of Europe and America, are empty—ultimately lies. He too is convinced that an individual cannot find meaning and worth in life by living *up* to and preserving the highest cultural achievements of the Christian West. He too requires a dramatic moment—the opportunity for the individual decision through which a man by the very act of deciding, infuses meaning, for himself, into an otherwise empty and absurd life. Better to wreak havoc and terror upon mankind through a frightful act—as long as we accept fully the credit or blame—than to save countless lives through a dutiful submission to the tenets of church or country; better to be a Genêt or Marquis de Sade than a Mother Theresa.

This is not the place to explore the pride that nourishes the existentialist's self-centered, closed vision of life; and it is not within our rights to assign guilt to those who succumb to existentialism's lures. God only knows why some turn to existentialism (and not all existentialists are in the same league as a Genêt, of course). But we can point out the socially damaging consequences of Thoreau's suggestions.

Once again, we must not take Thoreau's words at face value. He seems to be walking in the sunlit uplands: "The law will never make men free; it is men who have got to make the law free. They are the lovers of law who observe the law when the government breaks it."

So far so good. We call them martyrs—those who out of deep moral convictions refuse to yield to a Nero, a Caligula, a Stalin, a Hitler, a Mao. Thoreau continues: "Whoever can discern truth has received his commission from a higher source than the chiefest justice in the world who can discern only law."[26]

True enough. This is an expression of the great tradition of resistance to tyranny. It appears to be, that is, until we remember Thoreau's guidelines; his "different drummer"; his existential-like elevation of the individual conscience; his unbridled subjectivism. Where a Socrates or a St. Thomas would hold for the existence of a standard of right and wrong attainable by human reason acting in community—one that a dramatic resistance to law might illustrate to our fellow men—Thoreau makes the individual an authority unto himself, morally autonomous, fully entitled to *invent* the standards by which he will live his life.

The controversy that arose in New England after John Brown's raid on Harper's Ferry in the summer of 1859—a raid in which seventeen were killed—gave Thoreau an opportunity to make specific his perception of these things.

Let us ignore, for the moment, the question of whether Brown's action was heroically inspired or insane or evil. Our interest just now is in Thoreau's reaction, in the motives for *his* praise of Brown.

The trial? "He could not have been tried by a jury of his peers, because his peers did not exist." Why? Because only he realized that the good that was realistically achievable through the raid outweighed the possible suffering? These considerations are irrelevant for Thoreau.

> When a man stands up serenely against the condemnation and vengeance of mankind, rising above them *literally by a whole body*,—even though he were of late the vilest murderer, who has settled that matter with himself,—the spectacle is a sublime one . . . and we become criminal in comparison.[27]

And, in a line that one could easily mistake for part of the dialogue in a play by Sartre set in a dingy coffee house on the Left Bank, Thoreau speaks of what Brown's example has meant to mankind: "How many a man who was lately contemplating suicide has now something to live for."[28]

> Unless above himself he can
> Erect himself, how poor a thing is man![29]

And, if it needs be said, he does not mean by this, raising oneself through a greater-than-average loyalty to mankind's most exalted cultural norms. Man must raise himself above his cultural tradition, above his society's banal understanding of truth, by creating a character for himself, which takes shape in the dramatic existential act. Here is where one finds dignity and worth, whatever the choice. Thus:

> Those who are continually shocked by slavery have some right to be shocked by the violent death of the slaveholder, but no others.[30]

Apparently this is to apply to any slaveholder, including the compassionate masters who would have freed their slaves if a way could have been found to do something more constructive than simply destroy all of southern society; a way which would have helped the slave, not just wound the whites of the South, as if that in itself were a noble deed.

Thoreau proclaims "I speak for the slave when I say that I prefer the philanthropy of Captain Brown to that philanthropy which neither shoots me nor liberates me."[31] One wonders whether black slaves or white freemen had the right to be more offended, or confused. (But perhaps we have to keep in mind that, for the existentialist, the act must be meaningful only to the perpetrator.)

The Would-be Alderman

Admittedly, it is possible to overlook Thoreau's shortcomings in logic by viewing him as one of what someone once called mankind's "birds of paradise"—those sensitive and tortured souls who just do not belong in the company of men, and through no fault of their own. Thoreau, himself, understood that there was something "different" about him when he conceded that his neighbors, no matter how comparatively outraged they were about slavery or other shortcomings of American society, just could not afford to follow him into the perils of civil disobedience. A man with roots, he admits—with home and family and church ties—could find too many *good* things to lose; and "good" in the finest sense (although he does not go so far as to phrase it like that). A man with roots faces far more wounding consequences than does a Thoreau when he proclaims his willingness to watch American society come to an end rather than endure the presence of a social evil. He pays a far steeper price. He has a stake; as the rootless, childless, unmarried loner, Thoreau does not. Thoreau conceded that "the long and short of the matter is that they cannot spare the protection of the existing government and they dread the consequences to their property and families of disobedience to it."[32] So true. But rather than giving Thoreau second thoughts about his own moral "courage," this admission makes him even more self-congratulatory. Let the rest of mankind worry about the consequences of the fall of their social order; let them brood over broken lives, ravaged children, the end of learning and houses of worship. "For my part," Thoreau assures us, "I should not like to think that I ever rely on the protection of the State."[33] If Concord itself were to go up in flames, the sun would still rise over Walden, you see, the birds would still sing, and the gentle Thoreau would not bat an eye. Until he needed a new hammer.

Early in *Walden* Thoreau writes of the future he anticipated for himself in his salad days. Here he was—Harvard graduate, man of intellect, not at all crass like his neighbors, capable as they were not of appreciating the finer things in literature and art. Like cream, he was sure he would rise to the top, perhaps become a revered village philosopher in residence. But, well, it did not happen. He remained a prophet scorned, another of the Christs society is always crucifying. So he resigned himself to the fact that his "townsmen would not after all admit me to the list of town officers, nor make my place a sinecure with a moderate allowance."[34] He was not, after all, to be able to spend his days in deep thought. And all he wanted was a modicum of the creature comforts from his co-citizens. He would not, after all, be able to live like what Studs Lonigan might call your typical alderman.

In a melancholy mood, he compares himself to an Indian craftsman who pours his creative energies into weaving fine baskets, only to find to his disappointment that the white man's market would not reward his talents quite as magnanimously as it does the local lawyers and merchants. A parable. It was not enough to be the best at what you do; you had to be good at the "right" things, the marketable things, to earn the soft life.

> I too had woven a kind of basket of a delicate texture, but I had not made it worth anyone's while to buy them. Yet not the less, in my case, did I think it worth my while to weave them, and instead of studying how to make it worth men's while to buy my baskets, I studied rather how to avoid the necessity of selling them.[35]

Now certainly no one is going to say there is anything repugnant about an artist refusing to cater to the mass market. The reverse would be the less than noble act. It is what makes Richard Burtons out of potentially great actors. But to suggest that the artist scorned seek retribution by using his literary skills to provoke widespread disaffection from his society . . . well, it is not the stuff of greatness.

And a society that elevates the memory of a man who has done just that can very well become (if it is not already) a society without a perception of its identity; without an appreciation of a character worth defending against those willing to place their egos above its very life—to say nothing of enemies abroad. A society that does not want the responsibility of living on.

A Postscript

Permit me a short personal observation to illustrate another dimension to the Thoreau legacy. Not only does he glorify dissent without making clear the distinctions between what should be dissented against and what not, he also encourages the worst kind of self-serving tendencies in all of us. The man had no understanding of what is meant by Original Sin.

A few years back the teachers' union in a high school where I was employed at the time called a strike, an illegal strike in direct violation of state laws against public employee strikes and a specific court injunction. I did not want to strike for moral and practical reasons but decided to take the easy route: to go along with the crowd in the hopes that the strike would not be of long duration. (Eventually, as the strike dragged on, I felt enough shame to cross the picket lines.)

One morning on the picket lines, I was talking to one of the other striking teachers, a man I felt thoughtful enough to see the less than honorable nature of striking against the parents and children of a community. "You know, the fact that what we are doing is illegal," I said quietly, "should tell us something."

"Illegal!" he exclaimed. "Come on, Fitz . . . where would the Irish be today if they worried about breaking England's laws in 1916!"

It is a perfect example of what the Thoreau legacy promotes. Every act of civil disobedience takes on the same character. Breaking the law for a fatter paycheck becomes the equivalent of resistance to a foreign army of occupation in the streets of your homeland. If you applaud one, you must applaud the other. Greed on the same scale as heroism; venal contentiousness indistinguishable from steadfastness. Whatever your drummer.

VI

The Monkey Trial

It is one of America's best known tales. Grammar-school children are often introduced to its charms through a page or two in their American history textbooks with the assistance of a progressive teacher, whose commentary helps the students see the issues in context—as a chapter in mankind's escape from backwardness, medievalism, religious bigotry. With their horizons thus broadened, the young people are well-prepared for the day when a local theater group performs *Inherit the Wind*; or when Hollywood's successful film adaptation pops up on the late night movies. The 1925 Scopes trial. The Monkey Trial. Clarence Darrow, played by Spencer Tracy, against William Jennings Bryan, who will be remembered forever as a paranoid Frederic March. Bible Belt intolerance vs. the enlightened attitudes of our modern scientific age, which have made the world so much a better place.

The scenes are familiar. Dayton, Tennessee, a small shop-lined main street on a sweltering day in July; a court house, neat, brick, and a small belfry, surrounded by fundamentalist pickets, hot dog and lemonade carts, a sea of straw hats and galluses, vendors hawking commemorative bric-a-brac—banners, monkey buttons, books and handouts on Darwin's theories, atheism, free silver. A tent set up, where for a small fee you can get a closeup view of a caged monkey and make up your own mind about the evolutionary sequence. Holy Rollers, "blind" fiddlers, revivalist preachers on wooden platforms, newspaper-men, and the marvel of the time—the wireless radio receivers set up to transmit the momentous words to all four corners of the country. Store windows festooned with monkey posters, saloons with specials of the day, "Monkey Cocktails" of ingenious mixtures.

And the cast of characters. The courageous free thinker, Clarence Darrow. Attorney for the Damned. Deep-set eyes afire, white shirt, white string-tie, dark suspenders, leaning over to question a heavy-set bald man nervously waving a palm fan—a fat man confident and pompous at first, a smug saloon-keep from appearances, but soon to be turned to an exhausted and quivering, sweating mass of self-doubts, blinking wildly in disbelief in the wake of the destruction of his primitive religious beliefs by the archetype of undaunted twentieth-century man.

"And who did this Cain do his begetting with if Adam and Eve had only two children?" asks the Spencer Tracy character. And the bald fat man looks around at his supporters in horror. Gulp! He never thought of that one before.

"And before snakes were made to crawl on their bellies in the dust for tempting Eve, you believe they pranced about *how?* On their tails?" Darrow demands. And the fat man fumbles nervously on the witness stand looking for a hole to crawl into. Where he belongs for trying to forbid the human mind its natural rights.

And the mean-spirited hypocrites, the ignorant supporters of the fat man, who came to cheer, sit stunned, their little worlds broken by the march of time. For which we should be thankful. You can tell—the fanatic's sneer. They are the ones who once burned witches at the stake and persecuted the gallant Galileo, and lynched blacks, and would one day burn books in Germany. The Forces of Darkness.

And it is nearly all bunk. Not that William Jennings Bryan cut to ribbons Clarence Darrow on that July day. He was maneuvered artfully by Darrow, more than once, into statements that must have embarrassed Bryan himself when he read them after the trial. (Although one is hard-pressed to make a suggestion for how he could have avoided them, for reasons we shall examine shortly.) And probably there were as many unattractive people in the pro-Bryan faction at the trial as there were in Darrow's.

But, nevertheless, upon looking back on the trial, after viewing the exchanges between Bryan and Darrow, it can be said confidently that Bryan and his cause emerge far more suited to the applause of modern Americans. Except, that is, for those Americans still waging Darrow's battle to make religious belief a discredited and insignificant participant in the life of the nation.

The point is that the Scopes trial should not be viewed simply as a dispute over the accuracy of the account of creation found in the Book of Genesis. The stakes were higher indeed. The trial can be seen as one of the first public expressions of the profound cultural struggle that continues to be waged in our time: the battle for the minds and hearts of our people; a battle that will ultimately determine whether the empiricism and secular humanism set loose in Europe in the eighteenth-century Enlightenment will win a final victory over the older Biblical understanding of the nature of man and his role in history, the view associated with the Christian faith.

This larger picture should be kept in mind when considering the trial, for when Darrow "embarrasses" Bryan (as the *Inherit the Wind* myth would have us believe he did), he does so only because he manages to get the media of his time—as well as later historians—to look at his one-upmanship within the context of his own secular humanism. Time and time again at the trial, Darrow's arguments amount to no more than "Mr. Bryan, it would take a *miracle* for what you say happened to happen!"

And Darrow's defenders, then and now, view such an approach as telling, and Bryan's responses as childish, because they hold that such a demonstration closes the argument; that Divine intervention cannot be treated as part of life on this planet from an intelligent person's point of view. It is not only Genesis that is to be removed from our life then. The very notion of a personal God, a Lord of history, must go too. There is to be no serious consideration given to the will of a God who demands from us a willing acceptance of standards of thought and behavior superior in authority to man-made and man-centered alternatives. And, as a corollary, the secularists require that the Christian churches that hold to the older Biblical views must be downgraded in legitimacy and made into little more than groups like the Flat Earth or Loch Ness Research Societies, tolerated quaint folk with no real role to play in the formation of the public conscience. High stakes indeed.

Setting the Stage

That it shall be unlawful for any teacher in any of the Universities, Normals and all other public schools of the State which are supported in whole or in part by the public school funds of the State, to teach any theory that denies the story of the Divine Creation of man as taught in the Bible, and to teach instead that man has descended from a lower order of animals.

This was the law that started it all, the so-called Butler Act. Its intent was obvious: to stop the propagation in the youth of Tennessee of the evolutionist view of the origins of man; to prevent the academic displacement of the God-centered story of creation by the Darwinian view, which was becoming ever more an orthodoxy in the universities and urban centers of the country.

But notice: the law said that a teacher must not "teach" a view contrary to Genesis. It did not say "discuss" or "explain" or "mention." This is an important distinction. Without keeping it in mind, we cannot easily see why the Scopes supporters deserve to be remembered as the intolerant faction, rather than the Bible Belters. One of the standard dictionary listings of "teach" is "to make known and accepted." "Discuss" and "explain" do not, on the other hand, imply that the teacher is to act as a partisan, introducing the students to a thought that demands acceptance. It matters little whether the sponsors of the Butler Act had thought out these distinctions. Bryan, their champion, did, even though Scopes and Darrow and their supporters went to great lengths to build their case as if he did not. Indeed, this ploy of theirs became the keystone of Darrow's defense.

From the very seedbed of the case, Scopes and his supporters maintained the pose. Although, it is true, they may not have been fully aware of the level of their disingenuousness. Being a zealot usually includes a level of self-deception, or self-delusion, if you prefer. But, for whatever reason, Scopes viewed himself as a crusader in the cause of freedom of thought, a man entrusted with the mission of thwarting an attempt by backward Christians to destroy learning in America.

He thought this in spite of the fact that he had to be *told* that his freedom of thought had been taken from him. Yes, *told*. It must not be forgotten that the Scopes trial was a test case put in motion by Dayton merchants and politicians and pro-Darwin members of the school board. And for mixed motives, one of which was simply putting Dayton on the map in a booster-like bid for national publicity. John Scopes was invited to be the "martyr" because he was young and a bachelor and able to afford the possible risks. Hired by the school district as a general-science teacher and athletic coach the year before the trial, he was only *substituting* for the regular biology teacher. He was not a learned biologist who had reached conclusions about Darwin after long and arduous study. And he had had no perception at all of being persecuted for the way he went along with the young college graduates' then fashionable preference for Darwin by teaching evolution in his biology classes. There were no parents picketing his classroom or writing him nasty letters. In his memoirs he tells us of no students or parents voicing a single objection to his class discussions on evolution. The pot was stirred by the town boosters and pro-evolutionists who were eager to take advantage of an offer by a group that even then was right in the thick of the drive to remove all traces of the Christian faith from the public life of the nation—the American Civil Liberties Union. The ACLU had offered to pay all the legal expenses, as well as $1,000, to any teacher willing to take on the Butler Act.

We must not underestimate the implications of all this. Scopes *was* teaching evolution in his classes. So was the regular teacher he had replaced. The textbook in use for years in Tennessee contained a section on evolution. Yet the trial had to be initiated by the pro-evolutionists! What are we to conclude? Obviously that the parents of Dayton did not object to the theory of evolution being explained to their children as a *theory*, or as a fact that came across to their children as a theory. What they objected to was the idea of it being taught as incontrovertible, as a certainty, as an explanation which excludes all others for rational men. There are biology teachers all over America who know that evolution can be explained in a way that will not be offensive to fundamentalists. Darwin can be covered in full detail. All the teacher has to do is discuss Darwin's theory as *theory*, which is exactly what it is, without ridiculing or denigrating the Biblical account of Creation in the process.

But Scopes tells us he wanted more. He admits this; he is proud of it. He wanted the right to teach his students the *truth* of Darwin, and the error of Genesis; that Darwin's theories are the *only* intelligent explanation for the origins of man. He seeks to liberate his students' minds from the religious narrowness of small-town America. The trial, he tells us, "was a specific example of the universal conflict of the narrow-minded and intolerant against the broad-minded and tolerant."[1] "They tried to pass laws that would take it [evolution] out of biology. Of course, it was *impossible* [emphasis added] to teach biology without teaching evolution.''[2] It is not unfair or presumptive to note that he uses "teach" here to mean "encourage to accept."

So when Scopes tells us he believed the "fundamentalists had an inalienable right to believe what they did" and that he objected only "when they insisted that others hold these beliefs too,''[3] we must conclude that he is either confused or being less than honest with us. Clearly, what he wants is for the Bible-believing parents to have the right to proclaim their beliefs to their children, but only in private, at home, as some sort of archaic and suspect rite, but to give him the uncontested right to preach his beliefs to their children as *truth*—truth corrective of what they learned at home—in classrooms the parents supported with their tax dollars. "I thought Darwin was right," he tells us. "It was the *only* plausible explanation for man's long and tortuous journey to his present physical and mental development.''[4] (Emphasis added.)

Scopes was so unquestioning of Darwin that it might cause the most uncompromising of modern evolutionists to blush a bit. As we know, it is no longer heresy to question the evolutionist creed. Nowadays those who tell us evolution "has to be true" will concede that they stand a far distance from being able to *prove*—by their own empiricist standards—that Darwin was correct. (Where, for example, are the fossil remains of the transitional animals?) So many questions have been raised of late that the same types of Bible-discounting scientists who once created the consensus in favor of the theory of evolution can be found on television specials in their pipes and tweeds calmly discussing the reasons why they think human life might have been sent to earth by ancient astronauts from another galaxy. Others, after facing up to the literal leaps of faith required to accept that an accidental chain of events brought about the ordered complexity and variety of life on the planet, are talking of a "big bang" theory of creation which comes remarkably close to the Genesis account. Darwin is no longer unquestionable in the scientific world. It is that simple. One wonders how many modern readers of journals such as *Scientific American* would be willing to appear before a committee of their peers on a PBS broadcast and defend Darwin's *The Origin of Species* as near piously as John Scopes.

If men like Clarence Darrow had not come to my aid and had not dramatized the case to a responsive world, freedom would have been lost.

I had been taught from childhood to stand up for what I thought was right and I did not think the state of Tennessee had any right to keep me from teaching *truth*.[5] (Emphasis added.)

Admittedly, one ought not spend too much time on Scopes. He was an impressionable football coach used by the secularists of the time to move their ideas to center stage. It was Darrow who was the spokesman, his words the battle cry.

Even so, one should not pass over Scopes too quickly. Through him we can discover a great deal about the overall world view of those who pushed for the acceptance of Darwin in those years. Through his memoirs we can see why so much more was at stake than a scientific explanation for Creation. In his analysis of the trial he discloses the "package" that was so much a part of the pro-evolutionist: a haughty agnosticism, a self-congratulatory contempt for traditional morality, strong preferences for Eugene V. Debs and the socialist movement, a smug enjoyment of how H. L. Mencken used the trial as an occasion to tweak the noses of the Tennessee "booboisie." "In a way it was Mencken's show. . . . His biting commentary on the Bible Belt and the trial itself was one of the highlights of the entire event."[6]

Scopes, in short, reveals himself to be a recognizable type of the 1920s, a man we all know: the pretentious and arrogant college graduate, struggling to prove his degree means something (and to favorably scandalize the flappers) by affecting an "anti-Babbitt" brand of radicalism—a free-thinker, foe of the "swells," champion of the underdog. Consider: Before his own case came before the judge, Scopes had a chance to take in a portion of a rape case. The defendant struck Scopes as a victim of society. But

his accuser, a girl in her late teens or early twenties, . . . seemed to me a sophisticated bitch. . . . As she told her story, it was evident she was knowledgeable beyond her years.

I was sure she didn't know which lover was responsible for her condition and was seeking the easiest way out.[7]

He was "sure" of that (as sure of evolution?) after one observation in court. The man tells us more than he would.

Enter Darrow

That the ACLU and Darrow made financial sacrifices to "defend" Scopes should tell us something, too. Darrow had never before volunteered his services to the unfortunates he saved from society's wrath. Both understood the impact the case would have in the cultural wars. A victory—even a moral victory—at Dayton would be a dramatic step forward for their brand of libertarianism—for the logical positivist, behaviorist, secular relativist forces they favored. The New York *Post* of that era detected something in the wind:

> Greenwich Village is on its way to Rhea County. . . . The Scopes case teachers, research workers, biologists and other men of science are being smothered in the rush of long-haired men, short-haired women, feminists, neurotics, free-thinkers and free-lovers who are determined to shine in reflected glory.[8]

The long range objectives, as we would expect, were never fully articulated for the occasion by Darrow; not for Tennessee jurors he suspected of being in sympathy with Bryan. He argued as if the only question at hand was America's proud tradition of freedom of expression.

> Here we find today as brazen and as bold an attempt to destroy learning as was ever made in the Middle Ages. The only difference is we have not provided that they [pro-evolutionists] shall be burned at the stake. But there is time for that, your Honor; we have to approach these things gradually.[9]

We should not think such a statement a singular burst of sarcasm, an atypical verbal flourish meant to sway emotions. In his calmest moments he argued identically. Randolph Neal, one of the ACLU lawyers who teamed with Darrow, could be just as histrionic.

> The great question is whether the Tennessee legislature has the power to prevent the young minds of Tennessee from knowing what has been thought and said by the world's greatest scientists, and thus to prevent them from forming their own judgements in regard to questions of life and science.[10]

This was the heart of the Scopes defense, *exactly* the point that the defense team wanted to make to the jurors.

One yearns for a time machine to put the question to Neal: How would it work if he had his way? The students would be "free" to receive from their parents an understanding of Genesis, as long as Scopes was "free" to give them corrective "truth" (as Scopes would put it) in his tax-supported classroom? Was that what Neal meant by "forming their own judgements"?

Well, yes he did. The Scopes supporters talked of "freedom of thought" and "respecting the rights of others," but that in no way meant that they were calling upon biology teachers to give an equal and respectful hearing to Genesis as a plausible alternative to Darwin. Their goal was to give Darwin free rein; in the name of intellectual freedom to grant a monopoly-hold to evolutionist theory in the schools. Bryan was the one—as we shall shortly see—who would have been willing to live with a *genuine* neutrality.

Another Scopes lawyer proclaims: "For God's sake, let the children have their minds kept open—close no doors to their knowledge, shut no doors from them."[11]

It is this intellectual disingenuousness (conscious or otherwise) that proves so exasperating as one looks back on the case. Darrow can intone as if he meant it: "If men are not tolerant, if men cannot respect each other's opinions, if men cannot live and let live, then no man's life is safe."[12] Scopes can proclaim: "Unless we, as individuals and as a society, respect the other man's point of view, no matter how far out he seems and no matter how vigorously we disagree with him, we are not going to give full expression to our own laws that insure the right of the individual to be his own man."[13] They can say such things knowing full well that they wanted America's classrooms to be as closed on the question of evolution as any medieval seminary was on the existence of the Prime Mover. Scopes talked of Bryan's "fool beliefs."[14] Darrow called them "mischievous," "wicked," as well as "foolish."[15] He could argue that "the prosecution is opening the doors for a reign of bigotry equal to anything in the Middle Ages."[16] One of the other ACLU lawyers insisted that the logical corollary to Bryan's views would be a law that forbids "any theory that denies the Bible story that the earth is the center of the universe, as taught in the Bible."[17] He said that with a straight face, as if evolution were as verifiable as heliocentrism.

It is painfully clear: these people had no intention whatsoever of practicing the toleration they preached; no intention of granting legitimacy to any opinion but their own. Yet they persisted, playing up to the American disposition in favor of a free exchange of ideas, arguing as if all they were calling for was some good old American open-mindedness.

What was going on in their minds? Well, if they were not simply confused (as one would not expect Clarence Darrow to be), the only logical conclusion we can reach is that they were marching under the guidon of "freedom of expression" the way revolutionary totalitarians do when they conspire against democratic regimes—to get a hearing for their ideas, until they get control of directive power, at which time the greater concern becomes the teaching of "truth."

There is no reason to beat around the bush on this matter with Darrow. He acknowledges the stakes. "I am going to argue," he promises "as if it was a death struggle between two civilizations."[18] And not between civilizations of equal value, fully entitled to toleration and an equal hearing in American classrooms. His enemies, he tells us, "with flying banners and beating drums" were threatening to take America "backwards to the glorious ages of the sixteenth century when bigots lighted faggots to burn the men who dared to bring any intelligence and enlightenment to the human mind."[19] And he was going to stop them. Medieval Catholics, fundamentalist Protestants, revealed religion—the great obstacles to mankind's development. Getting their insidious ideas out of the schools was a mission worthy of the donated services of Clarence Darrow and his ideological allies, the ACLU.

The Cross-Examination

It has to be conceded: Darrow emerged triumphant in the courtroom confrontation.* Hollywood was not entirely in error. He had reason to be proud; as proud as whenever else in his long and glorious career he used a clever lawyer's techniques to blur the issues and carry the day for his client. Time and time again he demonstrated that Bryan believed in absolutely preposterous things. In miracles. And he created an atmosphere that made people—especially the reporters covering the case—react as if this demonstration were a thunderbolt from Olympus, sufficient in and of itself to discredit Bryan's mind, and even though such a conclusion is as clear a case of begging the question as one can find.

Before considering the critical exchanges between Bryan and Darrow, however, let us pause to examine Darrow's cross-examination of one other witness: Harry Shelton, one of Scopes'

---

*Scopes was found guilty, of course, and fined a minimal amount. The Butler Act stayed on the books. But we speak now of the intellectual confrontation as seen by the country as a whole, and by historians, not just twelve Tennesseeans.

students. It confirms for us that Scopes' desire was for more than the right to lead a spirited discussion on Charles Darwin's theories; that he wanted to act as an advocate, to *indoctrinate* his students with Darwin.

"Are you a church member?" Darrow asks the boy.

"Yes, Sir."

"Do you still belong?"

"Yes, Sir."

"You didn't leave church when he *told* you all forms of life began with a single cell?" (Emphasis added.)

"No, Sir."[20]

Notice: The student has been *told* that evolution is a scientific fact, the way he has been told that two plus two equals four. Darrow's defense rests on the fact that the boy has not left his religion even though his teacher *has* attacked his parents' religious beliefs. One wonders how far this can be carried for Darrow—this "no harm, no foul" approach to education, as they say in basketball circles. Would Darrow have defended the teaching of witchcraft as long as most of the students never joined a coven? Is that the point? Obviously not. Darrow wants only truth taught without hindrance; his perception of truth.

But on to Bryan.

Probably the three most celebrated portions of Darrow's cross-examination (it was Darrow's idea to call Bryan as a witness on the Bible) were his questions on the six-day sequence of Creation, Joshua at the battle of Jericho, and Jonah. In each case we see Darrow's mind working at its best, and Bryan embarrassed and in confusion because of the insightful questioning, or so say Darrow's supporters.

In fact, however, such a conclusion can be held only by those who accept Darrow's premise: that divine interventions —miracles—are impossible, and that a willingness to believe in them is the sign of a weak mind.

Actually, Bryan's overall position comes very close to that of some of the most sophisticated modern Scripture scholars.

Early in the cross-examination Darrow asks: "Do you claim that everything in the Bible should be literally accepted?"

Bryan's answer: "I believe everything in the Bible should be accepted as it is given there. Some of the Bible is given illustratively." He adds with a barb: "For instance, 'Ye are the salt of the earth.' I would not insist that man was actually salt."

In response to Darrow's specific questions on how the world

as we know it could have been made in six days when science indicates a longer span, Bryan answers that the word "day" in the Bible does not "necessarily mean a twenty-four hour day. . . . My impression is they were periods."

"Have you any idea of the length of the periods?" asks Darrow.

"No," responds Bryan. "But I think it would be just as easy for the kind of God we believe in to make the earth in six days or in six years or in six million years or in six billion years. I do not think it important whether we believe one or the other." He hastens to add, "I would not attempt to argue as against anybody who wanted to believe in literal days."[21]

Think of what the man has said. Grant the existence of a Creator—God—for starters. (Deny that and Bryan and all but the most exotic of Christians believe in a fairy tale, of course, and Darrow wins by default.) It is awesome, stunningly miraculous, whether that Creator put into motion and directed the evolutionary process or created in a six day period. If science has demonstrated satisfactorily for you that Creation could not have taken place within six days, Bryan says: fine. Believe that God worked through the evolutionary process. The Bible is not a text in earth science. If, on the other hand, you prefer to stay with the idea of a literal six-day Creation because modern science's conclusions on evolution appear too speculative, fine too. If you opt for the latter you are calling for a miracle modern scientists consider startlingly beyond the scientific understanding of today—most scientists. But more astounding than the idea of a Supreme Intelligence choreographing a billion-year evolutionary process, or Christ's resurrection from the dead or calming of the seas or healing of lepers? Miracles are difficult to grade. God cannot be against truth. But until the Darwinians give us proof of the evolutionary process (which they cannot), Bryan wants to leave Christians free to choose their preferred miracle of Creation.

The same situation arises in the exchange over Joshua.

"Do you believe Joshua made the sun stand still?" Darrow asks.

"I believe what the Bible says," answered Bryan.

"I suppose you mean that the earth stood still."

"I don't know. I am talking about the Bible now. I accept the Bible absolutely."

"Do you believe at that time the entire sun went around the earth?"

"No, I believe the earth goes round the sun."

"Do you believe that the men who wrote it thought that . . . the sun could be stopped?"

"I believe what they wrote was inspired by the Almighty, and He may have used language that could be understood at that time . . . instead of language that could not be understood until Darrow was born."[22]

A fascinating exchange. It is Darrow who tries to make the Bible a book of scientific theory. Bryan is content to say that the day was somehow miraculously prolonged to aid the Israelites. To their eyes the "sun stopped." How? Bryan does not know. He does not pretend to. It is a miracle. Did God freeze the sun in position and dampen its rays, suspending the laws of physics the way Christ did when he calmed the seas? Did He somehow create the illusion of continuing light in the area of the battle? Who knows? It is a miracle. The Bible does not tell us the *mechanics* of miracles. Believers do not claim anything of the sort. Darrow has—cleverly, we must admit—constructed a classic straw man. All through the trial he pokes fun at an understanding of the Bible which *he* defined, not Bryan.

And Jonah?

Darrow asks Bryan if he believes that God "made such a fish and that it was big enough to swallow Jonah?"

"Yes, Sir," said Bryan. "Let me add: One miracle is just as easy to believe as another. . . . A miracle is a thing performed beyond what men can perform. When you get beyond what man can do, you get within the realm of miracles; and it is just as easy to believe the miracle of Jonah as any other miracle in the Bible."[23]

Or—we may add—just as hard. It is the same thing actually.

Darrow smugly asserts that Bryan "makes the Bible the yardstick to measure every man's intelligence. . . . Are your mathematics good? Turn to One Elijah two. Is your philosophy good? See Two Samuel three."[24] But actually it is the other way round. Believers were asking the empiricists to respect their right to treat the Bible as a record of things not bound by the yardstick of science; as a volume where incidents of a miraculous nature may be recorded, and respected, without the school systems they support mounting an attack against them because they do not agree to think within the shallow confines of respectable Victorian era science—the H.G. Wells view of the universe; as a volume that treats things that cannot be explained by the standards of 1920's biology. They were asking that the people who refuse to accept the dreary belief that there is no more to existence than the knowledge men can grasp with their five senses should not be pictured as practitioners of a "fool religion," in Darrow's words.

It would not seem unreasonable to request that our modern, intelligent evolutionists concede this weakness in Darrow's case. It is so obvious. He did no more than repeat the kind of glib scientific analysis of the Bible that had been associated with Robert Ingersoll all through the last quarter of the nineteenth century. And it was old hat even then. Whom did Cain marry? How would you fit every animal in the world into Noah's ark? Henry Steele Commager, a man not usually thought of as a backwoods revivalist, quite perceptively noted that "Darrow and his colleagues" by relying so blindly on the old Ingersoll cliché thinking "made antifundamentalism almost equally ridiculous"[25] as the caricature of fundamentalism they were trying to associate with Bryan.

Darrow's much-applauded open-mindedness, to be direct, is a myth. When he tells us he is no enemy of religion, he is being, well, less than forthright. "I know there are millions of people," he says, "who

> look on it [the Bible] as being a divine book, and I have not the slightest objection to it. I know there are millions of people in the world who derive consolation in their lives of trouble and solace in times of distress from the Bible. I would be pretty near the last one in the world to do anything or take any action to take it away. I feel just exactly the same toward the religious creed of every human being who lives.[26]

He says that, but one does not have to look too closely between the lines to see that he means: "I'll respect your religion the way I would a mountain man's rabbit foot or a Delta black's mojo. If it makes you feel good, believe it. If the Easter Bunny helps, fine. No problem. Just don't bring your superstition into the formation of public policy. Don't expect it to make any difference in the way Americans live. Don't expect progressive men such as me to permit your beliefs an equal place in the schools. Don't expect us to slow down our march toward the secular humanist paradise that is man's destiny. Keep your ideas at home, in private, where we will let them die a slow and painless death. We are sincere about that. We are the champions of tolerance, remember."

The Bryan Not Played by Frederic March

Not all modern Christians are comfortable with Bryan at the Scopes trial, of course. Some find in his words an unacceptable degree of anti-intellectualism. Why, they ask, did he parry with Darrow as he did? Why did he not simply concede that some sections of the Bible, especially the early books, can be taken as parables, or at least that the possibility can be considered by modern and orthodox Christians? (And they are, despite fundamentalist warnings and objections. But even those fundamentalist objections seem to stress not that every event in the Bible had to take place exactly as reported, but that conceding a level of allegory in places where it is likely will lead to similar analyses of more essential sections—the New Testament, especially.) He could have derailed Darrow's attack in that manner, some hold, simply saying "Look, Clarence, old boy, the Bible is neither a history book nor a science book. What we object to is people like Mr. Scopes trying to take God out of our children's lives while on our payroll, and with a theory that is so problematic that it is likely to be revamped a hundred times before the century is over. Discuss evolution as a theory that is in vogue in many scientific circles and we won't object, but don't use it as a vehicle for your secularist ambitions." (This, by the way, is exactly the kind of thing Bryan would say when off the witness stand in his public comments about the trial.) Why even consent to discuss how snakes traveled about before Eve ate the apple?

It is a valid criticism, up to a point. But it depends too much on the advantages of hindsight to press too far. Moreover, it fails to consider the nature of the opponent; of Darrow, a man determined to make use of the trial as an attack on revealed religion.

In point of fact, Bryan was quite willing to discuss possible interpretations of the Bible, but with those he was confident were believing Christians. He had exchanged letters before the trial with Henry Fairfield Osborn, director of the American Museum of Natural History. Osborn's attempt to show a parallel between the six-day description of Creation and six corresponding stages in the evolutionary process excited and pleased Bryan. He applauded, too, work in a similar vein by Louis F. Post. "Did God use evolution as His Plan?" he asked. "If it could be shown that man, instead of being made in the image of God, is a development of beasts we would have to accept it, regardless of its effect, for truth is truth and will prevail."

But he understood well that, when talking to Darrow, it was not the same as discussing the Bible with Osborn: "But when there is no proof we have a right to consider the effect of the acceptance of unsupported hypotheses."[27] What is the goal of those who demand that this hypothesis be granted academic primacy?

Bryan, it is safe to say, knew; he had a firm grasp on the full ramifications of the trial, of the effect Darrow was trying to create. To concede on the stand that an individual was entitled to interpret the Bible would have given Darrow exactly the opening he wanted to portray the Bible as just another of the ancient books of religious folklore which have been handed down through the ages—a work in the same league as the *Koran*, *Gilgamesh*, the *Upanishads*, no better, no worse. It does not take much imagination to come up with the kinds of questions Darrow would have asked if Bryan had conceded room for interpretation of the Scriptures. "Now Mr. Bryan, *which* interpretation should my client have considered before teaching his science class? *All* of them? Why would not his own be as acceptable as the others?"

The "atheists," Bryan warned in a speech to the Dayton Progressive Club (a pro-evolutionist group) just days before the trial, "agnostics, and all other opponents of Christianity understand the character of the struggle, hence the interest in the case."[28]

To a more sympathetic audience in another pretrial speech he asserted that the Scopes backers were people who "come in from outside of the state and force upon the people of the state and upon the children of the taxpayers of this state a doctrine that refutes not only their belief in God but their belief in a Savior and belief in heaven and takes from them every moral standard that the Bible gives us."[29] He was right, of course.

Undoubtedly there were some sincere Christians who supported Scopes simply because they had become convinced that Darwin was on the right track and felt that they could reconcile that conviction with their religious beliefs (as Bryan seemed inclined to do) by talking of six periods of time and a God-controlled evolutionary process. But such folk would have to have been painfully out of touch with the cultural collision taking place in the courtroom. It is safe to say that the pro-Scopes forces, by and large, were in tune with the larger goals Bryan charged:

Our purposed, our only purpose, is to vindicate the right of parents to guard the religion of their children against efforts made in the name of science to undermine faith in supernatural religion. There is no attack on free speech, or freedom of the press, or freedom of thought, or freedom of knowledge, but surely parents have a right to guard the religious welfare of their children.[30]

Bryan knew the mentality of the Darrows of the world too well to be put off guard by their pose as the great defenders of freedom of expression. He saw clearly the challenge; that the "principle of evolution" was attractive to the secularizers not because of any overwhelming scientific evidence, but because "there is no place for the miracles in the train of evolution, and the Old Testament and the New are filled with miracles."[31]

He correctly perceived that ultimate questions were on the line: whether man was to be seen henceforth as a creature with "ancestors in the jungle," or one "made by God in His image and put here for His purpose as part of a divine plan."[32] "The facts are simple," he proclaimed to the court, "the case is plain. . . . These gentlemen want to enter upon a larger work . . . to banish from the hearts of the people the Word of God as revealed."[33] Darrow would phrase it differently, speak of his attack on the kind of reign of bigotry that burns men at the stake, but his motives were just what Bryan says they were. To "free" mankind by dealing Bryan's brand of religion a death blow. One might argue that organized Christianity should meet with that death blow, but not that Darrow was merely seeking an "equal hearing" for his own brand of secularism.

Academic Freedom

There are many reasons why it would be beneficial for America if a revival of scholarly interest in Bryan were to take place. But perhaps the most important for tradition-minded parents would be the discovery of the tool he offers for dealing with the fraud of "academic freedom."

If it were not so serious an issue, the modern educationist demand for "academic freedom" would be amusing. Evelyn Waugh could have done wonders with it.

Often one can get the impression that American teachers believe, or would have us believe, that they are a group of deep thinkers who are continually imposed upon by groups of young Americans, with parental encouragement, to join in discussions of intellectual matters, while they are returning from their days of research at the local libraries. These learned scholars, out of the goodness of their hearts and because of their concern for Truth, always agree to talk to the young folk. And "academic freedom," the story seems to go, is simply the natural demand these scholars make to insure that "outsiders" do not force them to take positions contrary to their beliefs. After all, if we want these scholars to participate in the discussions, we cannot tell them what to say. Certainly in a free society we would not want *that*.

Perhaps if schools were places where chance discussions, such as those described above, took place, the demand for academic freedom would be plausible. Perhaps the most we can do if we find our children involved in a discussion we deem dangerous to their moral health is to take them home and warn them about the dangers of bad companions. But since schools are nothing of the sort, the modern educationist call for academic freedom is without merit. Schools are institutions established by society, paid for by society, to give to the young the skills needed to make their way in life, certainly, but also to transmit to them society's cultural heritage—to preserve, protect, defend and extend the community's value system. Teachers are hired by society to provide these services. And a community, Bryan insists, has as much right as any individual teacher to *its* freedom of thought, and to the accompanying right to demand that paid employees perform the service for which they were hired: "The collective right is bound to protect itself from misrepresentation and is just as sacred as the individual's right to think for himself as an individual."[34]

Bryan had no intention to deny any teacher the right to think and read and write and assemble as he saw fit *as a private citizen* when he was off the community's payroll, when he was representing only himself and not the parents of the community. "We concede the right of any man to be an atheist or agnostic,"[35] states Bryan flatly. But one who accepts employment as a representative of a society to its young, when he accepts such a position, must not be allowed to operate as a public censor instead, as some high priest encharged with converting the children of his employers to his private perception of higher virtue. This does not imply that teachers are to act as dictating machines for some narrow communal consensus. An intelligent questioning attitude, perhaps even a healthy skepticism, has long been an attitude admired by the American people. But the teacher goes beyond his rights when he operates as an adversary to community values—as a true-believing, doctrinaire apologist for values contrary to the community's, as did John Scopes.

If classrooms ought not be turned into pulpits for the majority's beliefs, they certainly ought not become pulpits for the minority's. "They have barred the Bible from the schools—now all I ask is to have this heresy, this anti-Bible teaching, thrown out, too."[36]

In other words, if a *genuine* neutrality—Genesis and Darwin explained as conflicting explanations for man's origins with support among many Americans—were being called for by Darrow, Bryan would have assented. He was leading a public campaign for a law that would force just such a situation when he died. What he refused to accept, however, was the close-minded authoritarianism of a smug claque of pseudoscientists who were willing to impose upon American schoolchildren as dogma a scientific novelty theory, and for less than noble motives. Bryan, one last time:

> When the Christians of the nation understand the demoralizing influence of this godless doctrine, they will refuse to allow it to be taught at public expense. Christianity is not afraid of truth, because truth comes from God, no matter by whom it is discovered or proclaimed, but there is no reason why Christians should tax themselves to pay teachers to exploit guesses and hypotheses as if they were true.[37]

He is a thinker worthy of one of the top spots in the new pantheon which will be erected once Americans shake themselves free from the blinders of the eighteenth-century Enlightenment.

The Implications

Continuing our overall theme: Is Bryan's call for parental authority in the public schools a leftist or rightist stance? Continuing our theme: neither. Once again, it depends. In the modern public consciousness, the groups continuing Bryan's fight against "godless" and "atheistic" and "anti-Christian" books in the public schools are usually considered conservatives and rightwingers. Think of the Kanewha, West Virginia, brouhaha of a few years back, and the ongoing media treatment of parent groups protesting the presence of *Soul on Ice* or Kurt Vonnegut's novels on their high-school library shelves.

Yet, on the other hand, the black parents seeking "community control" and teachers and curricula in tune with the black American experience are considered radicals, as are the counterculture parents looking for alternative schools for their children lest their creative energies be deadened by the plodding Department of Education straights who live beyond—physically and spiritually—the confines of Haight-Ashbury and New York City's West Side.

All our flip-flops are at work. Those black parents, if they moved to the suburbs undoubtedly would be seeking state-mandated black-studies programs in spite of the local opposition from the community-control-favoring white parent groups—the same whites who fret over the courses in Swahili and ghetto slang, which they say black communities will mandate unless held in rein by the educational "experts" at the State Board of Regents who suddenly become defenders of Western Civilization instead of functionaries in the movement for world atheism.

And, once again, our response is the same. Community control is not a good thing in and of itself. It depends on what community is doing the controlling. *What* is found in a curriculum is more important than the level of authority that determines the content. In a society with a clear vision of its identity—one with the kind of well-established moral consensus we are told the First Amendment forbids—most communities would be healthy enough to be allowed wide leeway in setting up educational policy on the local level. Certain others, for a variety of reasons, might be considered aberrant and in need of checks and enforceable guidelines from a higher authority to insure that their schools will successfully introduce local young people into the ennobling national heritage.

In modern America, since (or so we are told) the First Amendment does not allow us to establish beforehand such a recognizable national identity, we end up arguing on the school issue over community control and academic freedom and parents' rights; as if *what* is being taught is secondary in importance to *how* we make the decisions on educational policy. Partisans seek the educational approach more likely to put people like themselves in decision-making roles, but then defend their choice as the result of an impartial analysis of educational theory. "It is not that people who agree with me will make your children better people, my friend. That's not why I want community control [or academic freedom for the local teachers—take your pick]; it is the principle of the thing."

Which is silly. Would Darrow have allowed in the name of academic freedom courses that insisted that mankind originated the way the Indian legends or Norse myths describe; or the way Genesis informs us? Would Bryan have waxed eloquent over parental rights if he were looking at a school on an Indian reservation that was promulgating a hatred of the white Christian devils who despoiled the North American continent?

One of the most striking ironies that results from all this is the fact that nowadays only *private* schools seem able to establish the moral and social atmosphere favored by the great majority of the American *public*. *Public* schools cannot. No matter how committed society as a whole may be to standards of propriety and performance, its public schools must operate as if that consensus has not been formed; as if they were the agents of a society that is no society; a society that encourages a discussion of social and moral questions but allows no conclusions. And parents have to sit back and resign themselves to the educational decay, unless, that is, they are willing to go to court and probably lose to the same opponent that took on William Jennings Bryan: the ACLU.

VII

McCarthyism

It has become clear of late—although it may take a later generation of historians and political commentators to make the public admission—that perhaps the only serious victim of "McCarthyism"* in America was Joseph R. McCarthy himself.

Think of the thrust of the case against the man: that he was a practioner of alleging "guilt by association," a "name-caller," hysterical, mean-spirited, cruel.

Well, at the present moment, in the official literature on our recent past, is there any other American historical figure as subject to that kind of treatment? John Wilkes Booth, John Dillinger, Bonnie and Clyde, Leopold and Loeb, Bruno Hauptmann, Caryl Chessman, Sacco and Vanzetti, Gary Gilmore, Ethel and Julius Rosenberg, even Charles Manson, find themselves the object of essays meant, at the very least, to mitigate their guilt. We have been instructed for generations now by progressive thinkers that we ought not condemn our fellow citizens too readily, especially when they are in pursuit of political justice. John Brown, SDS bombers, Nat Turner. But Joe McCarthy? No quarter with evil.

Richard Rovere tells us "no bolder seditionist ever moved among us—nor any politician with a surer, swifter access to the dark places of the American mind."[1]

"The effect" when McCarthy spoke "was that of a Nazi bully boy glaring at you from the television screen"[2] we are told in

---

*"McCarthyism," if you do not know, is now found in the dictionaries. "The practice of accusing another of wrongdoing without sufficient evidence; a witch-hunt" is the way you will find it listed in one of the more popular versions.

The Nightmare Decade, a book favorably reviewed in the journals sent into paroxysms by McCarthy's name-calling. Not until Spiro Agnew rose to threaten freedom of expression in America (he was silenced pretty quickly though, wasn't he), was there anything quite like McCarthy, that same book continues. Agnew "intentionally or not, had the old McCarthy legions baying. They never had gone away. They had subsided for a time because they had lost their leader, but now they were rallying to a new voice."

> A large number of Americans frustrated by the Vietnam stalemate, alarmed by the issues of race and the ghettos and the revolt of the young, were ready to follow the new Pied Piper, blaming all the nation's ills on such scapegoats as the "effete" and the "intellectuals" and some unnamed "conspirators" against the American way. This was the old McCarthyism resurgent, hate-filled, appealing to a blind superpatriotism; impervious to reason.[3]

Agnew threatened another "time of national paranoia" when Americans once again would look "fearfully over their shoulders, wondering whether *they* would be tapped next to explain themselves before the grand inquisitors" who were convinced there were "communists under every bed."[4] Remember those nerve-wracking years?

When Bertrand Russell in *The New York Times* Sunday magazine section fretted (from the safety of his English fastness) that "If by some misfortune you were to quote with approval some remark by Jefferson you would probably lose your job and find yourself behind bars."[5] When Bernard DeVoto warned that the "hardheaded boys are going to hang the Communist label on everybody who holds ideas offensive to the U.S. Chamber of Commerce, the National Association of Manufacturers, or the steering committee of the Republican Party."[6] When the *Times* editorialized of the "black fear in the country brought about by the witch hunters."[7]

Do you have any vague memories of those victims of the nightmare decade, all those who passed from sight, to the salt mines or worse, never to be heard from again? Bernard DeVoto, *The New York Times*, Bertrand Russell, Alger Hiss, Howard Fast, Norman Cousins, Archibald MacLeish, Arthur Schlesinger, Lillian Hellman, Dashiell Hammet, Paul Robeson? Surely there might never have been a better way to intellectual recognition than to earn the status of victim of anti-Communist zealotry.

This McCarthyism of McCarthy extends beyond McCarthy

the individual. It is not, apparently, a flaw in the man as much as the disease of anti-Communism that elicits the sledge hammer response from American liberals. Another well-received recent book on McCarthy takes aim at Louis Budenz, an ex-Communist whose testimony about his former comrades was used to support McCarthy's charges against Owen Lattimore. Budenz's testimony is to be doubted by thoughtful Americans, we are told, because he "had been in frequent contact with Alfred Kohlberg for some years." (Kohlberg was an American supporter of Chiang Kai-shek in his attempt to recapture the mainland.) "It is more than probable that all of Budenz's charges concerning the China question sprang not at all from the ex-Communist's facile memory, but rather from the fertile imagination of the China merchant," Kohlberg.[8] Notice, *all* of Budenz's charges.

Astounding but symptomatic of so much of the anti-McCarthy literature. Another writer, after deploring the atmosphere of fear and conformity that McCarthy threw like a pall over political discourse in the country, proceeds to condemn the newspapers of the era.

> Even McCarthy's strongest critics among the press may have given him unintended aid. The papers—the *New York Post*, the *Washington Post* and the *Capitol Times* (Madison) come immediately to mind—expressed an almost obsessive hatred of McCarthy. They exposed his past and denounced his present, and above all gave him column after column of coverage. They suffered what one critic described as phobophilia: they were in love with the enemy.[9]

Well, perhaps when the issues are important enough for the survival of decency you can have it both ways; when truth is not as important as what Walter Lippmann used to call the "battle for men's minds."

Losing the Peace

It ought to be conceded by those who seek to rescue Joseph McCarthy's reputation that his name can be cleared up only to a certain extent. There were unattractive things about the man (beyond any of his personal vices, which his critics would find irrelevant in anyone else). His public accusations were too broad, sloppy in fact, for his purposes. He used a battle-axe in just the right moments for a rapier. He could be thoughtless, cruel—there can be no denying that. His presentation of evidence left much to be desired. His flair for the dramatic, although appropriate for the headline-seeking which was in order, led him to overstate his case. And, most important, he failed to grasp the full significance of the term "fellow traveler," which he employed with some gusto. That is, he failed to grasp the fact that it is possible for a modern American to agree with Russia on almost all the crucial issues of the time, but not be in that country's employ or even a Communist Party member as such. That, sad to say, being a twentieth-century "liberal" is often enough to lead to that frame of mind. But more of this later. Let us proceed apace.

The point just now is that there is no necessary reason for modern "McCarthyites" to defend McCarthy when he speaks of Drew Pearson's role as that of a "Moscow-directed character assassin"; or refers to Adlai Stevenson as "Alger—I mean Adlai." Those were cheap shots. As was calling Dean Acheson "Red Dean," a man "Russian as to heart—British as to manner." And what intelligent reason could be served by referring to the State Department as a "crimson crowd" and a "lace-handkerchief crowd." If nothing else, it is counterproductive.

Hence the prudent course for a modern anti-Communist is to simply concede and condemn these excesses. But, then, adamantly refuse to concede that McCarthy's cause was unjust or wrongheaded. The battles for a noble cause can be fought incompetently and disreputably and be led by combatants better suited for the role of aide-de-camp than commandant. The great irony of the McCarthy years is that the American cavaliers, the well-educated upper-class legislators and bureaucrats of long standing, proved impotent. The polished representatives of the American elite, the Ivy League graduates and scions of the American money aristocracy—the men who would have known how to tone down the charges and present them in a more prudent and effective manner—were unwilling or unable to face up to the implications of the presence of Communists and Communist sympathizers in Washington in the years after World War II. And, as a consequence, a newcomer to Washington, a junior senator from Wisconsin, bit off more than he could chew. The question is why no one else moved effectively when they clearly should have. The Marxists were there.

They were. The Communist presence charged by McCarthy is now conceded, *by McCarthy's enemies*. It is a phenomenon that has not yet received the attention it deserves.

Think back, if you will, to the nightmare decade, to the most repeated anti-McCarthyite barb. Invariably, it was something to the effect that the lout sees "Communists under every bed." In other words, McCarthy was a menace, we were told, because he accused innocent people of being Communists when they were *not*; grossly exaggerated the numbers of Communist sympathizers in positions of importance; smeared good patriotic Americans because they disagreed with him; set off on a "witch-hunt." Correct? His opponents, then, it is fair to say, were arguing, in public in any event, as if they would not have opposed McCarthy if he had *had* the proof; that, in fact, they might even have been supporters of his—if he had been able to *prove* that the people he named actually were Communists.

Well, now, in our more progressive climate, Lillian Hellman admits to us in *Scoundrel Time* that the people in her circle threatened by McCarthy and his followers *were* actively involved in the Communist movement. In *The Front*, the character Woody Allen plays, finds himself in hot water when he takes the blame for a man who *was* a Communist. In *The Way We Were* Barbra Streisand plays one of those numerous urban intellectuals who worked for the Communist Party in the 1930s and later made their way into government jobs during the war years, or perhaps—as did Barbra's friends in the movie—secured positions in Hollywood with the Marxist cliques there waging the proletarian wars by turning out socially conscious movies and radio drama.

This is a remarkable change in stance. The message now is not that the McCarthyites were villainous for calling people Communists when they were not, but for being paranoid about people who *were* Communists, for failing to perceive the high-minded idealism that leads people to Marx; for viewing Communism as an enemy system, as if it were Nazism or Fascism, rather than a system that deserves to be the object of the politics of convergence; as one of the varieties of dictatorship that deserve to be warred against in pursuit of unconditional surrender.

Considering this new candor, one is struck all the more by the success of the anti-McCarthyites in maintaining so successfully for so long that only an irrational or dark psyche could have led McCarthy to be suspicious of a Communist presence in Washington. Actually—accurate or not—the charge that McCarthy was a Johnny-come-lately who jumped on the anti-Communist bandwagon for lack of a better attention-getter, is the more potentially telling blow. McCarthy hardly invented the early 1950s' suspicion that there were people in Washington suspiciously soft on Communism. Veterans of World War II, and those who waited for their return, were beginning to smell something fishy.

The most monumental and costly war in history had been fought to keep the small nations of Europe out of the hands of totalitarian dictatorships. Dresden and Cologne had been carpet-bombed into a rubble rather than accept German hegemony over Poland, Czechoslovakia, Hungary. The most devastating weapon of war ever developed was dropped on Japan to prevent it from establishing puppets in Korea, China, and Southeast Asia. Americans gave their lives by the hundreds of thousands for the cause of the Four Freedoms. But that was a price worth paying. Free men brook no compromise with the enemies of democracy. We had learned the lessons of Munich.

Yet by the 1950s almost all of the Eastern European and Asian land Americans had fought to keep out of the hands of German and Japanese dictatorships had come under the sway of Soviet Russian and Communist Chinese dictatorships. Yet, the same American policy makers who were willing to risk all, pay any price for victory against Germany and Japan, seemed to mind hardly at all. The Communists seemed "entitled" to what the Nazis and the Japanese were not.

Americans did not need Joseph McCarthy to start asking: *why?* And the answer was not—as one might argue in our time—that the Communists' military strength forced a spirit of compromise. In the early 1950s Russia and China had no atom bombs. They could resist, to be sure, any American demand that China and Eastern Europe be as free from Communist domination as they had been made from Nazi. But only in the same manner as the Germans and Japanese. Which means they could have been beaten. Not easily or painlessly, of course. But it could have been accomplished if American leaders had had the will to do so—a will comparable to that which they displayed against Germany. (In fact, if they had convincingly demonstrated that same level of determination, physical force might very well have been unnecessary, considering the clear-cut American and British military superiority at the time.) But they did not. The Communists were not viewed as a force as evil as the Nazis. The average American did not need Joseph McCarthy to ask: *why?*

What was it about Communism that was so less offensive? It was more totalitarian, more repressive of religion. Its expansionist urge was unlimited: The proletarian revolution, the Communists say, is to be worldwide. The very invasion that launched World War II in Europe—of Poland—was one in which the Communists collaborated through the Hitler-Stalin pact. And in 1950 the Communists had the Nazi share of the plunder too. The concentration camps? Genocide? Even then the world knew of the extermination of the Kulaks and the Gulag Archipelago, if not by that name.

So *why* were the Communists entitled to what the Nazis were not? Who was making the decisions in Washington that allowed the Russian domination of the satellite ring? Why did Harry Truman cut off arms supplies to Chiang Kai-shek at the very moment the Communists under Mao were gathering in their Yenan strongholds, preparing to uncoil into the Yangtze valley?

It was not unthinkable in 1950 to ponder the possibility that Communist sympathizers in Washington had something to do with the curious turn of events. In 1945 over a thousand stolen classified documents were found in the offices of *Amerasia*, a magazine openly committed to the overthrow of Chiang Kai-shek's government. In 1946 a spy ring was broken in Canada, one that had transmitted vast amounts of secret data to Russia, including samples of Uranium 234 and the information needed to build radar. In 1946, as well, Harry Truman set in motion a commission on employee loyalty and a Loyalty Review Board in response to the widespread belief that Washington during World War II had become a safe harbor for Communists and Communist sympathizers. In 1948 Whittaker Chambers and Elizabeth Bentley, admitted former Communists, appeared before congressional committees, giving the names of highly placed government employees who had been former comrades of theirs, including those of Alger Hiss, Harry Dexter White, and Lauchlin Currie, men at the very pinnacle of decision-making power during the Yalta days. In 1949 Judith Copolan was arrested while giving secret documents to Soviet intelligence agent, Valentin Gubitchev. In 1950 Klaus Fuchs was arrested in England for giving atomic secrets to Russian underground courier Harry Gould; their confessions led to the conviction and eventual execution of Ethel and Julius Rosenberg in the United States. The list went on and on.

Not only McCarthy was up in arms. Max Kampleman in his book *The Communist Party vs the CIO* writes of the purge of that labor organization conducted by non-Communist members. It was necessitated, he says, by the fact that the Communists controlled "at least 40 per cent of the CIO unions."[10] The United Electrical Workers union was expelled because the Communist domination was deemed too deeply entrenched for an effective reform.

Senator William Knowland, in 1949, spoke of the fall of China to the Communists: "If ever a government has had the rug pulled out from under it, if ever a non-Communist government in the world has reason to feel betrayed, that government is the Republic of China."[11]

General Patrick Hurley in November of that same year stated flatly that China fell because too many members of the State Department "sided with the Chinese Communist armed policy." They "engineered the overthrow of our ally, the Nationalist Government of the Republic of China and aided in the Communist conquest of China."[12]

Senator Robert A. Taft—whose title of Mr. Conservative, it is true, is enough to make him suspect in some circles—is nonetheless considered a "good" rightwinger by many of his ideological opponents, a man of reason and decency. Yet his estimate of Mao's takeover centered upon his conviction that "the State Department has been guided by a left-wing group who obviously have wanted to get rid of Chiang and were willing at least to turn China over to the Communists for that purpose."[13]

In fact, the Republican Party, as a party, in February of 1950 issued the following "Statement of Principle and Objectives":

> We deplore the dangerous degree to which Communists and their fellow travelers have been employed in important Government posts and the fact that information vital to our security has been made available to alien agents and persons of questionable loyalty. We denounce the soft attitude of this Administration toward government employees and officials who hold or support Communist attitudes.[14]

But, surely, McCarthy's critics would say, there is a difference between the above and the impassioned and irresponsible purple prose of McCarthy. To an extent, yes. But one cannot help wonder if McCarthy's rhetoric would have been anywhere near as offensive if it had been directed toward, say, the Ku Klux Klan or American neo-Nazis. The twentieth century, after all, is the century of mass politics. Politicians no longer address their speeches to House of Lord-type assemblies; not if they intend to generate the political backing required to succeed. Were McCarthy's words more offensive than those used by some of his oft- and highly praised contemporaries? Or was it that he was stirring up the *hoi polloi* for the wrong purposes? Consider some examples of apparently acceptable American political language cited by L. Brent Bozell and William F. Buckley in their book on McCarthy.

Harry Truman in criticism of the Republican supporters of the Taft-Hartley Act: "Powerful forces, like those that created European Fascists, are working through the Republican Party [to] undermine . . . American democracy."

John L. Lewis, on American management: "When we sought surcease from bloodletting, you proffered indifference, when we cried aloud for the safety of our members, you answered, 'Be content, 'twas always thus'. . . . When we spoke of little children in unkempt surroundings, you said—'look to the State'; . . . you are smug in your complacency; we are abashed by your shamelessness."[15]

And we all know of FDR's ringing denunciations of "economic royalists."

The point is, simply, that when a cause is deemed exalted enough by its supporters, verbal excesses such as the above, overstatements, even on occasional wounded innocent bystander, are deemed a price worth paying; just as Lieutenant Calleys are more likely to be covered up, with the active connivance of the press, when the war is fought against an enemy perceived to be truly villainous. Felix Frankfurter, a man hardly associated with McCarthy's side of American politics, made the point when he chided ideological allies fretting over the prospect of innocent and well-meaning businessmen being defamed in the reformist ardor of the Progressive Era.

> The question is not whether people's feelings here and there may be hurt, or names "dragged through the mud," as it is called. . . . Critics, who have nothing to say for the astounding corruption and corrupting soil which have been brought to light, seek to divert attention and shackle the future by suggesting restrictions in the procedure of future congressional investigations.[16]

Just so. One had to be in opposition to McCarthy's objectives to be scandalized by his methods.

It should be noted, moreover, that if McCarthy had had his way, he would never have been "guilty" of the charge that he defamed innocent people in public.

McCarthy, it is seldom remembered, specifically requested that his testimony, before the hastily gathered congressional committee (the Tydings Committee) charged with investigating his allegations, be given in private. He conceded that certain of the people on his list of security risks might come up with a "clean bill of health." It was the leadership of the Tydings Committee who wanted his testimony in public. Their concern was with demonstrating to their constituents that McCarthy was in error; that he had not been more vigilant than they, just ruthless and irresponsible. Only by exposing McCarthy as a fraud or scoundrel could they save face. Theirs was a poker player's move, calculated in the hope that McCarthy could not back up his words. And it was a clever move. It forced McCarthy onto ground he did not plan to defend. His position was not that his list contained manifest examples of subversion, but "security risks" crying for further investigation. He was calling on the Congress to begin those investigations, to review his evidence in closed sessions, to seek out further evidence and fire only those on his list who proved to be too serious a risk for a country on the verge of open conflict with Russia. McCarthy:

> I have enough to convince me that either they are members of the Communist Party or they have given great aid to the Communists. I may be wrong. That is why I said that unless the Senate demanded that I do so, I would not submit this publicly, but I would submit to any committee—and I would let the committee go over these in executive sessions. It is possible that some of these persons will get a clean bill of health.[17]

But Scott Lucas and Millard Tydings would have none of that. The names had to be named, in public.

Which is when McCarthy came up with egg on his face—or so we have been told. All the guilt by association. The lack of convictions. No one sent to jail for treason. Not one. McCarthyism.

Actually the charge makes use of one of our recent history's best examples of a straw man. McCarthy never did come forward with evidence sufficient to earn a conviction. That is true. But irrelevant. McCarthy's efforts were directed toward getting security risks *fired*, not imprisoned. (Although he certainly had no objection to convictions if warranted.)

There is an important distinction involved here. The crime of treason must be demonstrated as convincingly as any other. The accused must be proved guilty "beyond a reasonable doubt." He has a *right* to remain out of jail until the presumption of innocence is dispelled.

Government employment, however, especially in high-security positions, is not a right. It is a *privilege* that must be won and vindicated by the recipient to be extended. It can be taken from us, in other words, with evidence that merely "raises a reasonable doubt." *Prima facie* guilt is sufficient for dismissal, McCarthy argued—and almost all would agree in cases other than those involving McCarthy. If our continued employment presents too much risk for the country as a whole, especially in times of crisis (such as the nervous early days of the Cold War), the privilege ought to be revoked.

And the fact, quite simply, is that McCarthy had evidence sufficient to warrant firings. It should not be necessary to argue the point any longer now that there is such a willingness among American leftists, in the *Scoundrel Time* and *The Way We Were*-type offerings, to admit to the extent of pro-Soviet sympathy in American academic, media, and government circles in the 1930s and 1940s.

There is neither space nor should it be necessary here to catalogue the list of those accused by McCarthy. Buckley and Bozell's *McCarthy and His Enemies* (the one pro-McCarthy book no intelligent anti-McCarthyite can ignore without sacrificing his intellectual self-respect) provides a complete list of those accused and the charges made against them. The evidence is most persuasive, and no longer challenged. The modern leftist position is that, yes, what McCarthy said about the backgrounds of these people is true—but "so what?" That close associations with Communist groups during the 1930s and 1940s ought not necessitate that a man or woman be fired in the 1950s; that one can be a version of the character Barbra Streisand played in *The Way We Were* and still handle top secret documents at the State Department.

Even what could be called the "temperate" anti-McCarthyites display a perplexing willingness to treat the issue with smug condescension. Adam Ulam, a man who writes with conviction of the tragedy of the Yalta giveaways, for example, pokes fun at McCarthy for his use of the term "card-carrying" Communists. "Someone should have told the senator that it was a capital offense for Soviet spies to advertise their political affiliation."[18] As if McCarthy meant that Communist agents were issued membership cards of the sort earned by members of Captain Midnight's Secret Squadron! "Card-carrying" in the American vernacular means "official" and "active" and "conscious"—and Ulam would have recognized that in any other context.

Ulam's position—one that has considerable following in certain conservative circles—holds that the fateful policy decisions McCarthy attributed to Communist subversion were actually the result of "honest miscalculations, stupidity, or historical circumstances."[19] "Instead of a search for and removal of those who had proved incompetent and naive, there was a frenzied chase after the wicked and treasonous."[20]

Interesting. But it misses the point at least partially. After all, it is not as if McCarthy had something against firing incompetents. The question is whether, after looking at the evidence he presented, a reasonable man would find cause to suspect that the accused were something other than bumblers and Pollyannas; indeed, that they were more likely to have been hardheaded realists, cleverly manipulating American policy in the direction of Communist ends (whether because of direct Russian instructions or a general Marxist sympathy for the world proletarian revolution being promoted by the Soviets). Ulam can stand insouciant even in the face of the evidence against Alger Hiss.

> In the Hiss case . . . the most important question from the point of view of the *public interest* would have been whether the accused was ever in a position (a) to betray information of value to the Soviet Union, or (b) to influence American policies for its benefit. . . . The notorious "Pumpkin Papers" were of slight value. . . . If half the State Department had been in the pay of the U.S.S.R., this still would not have warped American foreign policy as much as did Roosevelt's conviction that he could "domesticate Stalin."[21]

One need not discount the effect of the naive American trust in Stalin's good intentions to take issue. What can he mean? That Hiss and his brethren should not have been hounded out of policy-making posts because they had not yet handed anything of value over to the Russians? Would we have shrugged at the presence of a Bund member in the State Department who was smuggling secret documents to German intelligence because the American Nazi had not yet seized any worthwhile information?

Of course, it is not Ulam's point that enemy agents should have been left on the payroll. His thesis is that stupidity and a lack of understanding of the demands of *realpolitik* were what led America to squander its moment of ascendancy in the world arena. But, nonetheless, he shows evidence of that all too typical disdain of the liberal intelligentsia for McCarthy's claim that—however much incompetency there was at work—there was evidence of the presence of enough subversive intent to warrant genuine concern; of the presence, once again, of the kind of pro-Communists the modern liberals are now describing with nostalgic affection in *The Way We Were, Scoundrel Time, The Front*, etc.

The Way Who Was?

Hence the critical issue—the cause of the liberal reluctance to admit to the dangers of the 1950s Communist presence in Washington. The *why*. What caused a man like Paul Appleby, an administrator of the Bureau of Budget, to state flatly that "a man in the employ of the government has just as much right to be a member of the Communist Party as he has to be a member of the Democratic or Republican Party."[22]

Now, granted, the above quote would be more meaningful if it came from someone in the State Department or Department of Defense. But it is germane. Appleby's attitude could be found, if not articulated as candidly, all through the more sensitive departments of the federal government in the early 1950s.

Is this last statement a shocking example of the "Mc-Carthyite" mentality at work? I hope not; and it is not—not on its own terms certainly. The point to keep in mind is that there were reasons why people in Washington in the post-World War II years could be "soft on Communism," besides orders from Moscow. The oft-revered dream of a permanent and enforceable world peace was one of them.

We are speaking of Woodrow Wilson's hope: the end of war; the brotherhood of man; peace and parliamentary democracy on earth; the favorite twentieth-century topic for people as harmless and well-meaning as church-wardens and women's club speakers, genteel and pipe-smoking folk of all sorts with their H.G. Wells-readings of history. As American as apple pie.

It is a dream intense enough to blind the visionary so obsessed to the political realities of his day; make him hope against hope, like a teen-age boy who has just been told that his dream hot-rod on the used-car dealer's lot needs a ring job. He'll want to buy it anyway. He'll scowl at the mechanic who shows him the fouled spark plugs and the black smoke from the exhaust pipe.

Certain otherwise intelligent Americans seemed to find themselves in such a position at the end of World War II. The bad guys had been beaten. Now all the good guys had to do was stick together as they had in defeating the villain, not make the same mistake that had derailed the League of Nations. It seemed possible: The U.S. and the U.S.S.R. joined permanently against the Fascist impulse—the United Nations.

For this dream to become a reality, of course, the Russians had to remain good guys. The aspirants for world peace could not face up to the fact that all the characteristics that had made the Nazis irreconcilable enemies in their eyes were present in the Bolsheviks, in spades—not without relinquishing the dream. When a Soviet "indiscretion" or two impinged upon the dream, for the greater good of mankind they had to be toned down into temporary aberrations caused either by the war or Soviet anxieties, which could be assuaged by a determined American effort to demonstrate uncompromisingly peaceful intentions.

It probably was such a hope that led Cordell Hull, for example, to assure Americans that "the Soviet Union had made up its mind to follow the course of international cooperation . . . because she would discover that any course other than cooperation was against her own interests."[23]

And it lead him to scold as unpatriotic those writers who would not let their fellow citizens forget the nature and history of Communism in Russia. "Malcontents in this country . . . were doing their best to drive Russia out of the international movement by constant attacks and criticisms. . . . Unless it was possible to prevail upon newspaper commentators and columnists to refrain from this line of activity . . . it would be difficult for any international undertaking, such as that offered by us [the U.N.], to succeed."[24]

And, feasibly, it was nothing more that led Harry Hopkins to proclaim that the Russians "trust the United States more than they trust any other power in the world, . . . are determined to take their place in world affairs in an international organization, and above all to want to maintain friendly relations with us."[25]

But there were other forces at work as well, forces which have become clearer in our time. And McCarthy was deemed dangerous because he was on a collision course with a good many of them; especially what we now call the New Left.

In McCarthy's time it was a view usually disguised or softpedaled. (The growing respectability of the New Left in the post-Vietnam and post-Watergate era is what prompted the candor of those caught up in the Lillian Hellman syndrome. That, and a fear of a new wave of McCarthy-like outrage over the defeat in Vietnam. "Recriminations" had to be defused before they took shape.) In the 1950s only overt Communists would openly declare that the path chosen by the Soviet Union, if not perfect, is nevertheless closer to the ideal than that of capitalist America; and that America's lingering and benighted attachments to private enterprise, Christianity, and the concept of the sovereign nation-state are the greatest obstacles to world peace. While in our day, it would not seem an overstatement to say that this position has become the consensus among younger college and high-school history and social science teachers; and that, correlatively, socialism, secular humanism, and a supra-national loyalty to "mankind" are the biases of the age with the American intelligentsia. Who would quarrel? Certainly no still sensate student who sits through the lectures.

It is a dream, an overtly Marxist dream, that first took root among urban intellectuals during the depression of the 1930s—the decade Eugene Lyons, an ex-Marxist himself, has labeled *The Red Decade* in his book of that name; a dream given vigor by the Russian-American alliance against the Nazis. Some now call it the politics of "convergence": Russia becoming more like the United States in certain respects, easing up on its restrictions on freedom of expression especially (what kind of Utopia can we have without the better grades of porn?). And the United States moving into political maturity by moving away from the market economy, private property, archaic theistic notions which affect the social order, and the atavistic nationalist fervors of the past. If only the wartime cooperation could be maintained, the dream seemed realizable, perhaps within the lifetimes of the idealists of the Red Decade; perhaps through the U.N.

But then, along came Joe McCarthy, treating all this, mankind's highest twentieth-century idealism, as *treason*, as if the desired subversion of the old order were motivated by something other than love for mankind. And he was finding increasing support among the American masses. (Believe it or not, considering the disgrace attached to his name in our day, at one time he was almost as popular as Richard Nixon before Watergate, according to the polls.) Not that it came as a surprise to the leftist intelligentsia that the American masses could be roused by his Neanderthal cries. They knew full well of the beasts in the hearts of the American people. They knew the *demos* would have to be eased into the politics of convergence.

Old myths die hard; new realities are sometimes born slowly and with pain. You just could not say to an audience of World War II veterans, many still in combat trim, the kinds of things about America that one says now to applause on the Dick Cavett show. Back then you could not paraphrase Walter LaFeber's explanation of the Marshall Plan; as an American attempt to dominate Europe in the interests of capitalism and surround our betrayed ally Russia. "The Marshall Plan served as an all-purpose weapon for Truman's foreign policy. It charmed those who feared a slump in American exports and who believed, Communist threat or no Communist threat, that American and world prosperity rested on a vigorous export trade."[26] Much less that the Cold War "sprang from the American determination to keep China politically sovereign and whole for purposes of exploitation by the burgeoning United States industrial complex."[27] It was this capitalist-imperialist drive, first described by Lenin, which forced Russia "to create buffer states between Russian soil and the ambitions of Great Britain, the United States, and especially Japan."[28]

You could not, as does Staughton Lynd, blame the Cold War on

> "the Ivy League graduates in Wall Street and government [who] are apparently prepared to destroy the world rather than let it become something they don't run.
>
> "What they fear, when all is said and done is socialism: management of the economy not by corporation executives selected by other corporation executives but democratically, by the people; . . . that incompetent common people in Mozambique or Muncie might take the rhetoric of the Declaration of Independence seriously and try to run the economy themselves. . . . If America can stay democratic I believe it will become socialist."[29]

Folks would get uptight about such truths in the early 1950s. They would have reacted unreasonably to Eugene D. Genovese's analysis of world politics too.

> The great political and moral problem for the world as a whole is the reconciliation of socialism, which has increasingly become the banner of the oppressed people of Asia, Africa and Latin America, with personal freedom and the tradition of free and rational criticism that have been the glories of Western civilization. Only the West can effect that reconciliation, and the West can do nothing without the United States.[30]

People in the 1950s would have (accurately) interpreted such remarks to mean that the United States should be striving to learn from the Soviet Union rather than hardening ourselves into an adversary relationship behind an "iron curtain." They might have interpreted such statements as giving aid and comfort to the enemy.

They probably would have reacted similarly to William Appleman Williams' words: "The rest of the world, be it presently industrial or merely beginning to industrialize, is very clearly moving toward some version of a society modeled on the ideal and the Utopia of a true human community based far more on social property than upon private property."[31]

They would not have felt confident with government employees who had absorbed from their favorite theologians the kinds of things Harvey Cox teaches modern Americans. That, for example, "we must now read Nietzsche, who coined the phrase 'God is dead,' in the light of Fanon, Mao and Ho Chi Minh, the diagnosticians of the decline of Western dominance. . . . Our nation now looms as one of the main barriers to the birth of the new World, and the religion of America still largely endorses our empire. . . . The time has come to change."[32]

Of course, modern Americans are now able to take the New Left analyses in stride, as acceptable participants in the formation of public attitudes, because McCarthy was prevented from forming a sturdy anti-Communist consensus that would have removed from consideration all the broad areas of agreement modern leftists in America share with the Communists. McCarthy was attacked so vigorously—and continues to be pictured as an unqualified scoundrel—because the American Left understood how a well-developed anti-Communist public psyche would destroy, perhaps forever, their hopes for converting America to their higher vision of the good life, that Utopia now openly proselytized in America's educational institutions by the New Left or New Left-influenced instructors. Mankind's best hopes could be have been killed because some redneck senator insisted on pointing out to Americans how much it looked like what Russia wanted for the world.

Whittaker Chambers called the forces that destroyed McCarthy the "movement for world socialism,"—that vision of man's future which rose to prominence in the eighteenth century Enlightenment; the hope of replacing the Old Regime's Christian perception of man's destiny (vertical and God-centered) with a horizontally-perceived secular paradise: a religion of humanity.

Marxism is just one branch of the movement; a wayward branch says the non-Communist Left. But it certainly is not in their eyes an enemy system to be destroyed. Some of its totalitarian excesses are to be tamed—perhaps. Its overly rigid disciples chided, cajoled, enlightened, brought back into the main stream. But not fought as Nazis or Fascists; not when their hearts are in the right place. Their dream is the noble one. Their extremism is understandable to those who share common Enlightenment roots. The great danger from the American Left's point of view was that McCarthy understood none of this. And he just might have formed a political base that would have brought more people like him to positions of power in government and the media. It was this prospect that had to be fought so consummately, with none of the gentlemanly codes of rational debate that are observed in political discussions over less crucial issues, among discussants who accept the Enlightenment perception of what is good and rational and progressive in life.

The Fronts

To deal with the mind of the anti-McCarthyite, one must first understand the nature of the Communist "front groups" of the 1930s and 1940s. The fronts, of course, were groups sponsored from behind the scenes by the Communist Party in an attempt to gain backing for their objectives from people who would not support the Communist Party as such. There were fronts organized to combat Nazism (after Hitler's invasion of Russia naturally; before that, during the honeymoon of the Hitler-Stalin pact, the American Communist Party was a great proponent of American neutrality in the European struggle); to combat Fascism in Spain; to stir up the anger of American blacks against the capitalist economic order in the name of civil rights. The *National Negro Congress* and the *American League Against War and Fascism* were just two of the most noteworthy laborers in these vineyards.

It was possible, then, for an individual to be a supporter of one or more of these groups without being a Communist himself or even aware of the extent of Communist control. Large numbers of American liberals, as a result, found themselves, consciously or not, in political collaboration with Communists during the Red Decade, especially the urban intelligentsia.

It should not be difficult to imagine the situation. The same experience was commonplace during the anti-Vietnam War years. Thousands of Americans now selling stocks or driving cabs or managing Burger Kings can reminisce about the marches and demonstrations when they stood shoulder to shoulder with Trotskyites and Stalinists of the Angela Davis breed and aficionados of the liberated lifestyle of Castro's Cuba and Mao's China, as well as the paradise to come when their heroes, the Viet Cong (remember, "Ho,Ho,Ho Chi Minh! the NLF is gonna win!"?), emerged triumphant in Vietnam. They remember the marches and demonstrations, which they learned later—or perhaps knew at the time and cared not—were organized by the Communist Party. (John Lindsay will be remembered forever in some Americans' minds speaking enthusiastically at one such demonstration in New York, with the Viet Cong flag flying above his head.) These same Americans can tell of friends—who may be one of those managing the Burger Kings now—who proclaimed themselves at social gatherings to be Trotskyites or Maoists or some other variety of Marxist revolutionary. (Many of these street-fighting men, it is true, first became aware of the magnitude of such a claim when National Guard units began to deal with them the way governments usually deal with revolutionaries, at places such as Kent State. It sounds cruel, but it is true. Kent State marked the time when authorities began dealing with the college kids as something more serious than college kids; began taking the kids as seriously as the kids demanded.)

Of course, there are others of these young people who have not joined the ideological mainstream. They are not selling stocks or real estate. They are teaching in American schools or manning posts at think tanks or the State Department, and are continuing to press for the New Left politics of their college days, the end of the "military-industrial complex," and the "American empire."

The same situation prevailed in the 1940s. In Washington, Hollywood, on the staffs of major newspapers and television networks, on the faculties of the leading universities and local grade schools were a garden variety of the 1930s' radicals, members of the old front groups. There were those who had outgrown their youthful infatuation with Marxism, some because of the horrors of Stalin's purges, others because of the enlarged vision of the world which comes with maturity. There were those who, by and large, retained their ideological commitment to Marxist goals, but who never allowed that enthusiasm to be transformed into a conscious collaboration with the Soviet Union or the American Communist Party as such. And then there were the others—the active Communist agents who had taken the bold step, committed themselves to the Moscow-directed pursuit of the Marxist world order their less steadfast comrades were content merely to talk about. Whittaker Chambers' *Witness* takes us into the agonizing soul-searching that led some Americans to this fateful decision.

And it all seemed cozy for a while, what with the Russians and Americans locked arm-in-arm against the Nazis. Why a man might feel himself a patriotic American, even while transmitting secret documents to a foreign power.

And then, the Cold War. The view the Red Decade radicals took of the Russian-American confrontation was determined largely by which of the above stages they had reached. Some were able to view the Stalinists as enemies—either perverters of Marx's exalted dream or proof that the dream could not be realized until far in the future when liberal educators would have better prepared mankind for the dramatic step forward. Others viewed the Cold War tension as a temporary aberration—a family feud, which a little time and patience and an American willingness to compromise (which they would have to teach to their fellow citizens) could repair. For this breed, the Russians were still closer to home than the United States, Stalin notwithstanding.

But those who were committed sufficiently to Marxism to have worked under Soviet direction up until the outbreak of the Cold War (with the exception of the headline-making penitents like Whittaker Chambers and Louis Budenz), tended to stay members of the Moscow directed network. From their point of view, it was clearly America—as the modern New Leftists argue so forcefully—that had strayed, not themselves.

But the point to keep in mind is that whatever variety of 1930s Marxist you were, you had a common enemy in Joseph McCarthy in 1950, a common sympathy with those likely to be hurt by his campaign, and a common fear that a successful upsurge of the McCarthy mentality would stall the world's progress toward enlightened political objectives. Even if you had learned to despair over Stalin, you feared McCarthy more. Stalinism was at worst a perversion of the Enlightenment goals, while what McCarthy championed was a political consciousness still rooted in benighted pre-Enlightenment soil, a step backward to the Middle Ages.

Even those American liberals who had turned their backs completely on Marxism, who saw the 1950s' Soviet Union as the vanguard of a world movement that warranted vigorous opposition, tended to be reluctant to treat their former ideological allies as villains worthy of the wrath of the McCarthyites. They *understood* too well what led a man to collaborate with the Russians. They knew the temptation from personal experience, recalled the idealism which can prompt it. Their reaction was very much like that of a modern Irish-American who learns that his neighbor is smuggling guns to the IRA, an American Jew who knows of a friend plotting violence against the PLO headquarters in New York with the JDL, a Puerto Rican New Yorker who knows the back room of a bar in the South Bronx where the FALN lays its plans. They might not agree with the men of violence, but they are not about to turn them over to the authorities either. They are more than forgiving; they associate with the anger of their brethren; associate closely with their "idealism," whether or not they genuinely deplore the extremes to which it has driven them. Such excesses can be forgiven. They come too close to the actions of the hallowed men-of-the-gun of the past to be condemned outright, certainly not by a McCarthy.

Is this an insinuation that only leftists of one sort or another seeking to cover up someone's past (maybe their own) were the anti-McCarthyites? No, there were others, but none that ought to be taken too seriously. There were the uninformed, for example, and the naive, who simply never looked at McCarthy's objectives and the nature of the evidence required for those objectives, or who blindly accepted the then fashionable contention that he "had no proof," without taking the time to see whether that was the case or not. And there were what Buckley and Bozell call the "melodramatic clubwomen" (they, I may add, come in both sexes) who tend to wear their social consciences on their sleeves as a sign of a rarefied character formation; who form those consciences the same way they acquire their tastes in modern art and experimental theater: by parroting the proclamations of the reigning *cognoscienti*, the *au courant* movie stars and foreign film producers and proudly neurotic playwrights—the kind of beautiful souls Tom Wolfe found such easy prey in *Radical Chic and Mau-Mauing the Flak Catchers*, the kind of folk who always do the "smart" thing.

The Hidden Fears

McCarthy was a threat. There is no question about that. He seemed to comprehend instinctively the fuller objectives of the American Left. For him, it was not just a problem of Russian sympathizers in our government working to aid the enemy in another of the typical Mata Hari balance of power struggles which had been part of European politics for centuries. Perhaps this was a result of his not having been educated in the American universities where the Enlightenment biases had become deeply entrenched orthodoxy. He had none of that liberal open-minded affection for the "good points" of Communism. The Communists were not former colleagues gone astray in his eyes.

The following are not the most quoted of McCarthy's words. But they should be. They show us how much times have changed. (Even born again Christians when they become President no longer perceive the American people as did McCarthy just over a quarter of a century ago.) Picture if you will, a New York leftist intellectual, conscious of the majority sentiment in America against his views, but confident nonetheless that he was on the eventual winning side, assured by the new consciousness he could perceive in the arts, education, and government after World War II. The wave of the future was flowing to the Left. He had few doubts about that. Until this Roman Catholic ex-marine from the American heartland, of Irish and German working-class parentage, came along to the increasing applause of the American masses, identifying the nature of the threat posed to America by Communism.

> The great difference between our western Christian world and the atheistic Communist world is not political, ladies and gentlemen, it is moral.
>
> The real, basic difference . . . lies in the religion of immoralism—invented by Marx, preached feverishly by Lenin, and carried to unimaginable extremes by Stalin, . . . this religion of immoralism will more deeply wound and damage mankind than any conceivable economic or political system.
>
> Today we are engaged in a final, all-out battle between communistic atheism and Christianity.
>
> Ladies and gentlemen, can there be anyone here tonight who is so blind as to say that the war is not on? Can there be anyone who fails to realize that the Communist world has said, "The time is now"; . . . that this is the time for the show-down between the democratic Christian world and the Communistic atheistic world?[33]

To corroborate his point, McCarthy quoted Lenin: "The existence of the Soviet Republic side by side with Christian states for a long time is unthinkable."[34] His description of the villainy of Alger Hiss followed suit. He was the man who "sold out to the atheistic world."[35]

The point, if it needs be said, is that a country which coalesces around such a viewpoint does not seek détente with the Communist world; nor does it move in the direction of a convergence with Marxism. And it does not treat as an intellectual elite those who seek to weaken its attachments to Christianity, the free market economy, and a patriotic longing for a separate and sovereign national identity among the family of nations. This is why McCarthy's "witch hunt" became so unforgivable. So unlike other acts of political zealotry. As William S. Schlamm perceptively noted,

> the liberal supercourt of columnists, editors, commentators and critics, of thinkers and comedians, of statesmen and account executives, of publishers and piccolo players, convened in permanent mob session and found: the atrocious misjudgment of the certified gentlemen, who have dropped (Oops, sorry!) half of the world into irrevocable perdition, are not merely forgiveable but downright honorable; while the erring young man from Wisconsin is the hound of hell.[36]

And so it became a time for stiffened sinews and summoned-up blood, not the gentlemanly and rational exchange of ideas the intelligentsia call for in other instances. No room for open-mindedness this time; no straining to see "both sides." No détentes with the American Right.

No More Crusades in Europe, or Asia, or Africa, or. . . .

The fact that American foreign policy is sometimes set by the victors over Joseph McCarthy or their protégés, by men unable to view the Communists as an enemy, has much to do with the apparent contradictions, and the demonstrated impotency, the piecemeal surrenders, which have characterized America's confrontations with the Communist powers.

It is what promoted the strange inconsistencies that bedevil American rightists, as well as most instinctively nationalist common folk: the calls to coexist with Ho and Mao in spite of their proudly professed totalitarianism, accompanied by denunciations and calls for nonsupport of Chiang Kai-shek and Premier

Thieu when they failed to realize the degree of political liberty to which Chiang and Thieu aspired. It is why the dynamics of world geopolitics have passed to Moscow and Peking, why they ponder their next intrusions into Africa, and whether it should be done openly or through Cuban janissaries, while America broods over the propriety of trying to stop them. It is why some want the United States to tiptoe around the world, seeking to be as unassertive as possible, apparently content with bringing off retreats with the minimum of embarrassment ("Peace With Honor"). It is why many now concede that direct American military involvement anywhere on the globe has become unthinkable. It is why some of our leaders find themselves in the position of a basically good-natured schoolboy who has teased a playmate a little more cruelly than is acceptable in playground circles. His friend is fighting mad now, moving in, pushing, shoving, demanding an apology. The boy who did the taunting does not like being pushed around, but he is not about to uncork any haymakers either. He does not want to raise the battle to any new levels. He knows that he was in the wrong; that if he wins he will have nothing to be proud of. He does not want to risk a broken nose in a dispute that lacks nobility. Better to ward off the punches for a while and hope for the best. He will hit harder only after his opponent does so. He concedes the initiative. It is not as if he were fighting a rapist or thug of some sort—the kind of opponent who has to be beaten no matter the cost, when escalation is not unthinkable but a noble course of action, as if he were fighting a Nazi. Indecisiveness, timidity, resignation are the order of the day.

Stalin knew how to play to this American liberal schizophrenia. At Yalta he responded to American and British protests over the establishment of Soviet puppet dictatorships in Eastern Europe with the observation that America and England too had established governments to their liking in France and West Germany, and that there had been suspensions of civil liberties in England and America during civil crises and times of war. He had no fear that he would be met with the flat assertion that there was a difference; that Russian influence in Eastern Europe was repugnant not because it was exerted, but because it was exerted in the name of Communism, something abhorrent; while the pressure applied by America and Britain was noble because it would result in the revivification of the Christian nations of Europe. Winston Churchill, a representative of a nation where some still savored notions of monarchy and the values of an aristocratic ruling class, could speak of such stakes. But not his successors, and not the progressive Americans, who were disarmed by Stalin's charge.

After all, how do we answer that one, Alger? Is not Stalin entitled to act energetically too? Could "Yes, sir, Mr. President, more so," have been the response, as we are now instructed by the New Left revisionists?

VIII

Separate But Equal Is Unequal?

There should be no further need to deal with outright racism in discussing the course of the civil-rights movement in America. The number of thinking Americans who still believe the black to be an innately inferior being suited only for slavery or the first boat back to Africa has shrunk to insignificance.* There have been too many black successes in the professions, sports, and business in general for any of the "they're only one step up from the jungle" talk to do anything other than make the speaker sound ridiculous. So let us just forget them. Their voices have to be dealt with in the political arena, but not in the intellectual. They have been beaten soundly on that ground—and that holds even if Shockley and Jensen-type scientists somehow manage to prove every one of their theories. Equality and human dignity do not hinge on IQ tests any more than they do on the numbers of your race represented on the NBA All Star team.

What is of ongoing interest are the things said by whites that *appear* to be racist to blacks; at any rate, the things that blacks tell whites they find racist. This is a crucial difference, of course. If black leaders tell us a senator who votes against open housing

---

*Which is not to say that they never were a force to be reckoned with. There was a time, and not that long ago, when even those who saw themselves as crusaders in the cause of racial justice thought of themselves as great white fathers of sorts entrusted with the care of a backward and childlike people who just would never be able to take care of themselves in the modern world.

is racist in order to more effectively lobby for favored legislation, it is one thing. If they believe it, it is quite another.

In some cases this misunderstanding is a result of the failure of white Americans to express themselves clearly—or perhaps to follow their thoughts to the logical conclusions. When, for example, a man says, "I'd never walk uptown alone at night. Are you crazy? Them coloreds'd slit your throat as soon as look at you," the odds are excellent that a little probing will reveal that the man would not be afraid to walk in black middle-class neighborhoods; that his distrust is of crime-ridden areas, not of blacks as blacks.

In other cases, the responsibility has to be laid at the door of American blacks. In recent years the tendency has become unmistakable—the tendency of blacks to ascribe any and all opposition to their demands to racism; to assume that a criticism of a proposed method for dealing with a black social problem is a symptom of a hatred for blacks or an indifference to their plight, rather than a criticism of the effectiveness and possible undesirable side-effects of the proposed vehicle for reform. Although, admittedly, more and more blacks (especially those climbing the ladder in business) are kicking out of the lock-step and suggesting, to take one instance, that it just might be better for unemployed blacks if a good chunk of the tax dollar now going into woeful poverty programs and ghetto make-work projects had been retained by the stockholders of America's corporations and directed into the business expansion which would increase the number of jobs—real jobs, not CETA-type placebos —available to aspiring black youths.

The point just now, of course, is not whether black Milton Friedman types are correct in this evaluation, but the tendency of too many blacks to conclude in a knee jerk that those *whites* who say such things are insincere; the tendency, in other words, to marry the cause of black Americans to the liberal, big government, leveling, welfare schemes, which are proving so manifestly ineffective with the passing of time.

The result of this unfortunate marriage of racial aspirations with ideology has been not only the demeaning of the motives of millions of white Americans but also the deadening of the resiliency and drive for personal achievement in large numbers of blacks. Petitioning Uncle Sam for public assistance has replaced in many cases the ethic of pulling oneself up by the bootstraps. And you do not have to be a subscriber to the Protestant ethic to see the dangers in that. Whether or not a self-disciplined, motivated, upward-striving Horatio Alger is a better man than Superfly is not the only question. Even if being a permanent ward of the welfare state were a fine thing for the human spirit, it is becoming clear that Uncle Sam will not be able to generate the needed largesse without crippling the economic system, the goose that lays the welfare checks and public housing. (Of course, to the extent that you are a true believer in liberal welfarism and its logical consequence—some form of socialism—that might not be all that unattractive a turn of events. More of this later.)

There Is a Difference

Now, admittedly, blacks have faced obstacles far more difficult than other immigrant groups. It is too easy to say, as some whites do, that if the Irish, Italians, Eastern Europeans, etc., were able to make it in America without the full panoply of welfare-state assistance, then blacks should be able to as well. Blacks do not overestimate the scars of slavery. Blacks were the only racial or ethnic group forced to come to America (although it is probably true that without the current immigration restrictions, large numbers of Africans would be emigrating today). They were the only ones whose families and family traditions were broken on the anvil of the slave block, the most devastating blow of all. They were the only ones who could not become indistinguishable from the rest of the population with a little education, the acquisition of new mannerisms, and the loss of an accent. They did have to deal with the earlier American superstitions about the lesser humanity of their race. All this is true. A criticism of the direction the civil-rights movement has taken need not begin with a discounting of the trauma of the black experience in this country. But the question for our time ought not to be whether modern blacks deserve the title of America's "most aggrieved victim"; whether we should feel sorry for them more than for anyone else. It should be what proposed solution will remedy the problems black Americans face, without unjustly penalizing white Americans for eighteenth- and nineteenth-century deeds done not by them or probably even their familial forefathers, who chances are were living under conditions of oppression in Europe at the time no less harrowing than those faced by slaves in the American South.

And also what solutions will *genuinely* help modern blacks, not those that will merely provide a comfortable floor of material comforts beneath which they will not be permitted to fall no matter how impoverished they become in spirit and backbone, how lacking in self-discipline, perseverance, ambition, and moral virtues.

It may sound cruel to say it, but it is nevertheless true, that the demands of certain civil-rights groups—for guaranteed incomes, government sinecures, federally provided and maintained housing, free child care, guaranteed and tax-financed education through the graduate school level, free health care, white-subsidized black cultural programs, for full financial security provided by someone else—are a call for a reinstitution of slavery, this time a plush and laid-back version, with an easygoing and undemanding master who even pretends to a deep interest in his charges tastes and lifestyle.

The Brown Decision

Ironically, and unfortunately, the famous Brown case—*Brown vs. the Board of Education of Topeka, Kansas* (1954)—has in many ways proven to be the source of the current problems. The details are familiar. Oliver Brown sued to prevent the Topeka school authorities from denying to his daughter, Linda, access to a neighborhood school on the basis of her color (using the logic, it goes without saying, employed nowadays by white parents protesting busing schemes). His case argued that such a denial was an infringement upon his Fourteenth Amendment guarantee to "equal protection of the laws."

The Court in making its decision was forced to deal with an apparently clear-cut and firm precedent in matters of this sort: the case of *Plessy vs. Ferguson*. This 1896 decision held segregated railroad cars to be constitutional as long as the facilities were comparable; that "separate but equal" facilities did not violate the letter of the spirit of the Fourteenth Amendment. Schools were assumed to be in the same category. Hence segregated restaurants, beaches, and other facilities, as well as schools, especially in the South, had become a long-established custom by 1954. As long as some semblance of "equal" accommodations could be alleged, or fabricated, there appeared to be no room for adjudication of the matter. The case seemed closed. It was this perception of the constitutional mandate which the Court had to find reason to overrule.

Basing its reasoning largely on the work of two social scientists prominent in the early 1950s, Dr. Kenneth B. Clark and the Swedish economist, Gunnar Myrdal, the Court held that "separate educational facilities are inherently unequal." *Inherently* unequal.

Clark provided studies that demonstrated that the educational achievement of black children in segregated (all-black) schools was significantly below that of white children of a comparable age. Myrdal's study, *An American Dilemma: The Negro Problem and Modern Democracy*, published first in 1944, was offered as a source of examples of the American failure to live up to its fundamental democratic ideals in dealing with its black population. Only by providing a racial mixture in society, starting with the schools, could the blemish be removed. To be equal, blacks could not go on living and working in an environment dominated by other blacks. All-black was "inherently unequal."

By now the logic has become embarrassing, implying as it does that while whites are harmed only in the most hypothetical of ways by an all-white experience (something about being denied the company of a variety of racial friends; a problem which, if real, is shared by all but the handful of multiracial societies on the globe), blacks were held back by an all-black experience; that separate facilities are inherently unequal because, well, because blacks are inherently unequal. Equality and dignity, in other words, were described as qualities of life bestowed by white America, *at will* when it opened its heart and lived up to the country's lofty democratic ideals. The solution was in white hands. Whites were the problem, the only problem.

Political action by black Americans, consequently, would be successful to the extent that it won more and more from white America. *That* was the job for black leaders. The only topic up for debate was whether appeals to the charitable and humanitarian impulses of white America (Martin Luther King's tactic) would work better than threats of physical violence and economic dislocation, or vice versa.

Now to a certain extent there was much truth in this perception. There were very real social stigmas from which black Americans could be freed only through a change of heart in white America. Jim Crow laws restricting blacks to specified areas and facilities could not be interpreted in any way other than as an indication that white society *as a whole* deemed blacks inferior, undesirable, second-class.

There are, it is true, ethnic and religious groups in America who even to this day must live knowing that they are not wanted in certain neighborhoods or clubs, and who seem to be able to live with that fact without burning down Detroit. But blacks were the only group that has had to live with *society as a whole* in some states defined openly, in the law, as a private club of sorts. Jews and Italians or Catholics might find themselves kept *from* certain limited areas. Under Jim Crow laws, blacks were confined *to* certain limited areas; and were barred from places where the still foreign speaking white immigrants off the last tramp steamer from Europe could go at will. Members of ethnic groups often chose voluntarily to live in neighborhoods where the sights and sounds and smells and places of worship would remind them of their unique Old World traditions; blacks had no such choice when faced with Jim Crow. Their isolation was not the result of pride, it was a lower caste status.

It should be clear to all by now that it was a situation that could not be allowed to endure. There were conservative spokesmen of the time, of course, who argued otherwise; but one strongly suspects, less than forthrightly. Those rightists who would not admit to an outright racism tended (continuing the overall theme of this book) to argue that "states rights," "constitutionalism," or "strict constructionism" was the issue at hand. Their line, it will be remembered, went something like: "I would not mind living next to a Negro or sending my children to a school attended by them, but what right does one section of the country have to overthrow local prerogatives and long-standing social custom. We must be patient in matters of this sort. Right or wrong, northern politicians simply have no right to set educational policy for southern school boards."

Once again, the emphasis was placed not on *what* social policy was most just, but on *how* we arrived at it. But probably everyone knows by now (if everyone did not at the time), not just the blacks who have always made the charge: Keeping the races separate *was* the goal of those who argued in defense of the states' right to preserve Jim Crow, not constitutional precision. Segregation was seen as a positive good, not as an unfortunately permissible side effect of our constitutional framework. The very busing techniques now deplored by whites, remember, were once employed by whites to maintain segregated education. The "neighborhood school" has been held sacrosanct only in neighborhoods of an acceptable racial composition.

The states' rights argument was employed as an "easy out," in other words, by whites who felt that acceptable educational and cultural standards for white American children could be maintained only in a segregated atmosphere, but who were uncomfortable making that admission; and defining those standards in our libertarian open society. For racists, of course, the absence of black faces was one of those standards. But there were others, not ignoble.

Would it have been better for whites in 1954 to state openly they feared the deleterious effects of an influx of blacks into their children's schools? Well, yes. And not only because it would have been the truth. The same can be said in our time about the opponents of busing, the defenders of the hallowed "neighborhood school." (Build a high-rise project for welfare clients in that neighborhood and see how sacred those local schools become. Although that project would not be built—for the sake of ecological balance, right?) Candor would have forced the high-minded of both races to deal with the problem of blacks and whites living in a truly biracial society.

But let us hold off on this point for a while longer. The issue just now is that the Brown decision *was* a healthy and necessary step for America because it made clear that our society in its public life would no longer through the law define a black as an undesirable *solely* on the basis of his skin color. Blacks were no longer to be faced with an official, legal stipulation that would ignore their personal, moral, and professional accomplishments. From the Brown decision on, and its offspring the Civil Rights Act of 1964, if blacks were to be held as undesirables, white America would have to come up with a reason other than pigmentation. (Would any conservative who wants to be taken seriously still want to defend the proposition that blacks who have achieved a high degree of personal refinement, professional excellence, and self-discipline should nevertheless be denied admission to our societal life? And, please, let us not quibble over the word "public." A family picnic is private. The town beach where everyone is a "member" except black families is not, except in the narrowest and most disingenuous use of the term.)

Our present difficulties stem from the fact that the civil-rights movement has moved far beyond this healthy stage—beyond the demand that the door to American society be kept open to blacks of talent and character; that blacks be judged in American society by standards comparable to those applied to white Americans. The other train of thought developed and took firm root—the one that held that what American blacks need is not the opportunity to realize the fruits of self-discipline and hard work, but a more generous dispensation of favors from white America.

Two unfortunate types developed within the ranks of workers for civil rights: those who sought to magnify the blacks' victim-status by maximizing white guilt and white charitable impulses; and those who attempted to coerce a redistribution of white income by labeling that income "capitalist" rather than "white"—the black Marxist. Quite different types to be sure. But they share the conviction that American blacks cannot be saved through their own efforts; that white America is the problem; that black failure is not a black responsibility to any appreciable degree, but a symptom of white racism. (The so-called Kerner Commission, called to investigate the causes of the black urban rioting of the late 1960s, learned this lesson well from black spokesmen. They would not even let black radicals—self-professed revolutionaries—take credit for their own riots. "White racism" was the cause. One wonders if the black leaders of the insurrections were more amused or insulted; or if they had so succumbed to the rhetoric of white guilt that they accepted such absurdities.)

Unquestionably, playing on white guilt in this manner has proven to be effective. Grades can be earned with less effort, jobs and promotions secured without as much preparation and training, welfare payments increased, jail sentences lessened or dropped, when a black finds himself faced with a morally disarmed white liberal determined to make up for everything from Kunta Kinte to the persecution of Angela Davis. (What Gulag, again, is she on?) In such confrontations the "victim" is at a tremendous advantage. He is at his most virtuous when demanding and hard and uncompromising, when he "stands up for his rights." While the "oppressor"—his conscience now aflame—is morally entitled to do no more than lower his head and mutter a heart-felt "do with me what thou will." For him, penitence is virtuous, as is surrender. Remember the faces of those college deans being hooted off the stage by black radical student protestors, or being escorted to their offices as if they were about to negotiate an exchange of ambassadors with the Court of St. James. Remember? They seemed ennobled by it all—the Suffering Servant.

But great though the material rewards of being a professional victim may be, the spiritual price the "victim" pays is high. One is tempted to prefer that the blacks who employ this victim-ruse be fully conscious of the nature of their ploy; that they be coldly and clinically aware of how they are "taking" whitey. Full and honorable integration could come easier for a rogue than a dormouse.

But, whatever the moral equations involved, that does not seem to be the case. Throughout the writings and public statements of black leaders, at protests for open housing or increased welfare payments or to free an Angela Davis or Joanne Little, time and time again the self-portrait is painted of a helpless people unable to make it economically or spiritually because of the "white establishment," because of someone else. Salvation—jobs, economic stability, self-esteem itself—is seen as in the hands of the slave master's descendants, not the freedman's, who we are told is still not responsible for what he does, or even thinks, the most demeaning form of servitude imaginable.

The urgency of the demand for integration is rooted, one is forced to conclude, in this self-perception of inescapable dependency. It is surprising the question is not asked more: Why do so many Chinese-Americans want predominantly Chinese schools for their children? Why do so many ethnic groups, other than blacks, want the same, the richness of a well-maintained and distinct heritage? *Why* is it only an all-black environment that holds back a child's academic and social development? Why do crime and academic decay thrive there and not in a predominantly Greek school in the Bronx or a predominantly Italian school in Bay Ridge, Brooklyn, or a predominantly Jewish school in Forest Hills? Most especially, why do blacks agree that these other communities can maintain standards in their ethnic isolation and call for the scattered placement of their children in schools where these ethnic groups predominate? Put another way, if it is segregation that is bad, why are not predominantly Italian schools, for example, asked to mix in some Germans, Irish, and Poles before blacks are mixed into the pot? Are we to conclude that it is only blacks who are unable to build and maintain a healthy community life?

The rhetoric of a good number of black spokesmen leads us to that conclusion, certainly. It is not money or the quality of the teachers or facilities that cause the problems. Ask in an area of the country embroiled in a dispute over a busing scheme—ask if anyone would be willing to accept a scheme wherein the children from the white community would simply swap places with the children from the black community. Everyone knows the answers. The whites would buy it. They would—and bring in their PTA's and Fathers' Clubs, and within a short time produce a school close to the one they left behind in educational achievement. And the children from the black ghetto community would make of the surburban school exactly what they make of many of the multi-million-dollar schools built in ghetto areas—a ghetto school. The failure, to be blunt, is one of the spirit, not of finances. Which is why black pro-busing leaders would vote down the scheme. Only a mixture, a blending, an assimilation into *white* society is seen as satisfactory.

It is too cruel to say these things? Well, for one thing, it is not racist. If the children from a hillbilly Appalachian community were substituted with the student body of a wealthy showcase suburban school, they would turn it into a hillbilly school. Actually, it is cruel *not* to say them. It is to accede to the ruse, or the self-hypnosis, that permits blacks to ignore the fact that at this moment in American history, the most troublesome obstacle they face in their pursuit of full and equal membership in American society is to be found not in the white community but in the black. American society has risen above the ugly prejudices of the past sufficiently—sufficiently, not completely, not satisfactorily—to offer a black with self-discipline, fortitude, training, and drive (the Puritan ethic, if you will) an open route to the middle class. And it will continue to do so unless taxation for useless government make-work schemes kills business expansion and along with it new job opportunities for upward bound blacks. Blacks with marketable skills and attitudes can make it; now, today. Examples abound, especially in *Ebony*. But those marketable skills come first. They are what allow one to pull himself up by his proverbial bootstraps, along with working part-time jobs, taking night courses, perhaps giving up significant creature comforts of the moment in order to educate your children—all the things, in other words, called for in the Horatio Alger myth; the things that worked for the white immigrant groups.

Yes, there was a time—to America's shame—when blacks would be denied opportunity even after having done all these things. There was a time when the American promise turned up empty for blacks. Let us admit that in capital letters. Okay, it was true. But not now. The opportunities are here and they can be realized. But it takes sacrifice, the price civil-rights leaders seemed determined to convince blacks they need not pay, leading them to think it is beneath them in fact. Would not large numbers of blacks be offended if they were told that their primary duty now is to make the sacrifices required to lift not them—no, perhaps *not* them—but their children up out of poverty; if they were told that they had to start living a family life comparable to that of old-time Jews and Italians and Bohunks; that a man who aspires to the lifestyle of "one mean dude" is not likely to raise a child who will be a doctor, lawyer, nurse, or teacher?

The need is not only for whites to start saying these things, but for blacks; for black leaders to reach the point where they feel free to admit that self-criticism is not a sell-out to the white establishment or a bout of Uncle Tomism. (Jesse Jackson is one black leader who, at least on occasion, understands. The man is so quotable one does not know where to begin. Who else in American would have the moral and physical courage to tell black high-school students to remove their Superfly hats when listening to him speak because he is a minister of God, and to assure them that "We can be best at our studies and still be the best in basketball.")

Black pride will not come from forcing whites against their will to let blacks into their schools or neighborhoods. At best, such victories will give the satisfaction of rubbing the white oppressor's nose into the dust and inconveniencing him into moving on to the next suburb or brownstone private-school enclave. Hardly the ideal aspiration for a high-minded people. More to the point, such goals will not allow a high-minded people to go on feeling very high-minded. It will strike home one day that it is inconsistent to deplore the bigotry of whites who try to escape having their children attend largely black classrooms when the blacks who are pushing for integration and busing are trying to escape precisely the same thing.

Black pride will come when blacks succeed in building black communities and schools in those communities successful and attractive enough so that blacks will not mind living and having their children go to school there. At which time whites will not mind a thorough integration.

It is true. Blacks can be assured of it. All over New York City, Catholic parents, the Irish and Italian and Eastern European ethnics Archie Bunker is meant to represent (whatever the show's pretense that he is a WASP), send their children by bus and subway to integrated Catholic high schools. Seventy-five percent of the children attending parochial schools in America attend what would be classified as integrated classes according to a poll cited by Andrew Greeley in his column (*Daily News,* Jan. 7, 1979). They do not mind a fig if their children sit next to blacks, as long as those children meet the same standards of decorum and academic achievement as their own. In other words, it is the *behavior* they associate with certain black schools that is deemed undesirable, *not* black skins. The same holds on the housing question. Whites who oppose new apartments in their area likely to house blacks are not, necessarily, racist. They want no part of the crime, the drugs, the prostitution, and a coarseness of style they have witnessed in ghetto areas; it's not black skin. Ask the seemingly ugliest of whites on this question, the ones who say they'll do anything to keep their neighborhood white, whether they really would mind a hard-working black family with well-behaved children and clean habits living near them, and they will almost always say *no;* that it is the "bad ones" they fear, kids on drugs, garbage out the windows, all night parties, etc., etc.

But again is it not racist to make such statements? To make the assumption that an influx of blacks means an influx of crime and social decadence? Is not this presumption why blacks cannot get ahead in our society? No, it is not bigotry. Not necessarily. It is arithmetic. The pattern is too well-established; the black crime rates, the drug addiction, too unmistakable. In city after city, neighborhoods and schools that reach a certain breaking point—a certain percentage of blacks—tend in short order to go downhill, to experience a rising crime rate, an increase in vandalism, drug use, prostitution, and all the rest of the usual urban ghetto ills. Whites who assume this process likely would have Jimmy the Greek on their side. It does not *have* to happen, true. But when a family is considering the education of their children and the fate of every penny they own tied up in a house, it is hard to find fault with them when they seek to lessen the chances of it happening to their neighborhood, unless equality is a goal to be purchased even if it requires making everyone equally bad off, lowering all neighborhoods and schools to the level of the ghetto.

When Martin Luther King took note of this "white flight" he

concluded that "However much it is denied, however many excuses are made, the hard cold fact is that many white Americans oppose open housing because they unconsciously, and often consciously, feel that the Negro is innately inferior, impure, depraved, and degenerate."[1]

He was wrong. Whites do not hold these failings to be "innate" to the Negro. Whites fear black neighborhoods and schools for the same reason they would fear and avoid a tavern where twenty Hell's Angels had pulled up at the bar. Maybe there will be no trouble. Maybe. They view them as *acquired* characteristics, even if they might not think of phrasing it quite like that. Or, at least, a patient discussion of the issue will draw that admission from the great majority of whites. (It is amazing to see how impatient white liberals and black Ivy League graduates can be with white working-class, high-school dropouts who do not immediately grasp the social significance of matriarchial homes, the cyclical theory of discrimination, and the charts in the Coleman or Moynihan reports. They jump all over whites not "open-minded" enough to understand black antisocial behavior, but refuse themselves to view in a spirit of compromise the "racism" of a white factory worker who can keep his Cicero, Illinois, home only because of his part-time job. Is it an assumption that whites should know better?)

Whites know, or can be reminded, that blacks are capable of building sound and virtuous homes, of maintaining neighborhood standards that would put many whites to shame, of achieving "respectability" (a much maligned word unfortunately, indicating the successful refinement of basic instincts, the conquest of natural inclinations toward dissipation), of striving for excellence, of attaining it, of punctuality, neatness, sobriety.* And by and large—the blacks who have broken into middle-class America can attest to the fact—once blacks achieve these qualities, whites do not mind having them as neighbors or as classmates for their children.

But is this not a picture of that "middle-class morality" enlightened moderns of all races have learned to scorn? Perhaps—but it is found all over those neighborhoods and schools that blacks want for their families. It is what builds and reinforces the standards that make those communities attractive. White dropouts from this stodginess, at least when they no longer have

---

*Do all middle-class whites possess these virtues? Of course not. But in general "middle-class morality" *is* required to maintain a middle-class home.

Daddy's checkbook to fall back on so that they can be radicalized in appearance and attitude but plump bourgeois in accommodations, end up in the sleazy counterculture enclaves of the East Village or Haight-Ashbury. One would not think high-minded blacks would want to enjoy the comforts of middle-class life the way spoiled hippy children of middle-class whites do—as patronized consumers of the fruits of the work ethic, who take from a community's largesse without helping either to increase or maintain it.

The thought, then, that tears at the hearts of decent and fair white Americans: How to open their neighborhoods and schools to blacks who have struggled to make the climb to respectability, while at the same time protecting themselves from the "bad," from welfare as a lifestyle, readily available drugs, vandalism, violence, sexual profligacy, from the ethos of so much of modern ghetto America?

Why?

We are left with perplexing questions. If the doors to better jobs and schools and neighborhoods will be opened to blacks who demonstrate their capacity to maintain existing standards, why do the leaders of civil-rights organizations fail to turn their energies to the development of the drive and initiative that would permit black youths to play out the Horatio Alger myth? Why do so many black youths continue to fall into a life of crime and drugs? Why does a gaudily dressed pimp continue to attract as a model instead of the successful black doctor, lawyer, teacher, or nose-to-the-grindstone businessman? Why is maintaining one's "cool" more important than studiousness and earnestness and perseverance? Why does not the number of black communities that would impress whites, rather than frighten and revolt them, grow?

The answer is no secret, even if it is not allowed to enter the public discussion. The failure of the black family. The absence of the father in the black home. The experience of ghetto children growing up under the care of a welfare mother in the company of brothers and sisters fathered by a wide variety of men, men who take sensual pleasure from their mother but refuse to stay to give love and discipline and character formation to the home.

The words, once again, seem harsh. But the time has come for candor. Moreover, blacks themselves have taken note of the problem, although unfortunately, for the purpose of blaming whites for the sorry state of affairs. Martin Luther King reminded whites that the American black's family instability can be traced to the scars of slavery. "Of those families who survived the voyage, many more were ripped apart on the auction block as soon as they reached American shores. Against this ghastly background, the Negro family life began in the United States."[2] And the conditions were not improved as white slaveowners continued to display a disregard for the family ties of the slave, buying and selling husbands and wives and children as separate commodities. "The shattering blows," Dr. King continues, "on the Negro family have made it fragile, deprived and often psychopathic."[3] The odds are that the American black of today, who often is the grandson or great grandson of a slave, grew to maturity in a family structure where the father's time-honored role as provider, protector and moral guide was not well defined. All this is true. America's shame ought to be great; it should be admitted and felt.

Okay. But now what? Does it do anyone any good to constantly inform (as did *Roots*) the black teen-ager cutting classes, shooting dope, and ripping off old ladies on the weekend, that he is becoming the kind of deviant he is becoming because of what whites did to his race's family structure; that he is not taking advantage of the wealth of opportunity afforded him to become a self-sufficient and proud black American because of eighteenth-century whites? The forefathers of certain American whites destroyed the family structures of his forefathers. Okay. One race can do that to another. But that white race cannot rebuild those family structures. The sound and healthy and warm and self-supporting black families of modern America are the products of black initiative and perseverance, not white liberal charity. Black men and women who decided to break the chain of welfare dependency, who decided to study and work and live clean lives instead of staying cool built the American black families that work. They were the ones who turned things around. No one else is able to, especially not white liberals in HHS. Dr. King knew what kind of families were needed.

> Many a Negro mother, after toiling from dawn until sundown, would spend the remainder of the night washing clothes and putting away pennies and nickels so earned until, with the passage of years, a few hundred dollars had been accumulated. Often she struggled and sacrificed to purchase not her own freedom but that of a son or daughter.[4]

But instead of pleading and scolding and encouraging black youth to do more of the same, too often the stress is placed only on the white guilt. Dr. King: "To grow from within, the Negro family—and especially the Negro man—needs *only* [emphasis added] fair opportunity for jobs, education, housing and access to culture."[5]

Wrong. Something "often psychopathic" needs more than that. Offering a young man a job will not get him off drugs and into the sack early enough the night before to enable him to show up often enough in the mornings to keep it. Building the biggest and most beautiful school with the most bountifully stocked library in the country will not guarantee that teenagers will attend it regularly, not vandalize it, or go anywhere near the books. (One surmises that Dr. King was mistaking the families of well-ordered southern black communities—minister's sons, for example—for the problem ghetto youth.) And free tickets to every play and concert and museum in the world will be of no use to a young person who has not been helped to see that there are better things than porn movies and coarse and raucous music blaring from a black shoulder-held radio as big as a suitcase. Homes and concerned parents do these things for young people. They refine and uplift and chasten the self-centered drives in us all. To suggest otherwise to the culturally disadvantaged—that whites hold the answer—is a cruel deception. One can see why black leaders who hold positions that are justified by the amount of tax dollars they are able to coax from the white establishment would not want to deny the efficacy of their efforts. But it is difficult to praise them. Narrow self-interest is not the stuff of heroes.

The Marxist Version

There are other reasons for stressing the need for big government welfare-state policies as the only workable answer to the problem. The same reason for proposing such solutions for the problems of farmers, teachers, mechanics, clerks, butchers, bakers, and candlestick makers. Socialist reasons, Marxist reasons; idological preferences.

It is not hard to imagine blacks with these preferences. Blacks are as liable to turn to socialist ideology for as many and as varied reasons as whites, and some have. The late Louis Lomax made the point for us.

The Negro revolt is a struggle between two segments of American opinion and action, with both Negroes and white people on either side. . . . George Scuyler, a Negro newsman [with conservative convictions], is just as much my enemy as, say, William Buckley. . . . There is a great temptation to invoke Spengler's prediction that, in time, the Western race problem would transmute into a class problem.[6]

In other words, blacks can only achieve full equality, in his eyes, when the socialist version of equality is established, which most Marxists argue, will be possible only through the instrument of revolution and dictatorship of the proletariat.

It is logical to conclude that for ideologues of this stripe, it would actually be counterproductive to encourage blacks to work for a climb into the successful middle ranks of American society. Better their anger be fired to increase the turmoil that will hasten the coming of the overthrow of capitalist society. It would not surprise us to hear these thoughts from a Che Guevara or Ho Chi Minh or any of the American white urban intellectual Marxists. It should not startle us to hear it from a black. It would be racist to think that blacks cannot become dedicated, thinking Marxists. It would be racist as well to "excuse" this ideological choice as merely the consequence of a deprived childhood. Whites who have opted for revolutionary socialism ask no such patronizing. They tell us they have made the better choice. Blacks deserve the same respect and the resulting adult condemnation from those of us determined not to allow our country to be turned into a Marxist society, even when the tool chosen to promote that end is the plight of our black population.

There are blacks who have openly announced their allegiance to Marx and their cooperative intent to work with his modern Russian or Chinese or Cuban heirs—Angela Davis, for one. What is of greater interest for our purposes just now are those who are less forthright, those who, purposefully but discreetly, seek to derail the effort to make American society work for blacks because their major interest is their leftist ideological goal, not the "bourgeoisification" of fellow blacks. Better their people suffer a generation or two more of anguish and poverty and spiritual decay than delay the coming of the revolution; better their condition worsen so that their anger will rise to hasten the revolution, which offers the only true end to racial and economic and psychological alienation—the Marxist utopia.

One can only guess at the extent to which such ideological

commitments have slowed down the rate of blacks moving into the mainstream of American life; at how many black youths—who view the work ethic, serious study, sexual self-denial, gentleness, compassion, and basic etiquette as somehow reflections on their manhood—do so because of a devious political tract (or the street-talk summary of it) specifically written to keep them *out* of the system, at odds with the "establishment," because of a leader who desires to *worsen* their plight. After all, it is probably true that a proletariat as purposeless, self-centered, uneducated, and violent as that found in the urban ghettos—a *lumpenproletariat*—can be converted into a disciplined work force only by the brutal regimentation of someone like Mao or the Khmer Rouge. Herbert Marcuse, the favorite pilosopher of the American New Left, has said just that in his books and essays; he encourages the outlaw consciousness in quite specific terms.

Still, there is hope. Marcuse is not the only one who speaks about these matters. Consider:

> Our goal must be to move beyond racism and create an Open Society—a society in which each human being can flourish and develop to the maximum of his God-given potential; a society in which ethnic and cultural differences are not stifled for monotonous conformity; a pluralistic society, alive, creative, open to the marvel of self-discovery.
>
> An Open Society is not merely an "integrated" society—one that grudgingly allows Negroes some of the privileges white people enjoy. An Open Society is, rather, one that offers choices and options. Some Negroes may prefer to live together in the psychological security that comes from close-knit enclaves that share similar traditions and culture—as just about every other ethnic group in America has done. But in an Open Society, the exercise of such a choice would not be penalized.[7]

Amen—if one adds that such a choice would not be penalized primarily because blacks will have succeeded in building those "enclaves" into such attractive communities that no one except the most Neanderthal racist would mind living as a neighbor with a product of one of them. Whitney Young wrote the above paragraphs. He is no longer with us, but it seems certain that, once the discredited liberalism which has thwarted progress for so long in this country emits its final rattling death gasp, more and more blacks will come forward with similar sentiments. They, too, echoing Burke, will propose "checks upon will and appetite" from within, which will make the Marxist checks from without not only unattractive but superfluous.

IX

Restating the Theme

Before going further, let us pause to seek a synthesis of the preceding eight chapters. What, to be specific, do our eight chapter topics have to do with each other and with the unfortunate results of the infusion of the secularist interpretation of the First Amendment into our political life?

Reconsider the course of events. The First Amendment is included in the Constitution to prevent sectarian strife in the New World; to insure the well-entrenched Christian churches of early America the right to practice their beliefs in an energetic manner. A freedom *for* religion is thus established to guarantee that the American Christian sects will be able to play the role expected of them: providers of the inner disciplines—Burke's "unbought graces"—upon which government by discussion hinges.

Yet in short order this agreement not to publicly define ourselves as a religious people, to leave our religious identity unsaid, to hope that a moral consensus would be maintained without a commitment at the national level to reinforcing it, begins to express itself in unfortunate ways. The discussion on the *method* of government comes to center stage. We find Jefferson feuding with Hamilton over whether states' rights or a strong central government would lead to a more just society, without telling us what ideals a just society should uphold.

Arguments over the degree of power appropriate for the Supreme Court grow in intensity—and continue to our day—but proceed as if we really did not have to know what kind of men were sitting on the Court before we made up our minds about whether to decrease or increase their directive hold on society.

John C. Calhoun devises an ingenious system to prevent a national majority from running roughshod over local minorities, without telling us why that majority's will was to be feared. Henry David Thoreau provides us with a poetic defense of the individual's right to civil disobedience, without explaining why his unqualified subjectivism was different from moral anarchy—or if it was, or if it mattered. Apparently Americans were not to ask such questions in public. Who defines moral values except religious leaders, and we all know that they are to play no role in a society with a progressive separation of church and state.

William Jennings Bryan accepts the label, Great Commoner, without pausing thoughtfully enough to consider whether his favored masses always were, or always would be, the safest repository for his cherished Christian values.

The problem became more obvious in the twentieth century, as advocates of alien cultural and political values found themselves able to maneuver effectively against an "open society" with no effective tool for branding them as unacceptable contestants for our society's mind and heart. Marxism especially became an apparently acceptable alternative future for America—once, that is, the residual resistance of the McCarthyites was overcome. The McCarthyites seemed unaware that the new and correct understanding of the First Amendment demanded not only that we not proclaim ourselves as a Christian people in our public documents, but also that we surrender all lingering perceptions that our moral convictions ought to play a role in shaping social policy—if those beliefs were rooted in the Christian religion, that is. Enacting laws based on other moral beliefs—those approved by the high priests of secular liberalism, to be specific—was to be applauded as a sign of a people with a social conscience.

The course of the civil-rights movement was diverted. Prompted by this American stress on the methods of politics—the *how*—as the answer to our problems, black leaders went from calling for equal opportunities to a plea for quotas and affirmative action to a call, in some cases, for totalitarian socialism. When getting the government out of the way (ending Jim Crow) did not bring salvation, government enforcement of racial balancing acts (Crow Jim) was demanded. And when that failed, totalitarian politics—so that we all would be forced to be equal, as in Cuba and Angola. And all the while, the need for blacks to discipline themselves and reach for moral virtue slipped further to the back of the bus. White leaders did not talk of such things, so neither would black. We have a separation of church and state here. You do not have to be good to get your rights.

But the saddest and sorriest and most poignant result of the American refusal to recognize the role religion plays in determining what is good about our society and worthy of a loving and dutiful patriotism was yet to come. In the 1970s we found ourselves unable to define why one of the most universally abhorred practices in the history of the West ought not become a basic human right: Abortion.

X

What Kind of Society?

Abortion? One wearies. If the issue were not fraught with such ominous implications for the country's future, the temptation would be strong to throw up the hands and never again bring up the subject. Really, what more is there to be said? Can anyone any longer believe that, except in the rarest of cases, the required preconditions for sincere and rational political discourse obtain on this issue? That we have disputants who can be won over by a demonstration of the accepted logical and moral imperatives; that the conflicting positions will be argued honestly, without deliberate sophistry, pretense, or hidden motives? Can anyone believe that the opponents will try to demonstrate the highmindedness of their cause rather than seek to secure a shyster lawyer's victory—a victory that depends more on the crafty and deceptive packaging of an argument than on being on the side of the angels; one where we seek to "get away with" as much as possible from an adversary rather than achieve a meeting of the minds with fellow members of our commonweal?

The urge, in other words, is to *plead* openly with the pro-abortion faction to "fess up," to admit that by all the standards of legality, ethics, and morality heretofore deemed integral to American society, abortion is a nightmare, an outrage, a national disgrace; that they are asking Americans to move to a radically new perception of human existence, one that will require those Americans who see themselves as part of the once-hallowed Judeo-Christian heritage to relinquish that perception, to give up the ghost, and concede to a clearly triumphant secular humanism.

And indeed, there are signs that the abortion dispute will prove to be just such a *pons asinorum* to our national development. States' rights, centralism, federalism, strict constructionism, loose constructionism—we see with abortion why it is all of secondary importance. We face the real world in a flash insight. *Metanoia*. We see that it is inconsistent only in the most formally legalistic—and in context, trivial—of ways to oppose the federal government's interfering in the way General Motors makes its cars and Mississippi runs its schools, while at the same time favoring federal legislation that would deny a woman the "right" to an abortion. And *vice versa*—to oppose, say, parental rights to keep their children out of the latest school-busing scheme while favoring every mother's right not to give birth to her eight-month-old fetus. Once again—but more acutely than with any other issue—we see that *what* we do, what truths we hold and preserve as a people, our national character, is what is of crucial importance, not the government machinery—the *how*—we employ to effect that character's historical development.

Roe and Doe

The day of reckoning was January 22, 1973. Many said it would never happen: that the Christian people of America would never permit the legalization of abortion, a practice which just ten years, more or less, before the Court's decision was considered one of the vilest of crimes. Remember? When abortionists were pictured in the movies as sleek villains who would—obviously—do anything for a price; or as sleazy backstreet hags who seemed from all appearances to enjoy the misery of the unfortunate girls driven to them in despair. Or as drunken and discredited doctors who had lost their licenses to practice and were now shamefully, in despair too, seeking to earn a living in this, the most disreputable of ways. Remember when doctors who performed abortions used to pop up every so often on the sensationalist talk shows, hooded or with their backs to the camera? And the tough-guy reporters who questioned them always wore a pained and incredulous look? "You mean you really earn a living killing babies and you are not ashamed?" seemed always to be the next question.

Remember the otherwise forgettable World War II movie, the one where we were introduced to the horrors of Nazism when a white-robed, German doctor (played by a Paul Henreid or Helmut Dantine type of actor) escorted a tweedy British reporter through a Third Reich hospital? He pointed proudly with Teutonic self-assurance to the room where the retarded and deformed were disposed of to better the Aryan race. And then, as the violins whined ominously in the background, he pointed to the room where—gasp! the British reporter, someone like Leslie Howard if memory serves, looked as if he had seen hell—the abortions were performed, most especially on the women of inferior races. Yessir, thank God they were beaten. A people who would kill babies would be capable of anything.

We've come a long way, baby, from all that to President's wives advocating abortion rights, to national Girl Scouts' leaders writing up sensitivity sessions for their young charges lest they go into adolescence with backward ideas about their bodies and their rights to "reproductive freedom"; to the eerie sight of the once-staid homemaker magazines featuring articles that would have the reader believe abortion to be a beautiful and altruistic act undertaken by sensitive women eager to save a marriage or an overcrowded world, or out of love for their already conceived offspring, who would be deprived of ballet lessons or a summer in Europe if a new addition were to enter the family's life—to say nothing of the dishearteningly self-congratulatory articles by women who abort lest they despoil their womanhood; to save themselves from diapers and soup for lunch so that they can become fully liberated women "in touch with themselves" and in "service to the community at large."

No one need ever again ask how the Nazis could have won over the people of the land of Brahms and Beethoven and Goethe. Whether you are pro- or anti-abortion, it has to be conceded; this reversal in American public opinion is nothing short of stunning. Just a few words from the right people in the right places, a movie here, a book there, and the populace stood in line.

The 1973 Wade and Roe decisions (*Roe v. Wade* and *Doe v. Bolton*) were remarkably straightforward on these questions, and remarkably contemptuous of the legal precedents and moral heritage of the American people. In summary, the Court held that a woman's "right to privacy" guaranteed that during the first three months of her pregnancy, no restrictions could be placed by state authorities on her right to secure an abortion. In the second three months, a state, if it so desired, in the interests of maternal health, could impose certain limitations on the practice—locations, facilities, licensing, etc.—but not in any way forbid it. In the final trimester, the Court held a state *could*—once again, if it so chose—prohibit abortions.* With one exception. An exception that resulted in abortion "on demand." An abortion could not be prohibited, even in the ninth month, when the "life" or "health" of the mother was in question. ("Mother?" Ought not scholarly standards, as well as decency, require that we come up with some other word to describe the woman who requests an abortion?) The term "health" was defined by the Court in line with the World Health Organization's standard: "state of complete physical, mental, and social well-being, not simply the absence of illness and disease." The result has been in effect to remove all restrictions since "mental and social well being" are interpreted by pro-abortion doctors to include the slightest, real or imagined, inconveniences alleged by the "mother." There should be no mistaking the implications. A woman just days away from a normal birth can allege psychological "problems" and secure an abortion by hysterectomy, the very same operation used to bring about Cesarean birth, except in this case the purpose is to kill the child rather than bring him into the world.

The consequences have been mind-boggling. If the story were to be shipped back through a time machine to the 1950s and beyond, Americans in those years would think it the wildest of science fiction. America has become the land of over a million abortions per year. In American hospitals, in one room infants prematurely delivered at the sixth month are spared no cost or effort to keep them alive, while in nearby rooms even more matured fetuses are dismembered and tossed into hospital refuse bins. Women who leave their newly born infants on doorsteps or garbage cans are hunted down as criminals, while those who end the lives of their children a few weeks before birth are interviewed on Public Television as if they were Florence Nightingales and asked to give helpful suggestions for "sisters" about to "terminate their pregnancies" too. In July of 1975, a New Jersey man was indicted for murder after shooting a pregnant woman—indicted for the murder of her child. In that same month the Massachusetts Supreme Court held in an automobile-bus collision that "an unborn but viable fetus is a person under

---

*Since many infants born in the sixth month of a pregnancy survive, the Court took recognition of their "viability."

the state's wrongful death statute."[1] That, in the state where a two- to three-month-old female fetus was heaved onto the ice at Boston Garden during a high-school hockey game. The American courts—which once ruled that a woman member of Jehovah's Witnesses was obliged to submit to a blood transfusion, in spite of her religious objections, to save the life of her unborn child, placing the "right to live" of the fetus above the mother's First Amendment guarantee of freedom of religion[2]—set about the task of knocking down legislation designed to save the lives of the unborn. Unborn infants, apparently, being deserving of protection (the United Nations "Declaration of the Rights of the Child" holds prenatal medical care to be a basic human right) from everyone and everything, except their "mothers."

At first, anti-abortion Americans reacted as if logic would prevail. But they soon found, to their surprise and disappointment, that even their *reductio ad absurdum* was taken in stride. No matter what, the pro-abortion people meant it. The answer was the same. "It is a matter that concerns only a woman and her doctor." Period. Could a recently widowed mother abort to avoid sharing an inheritance? Could parents abort repeatedly, fetus after fetus, to make sure that their next child would be a boy? Could a deranged and embittered woman abort her child simply to take revenge on her husband? Could a woman become impregnated for the purpose of allowing medical experimentation for a price on the fetus—take thalidomide voluntarily and then abort so that research physicians could measure the results? (And do not we need a word other than "physician" or "doctor" for one who aborts? Physician means healer.) The answer was the same. "It is a matter for a woman and her doctor to decide." Nothing else to be discussed. (Although one searches for the pro-abortion acceptance of the logical corollary of this position. If having a child is now the sole decision of the woman, is not it logical to hold that no man should be expected to provide support for a child that he has fathered? Why should he bear the burdens of this "quirky" decision by a woman?)

Not that the pro-abortion folk have not presented arguments to support their position. They have. But in all sincerity, it is impossible for a rational being to accept that any of them truly believe what they say.

It is not yet human life, they tell us. Well, it might be possible to take this argument seriously if those who express it were willing to place *some* limit on when the abortions may be performed; six months, seven months, eight months—twenty-two days, anything. But the pro-abortion folks will have no such compromises. It is a matter for the "mother" and the "physician." *Whenever.* There was a panel discussion on Public Television a year or so after the Roe and Doe decisions. A silver-haired, distinguished-looking, pipe-smoking, pro-abortion doctor in dulcet tones and with the sincerest of eyes explained how the child was not human until it took its first breath on its own. That was how he drew the line. That howl after its bottom is slapped makes the difference. Hanging there by the heels it is a fetus, nonhuman, subject to having its life snuffed out. Then one magic whack on the fanny by the doctor and *presto* we have a human baby, the taking of whose life might get you a life sentence. The doctor said it as if he meant it.

As if to accentuate this point, there were few serious defections within the pro-abortion faction in the now famous Edelin case. Edelin, it will be recalled, was the Boston physician who found himself in a graphic encounter with exactly what a doctor does when he performs an abortion. The child he aborted had the effrontery to survive the saline injection. He was breathing, witnesses testified, squirming about, until Edelin completed the task he was hired to perform by the "mother." He pressed on the windpipe until this fetus too "expired." The pro-abortion humanitarians rallied behind him.

How does one account for it? It is a good question. It is incomprehensible that the socially aware Americans, who assure us that they cringe at the thought of clubbed baby seals and harpooned white whales, could shrug off the idea of a fully grown man pressing his fingers down on the throat of a struggling infant. But one can see their problem. To concede that the "product of an abortion" is human would be to, well, give away the ball game. Rather than run that risk, the pro-abortion folk seem to have made an act of faith comparable to that which Catholics make when they assent to transubstantiation. They posit, hold as dogma and refuse to question again, that a fetus is not what science, reason, and common sense tell us it is: a developing human child. The pro-abortion partisan does not care what you say. It is not a child, not a child, not a child . . . six months, seven months, in Dr. Edelin's hands. I believe. . . .

Not likely, you say—this act of faith? Okay, probably not. It is more plausible to hold that those who favor abortion know full well what a fetus is and that they do not give a damn (for reasons we will examine shortly), but they are aware too that they cannot admit to such indifference when arguing their case in a country where the Christian religion, if waning, still holds the affection of enough voters to make a difference at the polls.

It is here, by the way, that we find the value of those "tasteless" pictures of aborted fetuses, which are found appalling even by some anti-abortion spokesmen. They make it impossible to assent to an agnosticism on the nature of a fetus. No one—really—no one can pretend that it is "marmalade," which is what pro-abortion spokesman Bill Baird calls the unborn child. Perhaps certain Right-to-Life types display an unhealthy, even morbid, enthusiasm for brandishing those pictures of scalded and dismembered tiny bodies. But, after all, that is what happens to the "products of abortion." (Sensitive moderns do not analyze the "morbid" minds of those Jews with pictures who are rightly determined to keep the horrors of Nazi concentration camps fresh in our minds.) If it were not for those pictures, I'm afraid, some who ought to know better just might find themselves open to compromise on the rights of a blob of marmalade.

The pictures serve admirably well as graphics for the findings of modern science. If the fact that the fetus's heart beats at eighteen to twenty-five days; that at thirty days it has eyes, ears, a mouth, and its kidneys and liver in place; that electroencephalographic waves can be received from its brain at forty-eight days; that the child has fingerprints at eight weeks; that the thyroid and adrenal glands function at nine to ten weeks; that the child can grasp an object at sixty-three days (at which time the baby also squints, swallows, moves his tongue, and begins to develop sex hormones); that at twelve to thirteen weeks fingernails are formed, the child sucks his thumb, and recoils from pain (including the abortionist's blade); if these scientific findings fail to stir the soul, then the sight of tiny legs and arms pulled apart by suction machines might. Or perhaps the sight of contorted infants dead from breathing in the salt solution injected into the sac on the instructions of their "mothers"; or fully formed infants, who could be asleep in a cradle, aborted by hysterectomy. (Do you know that after the saline solution is injected, the "mother" has to be held down because the thrashing child recoiling from the saline convulses violently the woman's midsection?)

No, it is a child. Everyone knows that Dr. A.W. Liley, professor of fetal physiology at the National Women's Hospital in

New Zealand, is stating the obvious: "Biologically, at no stage can we subscribe to the view that the fetus is a mere appendage of the mother. Genetically, mother and baby are separate individuals from conception."[3]

Which is why it is so frustrating to go through the arguments as if the pro-abortionists were sincere. (The weirdest of the arguments has to be the one where they say "How can you be in favor of war and capital punishment if you are against abortion?"—as if there were no difference between killing a wrong-doer or in self-defense and taking an *innocent* life; as if the anti-abortion advocates are unable to distinguish between permissible and impermissible taking of life.)

It has "no will or conscience" they say. But neither do three-month-old infants. "It could not survive on its own. It lives off the mother," they state triumphantly. We must assume them intelligent enough to know that the same could be said of a child five years old or the deformed and retarded of all ages. Moreover, the most self-sufficient and mature of adults could not survive "on their own" if parachuted into the Brazilian jungle or onto the polar ice cap. Humans at all stages of their development need the life support of others. Dependency does not lessen humanity; it is a concomitant. No man is an island.

"But the children will be unwanted and unloved and will live miserable lives if they are born to women who do not want them." Abortion for the well-being of the child. Apparently it matters not at all that the line of good parents eager to adopt children continues to grow. (Would it be a wiseacre remark to suggest that if we are worried about the quality of life of these children that we wait until they are old enough to know whether their life is miserable enough to warrant its termination by our country's conscience-elite, and then ask them, say at their eighteenth birthday, if they want to be dismembered or drowned in saline for their own good?)

No, it is killing. We all know it. If you keep your eyes open you can spot the pro-abortion folk—especially when they are talking to each other—making the admission. In *California Medicine*, for example, the official journal of the California Medical Association, the pro-abortion doctor-editors speak of the need for verbal finesse when describing abortions to the public. It is "necessary to separate the idea of abortion from the idea of killing," even though such a task will require "considerable semantic gymnastics." However, the editors continue, "this schizophrenic sort of subterfuge is necessary because, while a new ethic is being accepted, the old one has not been rejected." Those who cling to the older Judeo-Christian outlook are likely to spook unless great care is taken, since the "semantic gymnastics" required "to rationalize abortion as anything but the taking of human life would be ludicrous if not often put forth under socially impeccable auspices."[4]

There are some pro-abortion folk less devious than the good doctors at *California Medicine*, some who have decided to quit the charade and try to win over anti-abortion America with a more direct approach. Norman Mailer, for one. He aroused the ire of the abortionist camp when he fired both barrels at the women's lib types who keep a straight and pious face while arguing that the act of abortion is something other than the taking of human life. In his inimitable way, Mailer told the ladies in so many words to stop the nonsense; to admit that they were killing their children and face up to the horrors of their deed, honestly, existentially. He did not tell them to deny themselves abortions. He would not want the act restricted by law. He merely wants from the women greater honesty—for them to face up to the terrible deed (like a man?) and the "necessities" which warrant it instead of hiding their heads under the pillow and pretending that it is some of Bill Baird's "marmalade" which is being scraped from their wombs.

A less well-known pro-abortion spokesman, Michael Tooley, raised some hackles too when he urged fellow pro-abortion crusaders to be consistent and take the next step toward a rational "birth policy" for the country. He favors infanticide, you see, arguing perceptively that it is illogical to favor abortion for socially desirable ends or the women's psychological good, but then hold back after the child's birth. After all, it is only after birth that we are accurately able to judge the nature of the child's deformities and the mother's reaction to the blessed event in her life.

Tooley's candor, whatever else you can say about it, is indicative of the accuracy of another oft-demeaned Right-to-Life charge. How often have we heard it said, "How ridiculous! Arguing that abortion leads to Nazi death-camp experimentation. Let's talk about abortion, not some science-fiction fantasy of what *might* happen if we allow abortion. If abortion is wrong it is wrong on its own merits, not because it leads to euthanasia of infanticide."

Euthanasia? Infanticide? Eliminating deformed children? Putting the old out of their misery? Well, these things are no fantasies. People long associated with the abortion camp have begun to push for every one of them. The disrespect for life promoted by the abortion ethos has spread into a barnyard perception of how human life should be managed by modern man.*

Representative Walter Sackett, for example, has introduced a "death with dignity" plan in the Florida legislature, arguing "Now where is the benefit in these severely retarded, who never had a rational thought."[5]

Bentley Gloss has written in praise of a future social climate. "No parents in that future time have a right to burden society with a malformed or mentally incompetent child."[6]

Norman Podhoretz has written of a biologist he met who told him that each newborn child in the future should have to pass a test to measure its genetic endowment. "If it fails these tests, it forfeits the right to life."[7] For humanitarian reasons.

Nobel Prize winner, James D. Watson, discoverer of the double helix DNA, in an article in *Prism* magazine proposed that "if a child were not declared alive until three days after birth, then all parents could be allowed the choice only a few are given under the present system. The doctor could allow the child to die if the parents so choose, and save a lot of misery and suffering. I believe this view is the only rational, compassionate attitude to have."[8]

But It Is the Law!

To be sure, there is another angle to be considered. The issue can be argued with the constitutionality of abortion uppermost, rather than the morality. The most frequent pro-abortion line of attack in this regard is usually something to the effect that "Well,

---

*One can only guess at the additions to the list that the "Me Generation" will make when they become a tax-paying, middle-aged political faction. They threw America's colleges into turmoil in the late 1960s and 1970s, demanding state-subsidized access to every material and sensual pleasure ever imagined by man. Imagine what the "Do Your Own Thing," "There's Only One You" crowd will be demanding when they will be seeking not more of someone else's tax dollars to support their liberated lifestyles, but less demands on their net income from the sick and the elderly and the like. People who do not have children because they will lessen the chances for ski vacations and summers in Europe are not likely to take kindly to old folks and orphans who threaten to cramp their style. Keep your ears to the ground. We could find the sixties' "don't trust anyone over thirty" crowd the great tax-cutters of the eighties.

whether you think it is murder or not, you have no right imposing your religious convictions on others. The Supreme Court has established that American women have the constitutional right to an abortion whether you like it or not."

It is an interesting approach, curious, to say the least. Our American flip-flop at work again. Many of the liberal types who once spoke of "nine old men" on the Supreme Court holding back social progress or failing to protect freedom of expression when they allowed local restrictions on pornography, treat the great geriatric ward as the most important bastion of liberty against the threatening winds of religious liberty when abortion is at stake. Now, because seven judges say it is so, it is. A raw exercise of judicial power proclaims the inherited wisdom of twenty centuries of Western civilization to be in error, null and void, and for patriotic reasons we are supposed to acquiesce.

A Fourteenth Amendment "right to privacy," never mentioned in the Constitution, is conjured up by the Court to provide a right to an abortion—a right that was specifically denied by thirty-six states at the time the Fourteenth Amendment was ratified. (As Justice Rehnquist aptly observed, "the only conclusion possible from this history is that the draftees did not intend to have the Fourteenth Amendment withdraw from the States the power to legislate with respect to this matter.")[9]

But the seven judges who voted to legalize abortion decided to ignore legal precedents, to disregard the intentions of the framers of the amendment, and interpret the wording with a maximum of poetic license so as to put into effect a social change *they* deemed desirable. So much for a government of laws. It was a clear-cut assumption of legislative power by the judiciary, the audacity of which left Justice White uncharacteristically exercised. "I am not yet prepared to accept the notion that normal rules of law, procedure, and constitutional adjudication suddenly become irrelevant because a case touches on the subject of abortion."[10]

John Noonan, professor of law at the University of California at Berkeley, was equally taken aback by the Court's reasoning.

> Vague as to the exact constitutional provision, the Court was sure of its power to proclaim an exact Constitutional mandate. It pinpointed a doctrine of human life which had, until then, escaped the notice of the Congress of the United States and the legislatures of all fifty states. It set out criteria it said were required by the Constitution which made invalid the regulation of abortion in every state

in the Union, the District of Columbia, the Commonwealth of Puerto Rico, and the City of New York. None of these bodies had read the Constitution.[11]

Now, admittedly, Noonan is an anti-abortion spokesman. But if his partisanship leads some to question his logic and scholarly judgment (the way progressive thinkers tell us partisanship should not), there are others who argue in the same vein—pro-abortion people, men whose intellectual integrity and concern over flagrant flouting of constitutional procedures lead them to take issue with the Roe and Doe decisions. Perhaps we should be used to the fine art of disregarding the intentions of the Framers as a result of our experience with the Warren Court. But at least, as John Hart Ely, pro-abortion professor of law at Harvard, points out, the Warren Court justices made an effort to create the appearance that they were in some semblance of a line with the spirit of the Constitution as written:

> The Warren Court was aggressive in enforcing its ideals of liberty and equality. But, by and large, it attempted to defend its decisions in terms of inferences from values the Constitution marks as special.[12]

The abortion Court, on the other hand, proceeded with a "sheer act of the will," failing even to pay the usual homage vice pays to virtue.

Birch Bayh, too, one of the least favorite men in America from the Right-to-Life point of view, admits that the Supreme Court's decision was, well, extraordinary from a lawyer's point of view.

> The effect of these two cases was to rule unconstitutional every one of the 50 state laws regulating the practice of abortion. The Court held on a vote of 7 to 2 that, as a matter of law, an unborn child was not a 'person' within the constitutional definition of that term and the constitutional 'right to privacy' of a prospective mother barred any government, be it state or federal, from interfering with the absolute right of the woman to terminate her pregnancy up to the time of 'viability,' or the ability of the fetus to exist outside the mother's womb, which the court *arbitrarily* [emphasis added] defined as occurring only in the last three months of pregnancy.[13]

Of course, the Court did go through some of the motions we would expect from a judicial branch of government overstepping its established bounds. They sought to justify their actions. But the rationale comes across as nothing more than that; as a strained rationalization, an excuse. To be blunt, the attentive and open-minded reader finds himself repeatedly doubting the

Court's sincerity. You cannot help it. They could not have believed what they said. Roe and Doe will stand as the most contorted and invalid of all the modern Court's manipulations of its constitutional mandate. The Justices, in fact, sound very much like devious schoolboys attempting to explain why the gyp notes under their cuffs should not be held against them or detract from their "A" grade. What they say will not fool a soul, and they know it, but a man has got to make a try—especially when he does not think of himself as a schoolboy culprit, but as part of a conscience elite moving America beyond the limiting moral consensus of a backward-looking majority bound to outmoded Christian religious and cultural beliefs. Progress has to be made, in spite of the law and majority will in this instance.

This is not to say that the Court's *apologia* lacks ingenuity. The best of legal scholars would be hard-pressed to suggest a better line of defense. There is no denying it; they had a tough row to hoe. But nevertheless, if the majority justices ever take the time to review their decisions in Roe and Doe, they are bound to cringe. When their case is not weak, it reeks of disingenuousness.

In Roe, for example, they argue that "throughout the major portion of the 19th Century [abortion was] viewed with less disfavor than under most abortion statutes" and that "a woman enjoyed a substantially broader right to terminate a pregnancy than she does in most states today."[14] The Court's argument, and that of pro-abortion supporters, is that such anti-abortion laws as could be found on the books in the nineteenth century were designed not so much to prevent the procuring of abortions as to guard the health and life of the mother; and that the anti-abortion statutes legislated in the last half of the nineteenth century and on into the twentieth were the result of an unwise, untypical, and illegitimate intrusion of religious enthusiasm into the American legislative process. In addition, the Court stressed that abortion was never considered homicide in the English common-law tradition; and that, therefore, up until that strange religiously motivated anti-abortion zealotry of the late nineteenth century (because of all those Popish immigrants upsetting the apple cart?), the legal traditions of America and Europe did not consider the fetus human—a "person." Thus Roe and Doe are actually *traditional*, an attempt to return to the older and healthier American legal heritage, the one before the separation of church and state was breached.

It sounds logical enough, until you examine what the Court left unsaid. (We are speaking, it must be stressed, of information readily available to the Court, information of which they must have been aware.)

When the Court informs us that abortion statutes were not written until the last half of the nineteenth century, they are telling the truth. But that does not mean they are telling the whole truth. Abortion was not *legal* before the anti-abortion statutes were put on the books or morally acceptable to the American people. Abortion was *always* considered a reprehensible crime in the English and American common-law tradition. There was no need for a specific statute since the common-law precedents were long established. When the anti-abortion statutes were written, they were written to tighten up *already established* principles in the common law.

Admittedly, the common law did not view abortion as a crime punishable with the same degree of severity as homicide. And it is also true that an attack upon a pregnant woman that resulted in a miscarriage did not bring an indictment for the murder of the fetus in the common law. The fetus was not granted the same rights as a child. But there *were* censures against abortion in the common law, in medieval Europe, and beyond in ancient Greece and Rome. Miscarriages caused by an attack upon pregnant women were not indictable because it was impossible to prove that the death of the fetus was directly attributable to the attack; not because there was a consensus that the fetus was not human until its first breath. In other words, it is a novelty, pure and simple, to suggest, as did the Court, that abortion be considered a "private" act of concern only to the woman and her doctor. Such was never the norm in the civilized West.

And when the anti-abortion statutes were written in the late nineteenth century, it was not because of the imposition of an alien religiously inspired belief. Far from it. The vanguard of the nineteenth-century American anti-abortion movement was the nineteenth-century American Medical Association, armed with the most up-to-date findings of modern science: evidence that the fetus was indeed an individual human life.

The irony is powerful and poignant. The pro-abortion forces in America today, it will be readily conceded, are those who pride themselves on their modern secular, empirical, "scientific" evaluation of issues. They tend to argue most excitedly against those who attempt to bring questions of "faith" and "religious belief" into the public arena. To hold a position contrary to the findings of science and observation of the senses—say that the consecrated host is the body and blood of Christ or that total immersion in a Georgia river forgives sin—is seen as "irrational" and "medieval" and "naive."

Yet these same folk now constitute the pro-abortion faction in America. They call upon us to disregard the findings of science; to ignore what our eyes tell us when we look at those pictures of dead tiny children in the hospital trash; to go back to the time when less-informed societies in Europe and America were more doubtful that the fetus was human life, and therefore less willing to treat abortion as a crime comparable in gravity to murder, even though those same societies were less condemnatory *only* because they were not as certain as we are about the nature of the fetus. We are to overlook that those societies wrote the deplored anti-abortion statutes in the quickest reaction this side of a knee jerk once science presented them with the evidence (even more conclusive in our time) that the fetus was indeed human life.

It should be noted, if only in passing, that the early feminist leaders had no doubts on this issue. They saw abortion as another attempt by men to exploit women, to use them as sex objects, as we would say it today, from whom pleasure could be taken without a commitment of love. *Revolution*, the magazine edited by Elizabeth Cady Stanton, condemned abortion as a "threat to and exploitation of women," and applauded the New York State legislation to "prosecute it more vigorously."[15]

Equally disorienting is the Court's juggling of the concepts of the "viability" of the fetus and their newly minted woman's right to "privacy." This right to privacy, although never before enumerated in a constitutional provision, was held to be "so rooted in the traditions and conscience of our people as to be ranked as fundamental" and "implicit in the concept of ordered liberty."

It might be waggish to ask how come such a fundamental right was never discovered before 1973. The more valid observation is to note that the Court's analysis begs the question. It certainly is true that a "right to privacy," if not in so many words, has always been considered part of the American tradition. "A man's home is his castle." There has been an American aversion to big government overseers intruding upon a citizen's personal life in our common-law tradition, from the days when the Star Chamber presided in England to the time when George Orwell's warnings about a coming "Big Brother" struck the public imagination. But—it should go without saying, but does not when abortion is at issue—obviously this "right to privacy" was never seen as a right to privacy while committing murder or robbery or any other felony. A right to privacy in carrying out an abortion would be part of our heritage *only* if abortion were a morally neutral or ambiguous act. Which, of course, is what the Court says it is. The only problem is that the Court can adduce as proof only its own words, in the face of the moral consensus of the American people in 1973, the legislators of the individual states, and the legal and moral tradition in Europe and American up until Roe and Doe. To be blunt, the Court created the aura of moral uncertainty about abortion, required to justify their alleged right to privacy, by judicial fiat.

The Court further complicated things by declaring this fundamental right to privacy less fundamental in the final three months of a pregnancy, at which time, remember, the states were allowed to restrict abortions except when the life or health of the mother were imperiled. How can so fundamental a right be washed away by a month or two in a woman's life?

The Court's answer was the concept of "viability" of the fetus. Since children prematurely born at a time as early as the sixth month of the pregnancy survive often enough, the Court held that states had a legitimate interest in acting to protect their lives. State regulations, as a result, at this point could have "both logical and biological justifications." But just a few passages later the Court informs us that abortions have to be permitted because "we need not resolve the difficult question of when life begins. When those trained in the respective disciplines of medicine, philosophy, and theology are unable to arrive at any consensus, the judiciary at this point in the development of man's knowledge, is not in a position to speculate as to the answer."

Nevertheless, they *did*. They speculated that life was present sufficiently in the final trimester to suspend the woman's fundamental "right to privacy." But then again, not present clearly enough to require stringent limitations on abortions, even when only an alleged psychological problem of the "mother" is at stake. If human life is present one would think that it would take more than a woman's psychological problem to warrant its extinction.

We are left with the conclusion that the Court made up its

mind by speculating that American society was changing in such a way as to make it likely that the Judeo-Christian abhorrence of abortion was about to die; that a new secular humanist view on this matter was on the horizon; and that it was the Court's (most unprecedented) role to clear the ground of the old restraints to prepare the way for the future consensus in favor of abortion (a consensus which very likely prevailed in the secularized upper-class circles from which the Supreme Court Justices tend to come). So they sought to change the law rather than demand its proper enforcement. Their vindication, they hoped, would come from future generations. They were betting on their proper perception of mankind's evolving conscience; on "progress." As Alexander M. Bickel, another pro-abortion critic of Roe and Doe, put it:

> The Court's decision was an "extravagant exercise" of judicial power, said Justice White; it was a legislative rather than judicial action, suggested Justice Rehnquist. So it was, and if the Court's guess on the probable and desirable direction of progress is wrong, that guess will nevertheless have been imposed on all fifty states.[17]

Now we must not read Bickel wrong. Once again, he is pro-abortion. His concern is with the damage Roe and Doe could do to our constitutional framework, not with aborted fetuses. He is concerned with that cherished myth that we are a "nation of laws"—if we one day are faced with a moral consensus that is not pro-abortion, and thus not inclined to overlook the inconsistent and conniving and successful manipulation of the Constitution by the 1973 Supreme Court—a government of men.

Whether or not Bickel's nightmare comes true (shall we keep our fingers crossed?), he has put his finger on the problem. We are faced with a Supreme Court decision that attempted to impose a new moral norm upon our society, one that acted with the audacity Bickel fears could present problems for future defenders of our constitutional order.

Bickel will have to forgive the enemies of abortion if they find this the perfect moment for an impatient "first things first." We should never forget that a Supreme Court decision not only settles a specific dispute. It teaches; establishes norms for society and for future generations. The longer Roe and Doe stay on the books, the more acceptable abortion will become in the public conscience—which is, it seems safe to say, exactly what the pro-abortion clique desires. The worst moral outrage can become a "right" when it is protected in the marble chambers of the highest court in the land and defended by the more sophisticated of our fellow citizens; and the opponents quickly becomes either quaint or un-American. It is far more difficult to take back such a "right" than to deny its extension. As John Noonan, once again, observes, the lesson for all future generations will be that

> the judge as teacher teaches the men and women of the fifty states that they were wrong in all their past teachings which viewed abortions as unique [among medical practices] because it involved not one human body but two.[18]

A World Upside Down

Malcolm Muggeridge wrote that

> the abortion issue raises questions of the very destiny and purpose of life itself; of whether our human society is to be seen in Christian terms as a family with a loving father who is God, or as a factory farm whose primary consideration must be the physical well-being of the livestock and the material well-being of the collectivity.[19]

Muggeridge is a man whose literary skills and understanding of, disenchantment with, and revulsion by the secular humanist world for which he was once an enthusiastic supporter, have made him one of the most important of modern writers. In his old age, he has become a born-again Christian of sorts; an idiosyncratic and non-institutional Christian to be sure, (Muggeridge has recently converted to Roman Catholocism) but, outside of Solzhenitsyn, the one who is delivering the most telling blows against the madness of the Godless and materialistic West, the crumbling shell of what once was called (remember?) Christendom.

He, anti-abortion advocate, is right on target of course, as are the pro-abortion editors of *California Medicine*, in the same editorial quoted earlier.

> The controversy over abortion represents the first phase of a head-on conflict between the traditional Judeo-Christian medical and legal ethic—in which the intrinsic worth and equal value of every human life is secured by law, regardless of age, health or condition of dependency—and a new ethic, according to which human life can be taken for what are held to be the compelling social, economic or psychological needs of others.[20]

The conflict is, in other words, a symbolic battle (as well as a very real one, of course, on its own terms), the outcome of which could well determine once and for all whether the secular humanism of the twentieth century will secure its final victory over the God-centered understanding of life associated with the Christian faith; whether the one-dimensional, rootless, Godless, hedonistic, utilitarian, narcissistic man extolled in the pages of *Playboy* and its imitators will replace as the norm, the God-fearing, self-disciplined, self-sacrificing man of the Christian West who aspires to a higher morality—one who views with alarm the much-heralded moral subjectivism of today; whether the Christian knight will be supplanted by the smug and cloying shells of men we see in the popular media of our time.

A quite ingenious ploy has been used by the secularizers in promoting the new morality on the abortion issue. We all have heard it dozens of times. "The main issue in the abortion question is whether or not one religious group has the right to impose its religious beliefs on the rest of us." They, of course, mean Roman Catholics, members of a church whose clear chain of command and demand that its members adhere to moral truths established and defended by a hierarchical authority and rooted firmly in tradition, makes it more immune to the *Zeitgeist* than the Protestant sects, and thus less less vulnerable to the secularist advances. (At least in theory, the polls seem to indicate that Catholics are falling to the secularist advance as easily as Protestants.) It is for good reason that anti-Catholicism has been called the "anti-Semitism of the intellectuals." If the Catholic Church manages to retain its position of opposition to the secularist advance (which, once again, is not all that likely, at least on the level of the average Catholic), Catholics and secularist intellectuals (and their ideological retainers in the political world and the media) just might find themselves in as tense an adversary relationship as these same factions found themselves in at the height of Jacobin rule in France.

The secularizers' current tactic, however, is to avoid the possibility of such unpleasantries by trying to cast doubts on those who speak on abortion—and, by implication, anything else—in a manner that results from their religious background. Thurgood Marshall, for example, has criticized those who "have attempted every imaginable means to circumvent the commands of the Constitution and impose their moral choices on the rest of society."[21]

Well, there are two possible reactions. You can either shake your head and wink in admiration at the man's audacity—that, if you are a pro-abortion activist. Or step back and steady yourself while you try to recover your breath. A 1973 decision by seven judges, which overrode the legislation of fifty states and ignored hundreds of years of judicial precedent (and which continues to be challenged by some of the best of the country's legal scholars, including many who are pro-abortion), suddenly becomes "commands of the Constitution." A man who owes his seat on the Court to the role he played in seeking to force a new perception of racial equality—a perception based on the religious notion of human equality, in spite of the resistance of substantial local southern majorities (and perhaps national as well), whose religious training (mistakenly or not) led them to disagree—now finds moral fervor out of line. The same kind of moral fervor that was called for to stop the war in Vietnam, to promote the busing of schoolchildren for racial balance, to bring down the government in Rhodesia, or boycott those farmers who do not bargain with the right grape-pickers union.

It is so flimsy an argument that it is surprising the pro-abortion folk have managed to get away with it for as long as they have. In fact, it is surprising they ever thought the line worth using at such an important stage in the culture wars. Their decision to do so indicates either their contempt for the intelligence of the American masses (whose tendency to give credence to the secularizers' case just might warrant that contempt); or self-delusion; or, perhaps, simply desperation—a willingness to try *anything* in their attempt to win an argument they themselves know is doomed to failure if the accepted rules of logic apply.

We are not talking of forcing Americans to go to confession, or wear yarmulkes, or submit to river baptisms; forcing them to act as if they were practicing members of a particular religious group. There is a vast and crucial difference between these things and demanding that our fellow citizens not sell their services as gangland assassins (even though there is a Commandment, "Thou shalt not kill"); or knock over Chase Manhattan or steal pocketbooks (even though there is a Commandment, "Thou shalt not steal"); or expose themselves on the commuter train (even though we learned of sexual proprieties in religious-training classes); or have five wives or enslave our next door neighbor, etc., because these things are defined as evil by our religious educators. It just is not the same thing. The basic standards of vice and virtue embodied in the laws of Europe and America—all of them—are expressions of the consciences of the people of the West; consciences formed by their immersion in the Christian

Faith. Forbidding the killing of unborn infants was one of the expressions of that conscience until the Supreme Court declared it unconstitutional. Abortion, in other words, was illegal for the same reasons that theft and bigamy were illegal, and rape and wife beating, and child molestation.

No one accused the Nuremberg trials of being a Roman Catholic revival of the Inquisition, if memory serves. Yet at Nuremberg, one of the Nazi crimes condemned was the practice of forcing abortions on Eastern European women. The indictment read in part that "protection of the law was denied to unborn children of Russian and Polish women." In fact, the Nazi justification for their abortion laws spoke disparagingly of the "objections of a minority of reactionary Catholic physicians."[22] The judges at Nuremberg did not mind at all that in this instance, their judgments coincided with that of Catholics.

As incredible as it sounds in retrospect, the majority judges in *Roe v. Wade* conceded that abortion has long been considered a crime in the West; but they argued that this was so only because the Christian churches managed to secure positions of influence, and hold them, after the fall of Rome. Think about it. To get to valid social and legal norms, we must cancel out the history of the West and go back to pagan Greece and Rome and beyond. Their norms, apparently will be valid because . . . because, well, because they were not Christian. What else are we to conclude? That we ought to accept ancient beliefs on infanticide, the paterfamilias, slavery, harems, sacrifice to Moloch, too?

No. It is obvious. Only those portions of the Christian heritage that are judged unacceptable by the reigning secular liberal consensus are judged to be violations of our precious First Amendment guarantees of religious liberty.

Abortion, then, has become (it is surprising it did not happen earlier—an indication of the Christian residue in the developing secular world) an integral feature in the Enlightenment's man-centered and man-controlled world. It is quite appropriate, even necessary, for a world where "self-fulfillment" and sensual pleasure are seen as values of the highest order. Those cumbersome nuisances that often follow upon sexual pleasure (whose idea was that anyway?) could not be allowed to go on inhibiting enlightened moderns. There is to be no price attached to that pleasure. No sacrifice, no pain. Why? For what purpose in a world dedicated to "getting it all" because "you have only one life to live."

Abortion was a quite logical development in the pursuit of a world controlled by man; where man is autonomous, the creator of moral value, master of nature; where "nature" is to be periodically re-created by mankind in its existential encounter with itself. Hence the fetus—*presto!*—becomes nonhuman. The best and the brightest have spoken. Who is to say no?

We end up with that strange religion of sentimentality we see in the pro-abortion ranks. The same people who sponsor UNICEF neighborhood fund-raisings for starving Ethiopian children and show pictures of the skeleton-like unfortunates to win our support, favor abortion and deplore the pro-life pictures of aborted fetuses.

We find enlightened moderns speaking in the kind of reverent tones we used to associate with those about to embark on dangerous missionary adventures in the far corners of the world, of how "I've gotta be me" and of the need for "self-realization" in order to become "the kind of person I want to be," no matter what society says. The "me generation." And no babies are going to get in the way. (I once was in the same room with two high-school teachers talking about abortion. One, a woman, stated flatly that there was a time when she feared she might be pregnant after taking her new teaching job. "There was no choice. I wasn't about to give up my career." It turned out that she was not pregnant, but if she had been—abortion. The other, a man, agreed. "Hell," he said, "my sister-in-law got pregnant a few summers ago, just after my brother bought a new camper. I told her to get an abortion. It would have ruined the whole trip. But she wouldn't. She still was into the Catholic thing." But the point is that there was a moral superiority in their voice, a self-congratulatory air. They were part of a developing American moral elite, a vanguard able to perceive that there is nothing finer than self-centeredness.)

In fact, you can get the impression that the fetus has become a villain, a nasty thing that threatens a woman's right to climb to the lofty things in life—her right to be the grandest of all moderns, the Liberated Woman, the *Cosmopolitan* girl, a genuine *Me*; that the child is about to take the *goodness* out of the "mother's" life; that abortion is a modern version of slaying the dragon.

Paul Ramsay reported in amazement a panel discussion of the Edelin case where the male discussants attempted to resolve the case by deciding "what women expect" in cases like this.

Should the products of abortion be terminated if delivered alive? Simple. Whatever the woman wants.

Ironically, it would seem that a Christian residue in America accounts for such decadence, a secularized form of Christian charity, a concern for the downtrodden. Women, apparently, in certain circles, have succeeded in picturing themselves as an aggrieved minority, as victims, and thus entitled to the same suspension of standards of thought and decorum given blacks and Chicanos by those who feel the pangs of liberal guilt. Abortion, hence, like Black Studies, cannot be denied.

James Buckley, who served the prolife cause admirably during his time in the U.S. Senate, has been to the top of the mountain. (His defeat, by the way, goes a long way toward answering his first question.)

> What kind of society is it that will abide this sort of senseless destruction? What kind of people are we that can tolerate this mass extermination? What kind of Constitution is it that can elevate this sort of conduct to the level of a social right, presumptively endowed with the blessings of the Founding Fathers, who looked to the laws of nature and nature's God as the foundation of the Nation?
>
> Abortion, which was once universally condemned in the Western World as a heinous moral and legal offense, is now presented to us not only as a necessary, sometime evil, but as a morally and socially beneficial act. The Christian counsel of perfection, which teaches that the greatest love consists in laying down one's life for one's friend, has now become, it seems, an injunction to take another's life for the security and comfort of one's own . . . a world upside down . . . a world in which the child's natural protector, his own mother, becomes the very object of his destruction.[23]

No doubt about it. It is the crucial issue of our time. If abortion is not stopped, it is safe to say that our children will be living in a world where practices as horrifying as abortion was to us only a short time ago, will be commonplace. Those are the stakes. If we do not find a way to reinvigorate the Christian moral consensus upon which our Constitutional order was built—if we cannot act upon that consensus even in a case as clear-cut as abortion—future Americans, instead of "dreaming of systems so perfect that no one will need to be good" will have no remaining notions of the good and the bad. They will live in a brave new world even Aldous Huxley, on his best nights, would have been unable to fantasize.

Notes

Chapter I
The First Amendment—Then and Now

1. Quoted in Willmoore Kendall and George W. Carey, *The Basic Symbols of the American Political Tradition* (Baton Rouge: Louisiana University Press, 1970), 31–33.

2. John E. Walsh, *The Mayflower Compact: The First Democratic Document in America* (New York: Franklin W. Watts, 1971), 33.

3. Ibid., 29.

4. Quoted in Winthrop S. Hudson, *American Protestantism* (Chicago: University of Chicago Press, 1962), 5.

5. Ibid., 63.

6. Quoted in George M. Waller, *Puritanism in Early America* (Boston: D.C. Heath Co., 1968), 23.

7. Ibid., 24.

8. Ibid.

9. Ibid., 25.

10. Ibid.

11. Ibid.

12. Ibid.

13. Ibid.

14. Ibid.

15. *The Basic Symbols*, 44–45.

16. *American Protestantism*, 62.

17. Ibid., 62.

18. Quoted in Theodore P. Greene, *Roger Williams and the Massachusetts Magistrates* (Boston: D.C. Heath Co., 1964), 34–35.

19. Ibid., 36.

20. Quoted in Andrew M. Scott, *Political Thought in America* (New York: Holt, Rinehart and Winston, 1960), 29.

21. Quoted in Edwin Scott Gaustad, *A Religious History of America* (New York: Harper and Row, 1966), 67.

22. *Political Thought in America*, 97.

23. Ibid., 98–99.

24. Ibid., 101.

25. *American Protestantism*, 13.

26. *Puritanism in Early America*, 34.

27. *American Protestantism*, 4.

28. Ibid., 18.

29. Ibid., 34–37.

30. Ibid., 45.

31. Ibid., 40–43.

32. *A Religious History of America*, 113.

33. Ibid., 113.

34. Ibid., 177.

35. Ibid.

36. Ibid.

37. Ibid.

38. Ibid., 119.

39. Ibid., 71.

Chapter II
Hamilton v. Jefferson

1. Samuel Eliot Morison, *Oxford History of the American People* (New York: Oxford University Press, 1965), 340.

2. Quoted in Jacob E. Cooke, *Alexander Hamilton: A Profile* (New York: Hill and Wang, 1967), xx.

3. Ibid., ix.

4. Vernon L. Parrington, *Main Currents in American Thought* (New York: Harcourt, Brace, 1954), 142.

5. *Hamilton: A Profile*, xiii.

6. Ibid., 137.

7. Ibid., 29, 38.

8. Quoted in John Roche, *American Political Thought* (New York: Harper and Row, 1967), 14.

9. Ibid., 21.

10. Ibid., 18.

11. Ibid., 26.

12. Ibid., 18.

13. Ibid., 26.

14. Ibid., 24.

15. Quoted in Dumas Malone, *Jefferson and the Rights of Man* (Boston: Little, Brown and Co., 1951), 155.

16. Quoted in John M. Blum, *The National Experience* (New York: Harcourt, Brace and World, 1963), 166.

17. *Jefferson and the Rights of Man*, 160.

18. Quoted in John Dos Passos, *The Men Who Made the Nation* (New York: Doubleday, 1957), 260.

19. *The National Experience*, 143.

20. Ibid.

21. Quoted in Andrew M. Scott, *Political Thought in America* (New York: Holt, Rinehart, and Winston, 1960), 100.

22. *Jefferson and the Rights of Man*, 132.

23. *American Political Thought*, 23.

24. *Hamilton: A Profile*, 159.

25. Ibid., 158.

26. Ibid., 160.

27. *Political Thought in America*, 52.

28. Ibid., 59.

29. *Hamilton: A Profile*, 204–205.

30. Ibid., 173.

31. *Political Thought in America*, 53.

32. *Hamilton: A Profile*, 33.

33. *Political Thought in America*, 127.

34. *Hamilton: A Profile*, 12.

35. Ibid., 13.

36. *American Political Thought*, 16.

37. *Political Thought in America*, 116.

38. *Hamilton: A Profile*, 52.

39. Ibid., 143–144.

40. *Political Thought in America*, 59.

Chapter III
The Changing Court

1. James J. Kilpatrick, "A Very Different Constitution," *National Review*, Aug. 12, 1969, 799.

2. Lino T. Graglia, "The Supreme Court's Abuse of Power," *National Review*, July 21, 1978, 894.

3. Quoted in L. Brent Bozell, *The Warren Revolution* (New Rochelle, N.Y.: Arlington House, 1966), 317.

4. Quoted in Jacob E. Cooke, *Alexander Hamilton: A Profile* (New York: Hill and Wang, 1967), 160.

5. *The Federalist*, 2 vols. (New Rochelle, N.Y.: Arlington House, 1900), 1:254, 507 (No. 81).

6. Ibid., 526 (No. 81).

7. Ibid., (No. 78).

8. Quoted in Max Farrand, *The Records of the Federal Convention of 1787*, 4 vols. (New Haven: Yale University Press, 1911), 2:78.

9. Quoted in Raoul Berger, *Government by Judiciary* (Cambridge, Mass.: Harvard University Press, 1977), 301.

10. Quoted in Lino T. Graglia, "The Supreme Court's Abuse of Power," *National Review*, July 21, 1978, 893.

11. *Federal Convention*, 1:97–98.

12. *Federal Convention*, 2:298.

13. *Federal Convention*, 1:108.

14. *Federal Convention*, 2:300.

15. *Government by Judiciary*, 303–4.

16. Quoted in James J. Kilpatrick, "A Very Different Constitution," *National Review*, August 12, 1969, 796.

17. *The Warren Revolution*, 238.

18. Marbury v. Madison, 1 Cr. 137 (1803).

19. 17 U.S. (4 Wheat) 316, 402 (1819).

20. Osborn v. Bank of the United States, 22 U.S. (9 Wheat) 738, 866 (1824).

21. 29 U.S. (4 Pet.) 514, 563 (1830).

22. Home Building and Loan Assn. v. Blaisdell, 290 U.S. 398, 442, 443 (1934).

23. *Government by Judiciary*, 262.

24. Lochner v. New York, 198 U.S. 43 (1905).

25. Tyson v. Benton, 273 U.S. 418 (1927).

26. Quoted in Andrew M. Scott, *Political Thought in America* (New York: Holt, Rinehart and Winston, 1959), 429.

27. Archibald Cox, *The Role of the Supreme Court in American Government* (New York: Oxford University Press, 1976), 34.

28. Fred Rodell, *New York Times Magazine*, March 13, 1966.

29. *Government by Judiciary*, 350.

Chapter IV
John C. Calhoun—Patriot?

1. Quoted in Richard N. Current, *John C. Calhoun* (New York: Washington Square Press, 1966), 41.

2. Ibid.

3. Ibid., 47.

4. *The Works of John C. Calhoun*, 6 vols. (New York: D. Appleton and Co., 1851), 4:507–509.

5. Quoted in Andrew M. Scott, *Political Thought in America* (New York: Holt, Rinehart and Winston, 1960), 268.

6. *John C. Calhoun*, 45.

7. Ibid., 45.

8. *Works of Calhoun*, 1:1–7, 56, 57.

9. Ibid., 7:13–24.

10. *Political Thought in America*, 231–232.

11. Quoted in Avery Craven, Walter Johnson, F. Roger Dunn, eds., *A Documentary History of the American People* (Boston: Ginn and Co, 1951), 382.

12. *Works of Calhoun*, 7:13–24.

13. Quoted in Henry Steele Commager, *Living Ideas in America* (New York: Harper and Brothers, 1951), 224.

14. *John C. Calhoun,* 62.

15. Ibid., 65.

16. Ibid.

17. Ibid., 67.

18. Ibid., 51.

19. Ibid., 69.

20. Ibid., 81.

21. Ibid., 54.

22. Ibid., 70.

23. *The Works of Daniel Webster,* 18 vols. (Boston: C.C. Little and J. Brown, 1851), 3:333.

24. Quoted in Richard N. Current, *Daniel Webster and The Rise of National Conservatism* (Boston: Little, Brown and Co., 1955), 67.

25. *Political Thought in America,* 245–247.

26. Ibid., 244.

27. Ibid.

28. Ibid., 265.

Chapter V
Henry David Thoreau—Idealist?

1. Quoted in Brooks Atkinson, *Walden and Other Writings* (New York: Modern Library, 1937), 642.

2. Ibid., 645.

3. Ibid., 638.

4. Ibid., 639.

5. Ibid., 643.

6. Ibid., 647.

7. Ibid.

8. Ibid., 640.

9. Ibid., 635.

10. Ibid., 8.

11. Ibid., 654.

12. Ibid., 10.

13. Quoted in T. Morris Longstreth, *Henry Thoreau: American Rebel* (New York: Dodd, Mead and Co.), 46.

14. *Walden and Other Writings,* 7.

15. *Henry Thoreau: American Rebel,* 125.

16. *Walden and Other Writings,* 685.

17. Ibid., 653.

18. Ibid., 151.

19. Ibid., 12.

20. Ibid., 28.

21. Ibid., 63.

22. Ibid., 659.

23. Ibid., 644.

24. Ibid., 699.

25. Ibid.

26. Ibid., 669.

27. Ibid., 695.

28. Ibid., 704.

29. Ibid.

30. Ibid., 702.

31. Ibid.

32. Ibid., 648.

33. Ibid.

34. Ibid., 16.

35. Ibid., 17.

Chapter VI
The Monkey Trial

1. John T. Scopes and James Presley, *Center of the Storm* (New York: Holt, Rinehart and Winston, 1967), 46.

2. Ibid.

3. Ibid.

4. Ibid., 53.

5. Ibid., 49.

6. Ibid., 6.

7. Ibid., 93.

8. Ibid., 80

9. Quoted in Louis W. Koenig, *Bryan* (New York: G.P. Putnam's Sons, 1971), 638.

10. *Center of the Storm*, 113.

11. Ibid., 65.

12. Ibid., 153.

13. Ibid., 116.

14. Ibid., 276.

15. Ibid., 204.

16. Quoted in Arthur Weinburg, *Attorney for the Damned* (New York: Simon and Schuster, 1957), 176.

17. Quoted in Irving Stone, *Clarence Darrow* (New York: Doubleday, 1941), 437.

18. *Center of the Storm*, 111.

19. *Attorney for the Damned*, 177.
20. *Clarence Darrow*, 441.
21. *Center of the Storm*, 134.
22. Quoted in Ray Ginger, *William Jennings Bryan: Selections* (New York: Bobbs–Merrill, 1967), 243.
23. *Clarence Darrow*, 457.
24. *Center of the Storm*, 169.
25. *Clarence Darrow*, 441.
26. Quoted in Henry Steele Commager, *William Jennings Bryan: A Profile* (New York: Hill and Wang, 1968), 242.
27. *Attorney for the Damned*, 179.
28. *William Jennings Bryan: A Profile*, 226.
29. *Bryan*, 639.
30. *Clarence Darrow*, 453.
31. *Bryan*, 641.
32. *Clarence Darrow*, 453.
33. *William Jennings Bryan: A Profile*, 232.
34. *Center of the Storm*, 146–47.
35. *Bryan*, 631.
36. Ibid.
37. *Center of the Storm*, 47.
38. Ibid., 50–51.

Chapter VII
McCarthyism

1. Quoted in Allen J. Matusow, *Joseph R. McCarthy* (Englewood Cliffs, N.J.: Prentice–Hall, 1970), title page.
2. Fred J. Cook, *The Nightmare Decade* (New York: Random House, 1971), 6.
3. Ibid., x.
4. Ibid., 3.
5. Quoted in William F. Buckley and L. Brent Bozell, *McCarthy and His Enemies* (1954, rpt. New Rochelle: Arlington House, 1970), 310.
6. Ibid.
7. Ibid.
8. Robert Griffith, *The Politics of Fear* (Lexington, Ky.: University of Kentucky Press, 1970), 83.
9. Ibid., 142.
10. *Joseph R. McCarthy*, 2.
11. Ibid., 8.
12. Ibid.
13. Ibid.
14. Ibid., 9.

15. *McCarthy and His Enemies*, 304.

16. Ibid., xvii.

17. Ibid., 70.

18. Adam B. Ulam, *The Rivals: America and Russia Since World War II* (New York: The Viking Press, 1971), 173.

19. Ibid., 141.

20. Ibid., 174.

21. Ibid., 143.

22. *McCarthy and His Enemies*, 7.

23. *The Rivals*, 18.

24. Ibid., 22.

25. Ibid., 87.

26. Walter LaFeber, *America, Russia and the Cold War* (New York: John Wiley and Sons, 1972), 52.

27. Ibid., 3.

28. Ibid.

29. Staughton Lynd, " 'Again—Don't Tread on Me,' " *Newsweek*, July 6, 1970, 31–32.

30. Eugene Genovese, "A Massive Breakdown" *Newsweek*, July 6, 1970, 27.

31. William Appleman Williams, *The Contours of American History* (Chicago: Quadrangle, 1966), 487.

32. Harvey Cox, *The Seduction of the Spirit* (New York: Simon and Schuster, 1974), 174.

33. *Joseph R. McCarthy*, 21.

34. Ibid.

35. Ibid., 26.

36. *McCarthy and His Enemies*, xviii.

Chapter VIII
Separate But Equal Is Unequal?

1. Martin Luther King, *Where Do We Go From Here?* (New York: Harper and Row, 1967), 119.

2. Ibid., 104.

3. Ibid., 107.

4. Martin Luther King, *Why We Can't Wait* (New York: Harper and Row, 1963), 137.

5. *Where Do We Go From Here?*, 108.

6. Louis E. Lomax, *The Negro Revolt* (New York: Harper and Row, 1962), 179.

7. Whitney M. Young, *Beyond Racism: Building an Open Society* (New York: McGraw–Hill, 1969), 151.

Chapter IX
What Kind of Society?

1. *Human Life Review*, 2, no. 1, (Winter 1976) 58. The *Review* is published at Room 540, 150 East 35th St., New York, N.Y. 10016.

2. 42 N.J. 421, 201 A2nd, 537 (1964).

3. *Human Life Review*, 1, No. 1 (Winter 1975), 18.

4. Ibid., 2, no. 4 (Fall 1976), 39.

5. Ibid., 71.

6. George Will, *Newsweek*, Sept. 20, 1976.

7. *Human Life Review*, 1, no. 3 (Summer 1975), 41.

8. Ibid., 1, no. 4 (Fall 1975), 85.

9. 410 U.S. at 174–175.

10. Wolfe v. Schroering, 380 F. Supp. 631 (W.D. Ky. 1974).

11. *Human Life Review*, 1, no. 1 (Winter 1975), 26.

12. Ibid., 57.

13. Ibid., 3.

14. Roe, 410 U.S. at 140.

15. Quoted in James C. Mohr, *Abortion in America* (New York: Oxford University Press, 1978), 111.

16. Roe, 410 U.S. at 159.

17. *Human Life Review*, 1, no. 4 (Fall 1975), 7.

18. Ibid., 3, no. 3 (Summer 1977), 12.

19. Ibid., 1, no. 3 (Summer 1975), 4.

20. Ibid., 1, no. 1 (Winter 1975), 12.

21. *Human Life Review*. After a search I have been unable to find the exact issue from which I took this quote of Thurgood Marshall's. There should be no quarrel, however, that the words are Marshall's. They contain nothing he has not said many times before in public.

22. Ibid., 1, no. 2 (Spring 1975), 62.

23. Ibid., 1, no. 1 (Winter 1975), 19.

Index